OUTBA

HIGHWAYS

Books by Len Beadell:

Too Long in the Bush
Blast the Bush
Bush Bashers
Still in the Bush
Beating About the Bush
End of an Era

OUTBACK HIGHWAYS

THE GUNBARREL HIGHWAY
STORY AND MANY MORE

LEN BEADELL

NEW
HOLLAND

To the members of the Gunbarrel Road Construction Party . . .

Doug Stoneham	— Bulldozer
Scotty Boord	— Grader
Rex Flatman	— Fitter
Bill Lloyd and Frank Quinn	— Fuel, rations, and water supply
Paul Christensen	— Cook
Willy Appleton and Eric Graefling	— Drivers
Whiskey and Lassie	— The dogs

. . . without whose resolution and hard work, despite extreme conditions, the 6000 kilometres of loneliest roads in the world which opened up 2.5 million square kilometres of the waterless wastes of Central and Western Australia could not have been made

Published in Australia by
New Holland Publishers (Australia) Pty Ltd
Sydney • Auckland • London • Cape Town

14 Aquatic Drive Frenchs Forest NSW 2086 Australia
218 Lake Road Northcote Auckland New Zealand
86 Edgware Road London W2 2EA United Kingdom
80 McKenzie Street Cape Town 8001 South Africa

Copyright © 1979 Len Beadell

First published 1979 by Rigby Publishers
Reprinted 1983, 1985, 1986, 1992
Reprinted by Lansdowne Publishing Pty Ltd 1997, 2000
Reprinted by New Holland Publishers (Australia) Pty Ltd 2001

10 9 8 7

A CiP record of this title is available from the National Library of Australia

ISBN 1 86436 786 5

Typeset in Hong Kong
Cover design by Sue Hawkins
Printed by Everbest Printing Co Ltd, China

Contents

Foreword

With the successful firing of the first British atomic device in the Monte Bello Islands, off the Western Australian coast, in 1952, there arose an urgent need to test two low yield devices as part of the weapon development programme.

On my way back to England I presented to the Australian Government Departments responsible the difficult task of finding a remote area and providing the logistic support for these tests within less than a year. It was apparent that this requirement would involve a considerable airlift, and that a flat clear area had to be found capable of taking medium size freighter aircraft and with a high guarantee that it would not be flooded by rain during the operation.

I can imagine now that, faced with the problem, someone in the Department of Supply must immediately have said, 'Send for Lennie.'

It has often been remarked that, with the uniformity and conformity that modern day civilization imposes, the individualistic characters of past ages no longer emerge. But Lennie, who was at home in the limitless boundaries of the Australian bush, and whose heavy field boots seldom tramped a pavement, developed and retained his own unique character. This I learnt as soon as I arrived in August 1953 to direct our tests at the site he had chosen, known as the Emu Claypan.

A short time after Lennie had chosen the site, an Australian Task Force had moved in under the direction of Brigadier Lucas and, with nothing to spare in time or equipment, had with great resource and sheer physical effort built the scientific and administrative facilities needed for the tests.

7

Despite the magnitude of the job, the Task Force found time to consider how they could welcome, and make bush life a little easier for, the 'Boffins from England.' As part of this process they prepared a booklet called 'Welcome to the Claypan' illustrated by Lennie, a talented cartoonist. The cover showed a Bristol aircraft that had landed on the Claypan. From behind mulga trees some of the Task Force, each with the attendant cloud of flies that one had to learn to live with, peered out in astonished horror at descending Boffins arrayed in a variety of garb ranging from natty city suiting with bowler hat to riding boots, breeches, and topee, and surrounded by a paraphernalia of cabin trunks, golf clubs, and even a pair of skis. I believe that, at the time, one was actually seen carrying an umbrella. On the walls of the nissen hut used as a dining room, Lennie had drawn two large charcoal murals. One, representing Australiana, was the head of a grinning Aboriginal. The other was Lennie's caricature of the average Briton and was of a half-bald, moustached, long-nosed character wearing half-moon spectacles. In one detail Lennie's imagination had failed: he had tried to include a butterfly collar but had drawn it upside down. These murals were carefully preserved when the tests were over and now adorn a laboratory at Aldermaston in Berkshire.

These gentle leg pulls were a happy beginning for the scientists who, although having a pallor from the long hours in their laboratories preparing for these experiments, were a young adaptable bunch and were soon indistinguishable from their Australian colleagues.

In the improvised beer garden on cool starlit evenings, Lennie would inevitably become the centre of a crowd of Britishers questioning him on all aspects of his bush pioneering experiences — a life so different from their own.

I should mention, for the non-Australian reader, that the country surrounding the Claypan, 16 kilometres from which we were to conduct the tests, was a featureless plain of wooded country. Through this had been cut roads and tracks, along which were arrays of instruments. The following rule was written in 'Welcome to the Claypan':

> When travelling from point to point keep to existing tracks or roads. Short cuts through mulga scrub (known as 'bush-bashing') can be an interesting experience but is attended with real dangers, and in any event becoming lost is a simple matter.

Interesting though it was to look for local fauna and flora, this rule had to be strictly obeyed, and it is understandable that Lennie was flooded with offers of assistance as soon as it was known that he had to make a sortie into the bush.

During the tests Lennie was given a week's leave to Adelaide, and somebody found his shopping list which, it was said, went something like:

> new boot laces
> new tooth brush
> new car
> new shirt
> new belt

The story goes further that he had heavy duty springs fitted to his car, so that on his rare returns from the bush to Adelaide he could organise outings with a full car load of children, for yet another characteristic of Lennie is his love of children and the complete reliance parents and children place on him.

While the operation at Emu Field was being mounted, a search was made for a permanent trials site. It was essential that this site should be clear of trees, to permit unimpeded lines of sight for instrument layouts.

We received a report that a reconnaissance aircraft had spotted two such sites about 190 kilometres south of Emu. Dr Butement, Chief Scientist, Department of Supply, organized a search from Emu, a search heavily relying on Lennie's bush sense.

They found the area, although not without difficulties, especially when they afterwards continued southwards heading for the Trans Australian Railway and encountered a range of high and almost impenetrable sandhills.

However, a return to this area was organised almost immediately, a camp established, a runway of sorts dragged out by a length of railway line towed behind a Land Rover, and I was invited to fly down from Emu to stay at the camp for a few days and survey the area. While there, a party led by Lennie made a sortie to search for the other clear area which had been reported over a hundred kilometres to the west. It was a four-day journey through dense bush. Everybody had complete confidence in Lennie's navigational prowess and bush craft.

Back at the camp in the chosen area (which was subsequently christened Maralinga, Aboriginal for 'Thunder') life with Lennie was not without incident. In the bush, he had acquired a degree of proficiency in such skills as hair cutting and dentistry. I fortunately had no need of the latter but was badly in need of a trim and still have a photograph of myself sitting on a pile of car tyres with Lennie performing. The size of the clippers suggested that they were intended for sheep clipping, and Lennie completed the job in about four minutes flat. I took some comfort from the thought that I would not reappear in civilization for a week or two by which time some of the more obvious discontinuities would have smoothed out.

9

One evening Lennie talked to us about the Aborigines, the way they live, and the strange things they eat. Among these were wichetty grubs that they found in the roots of old mallee trees. As I emerged from my tent the following morning I was confronted by Lennie with a plateful of these large white squirming maggots, and I was asked how I would like them cooked. I had lost my appetite for breakfast, but Lennie ate a few with real or simulated relish.

When, three years later in 1956, I flew into Maralinga, it was then a village of gleaming aluminium, and out to the distant horizon led straight ribbons of roads and instrument lanes, the accuracy of which had the imprint of Lennie's surveys.

We then conducted our first series of tests at Maralinga. People will have different views on the purpose of this operation, but I need not dwell here on these profound and difficult questions. Whatever the purpose, they were unique, in that they drew together so many different people — Australians, Canadians, and British from all three Services and from a variety of civilian professions, skills, and crafts — and they all believed so whole-heartedly in the importance of what they were doing.

In wishing Lennie well in this latest venture and thanking him for the invitation to write this Foreword, I do not think he will mind my taking the opportunity of thanking again all those Australians who joined with us in those days and who, by their efforts, ensured the success of the work which we had been required to undertake.

LORD PENNEY

Introduction

Everyone knows the world is round. Most people believe that it is spherical and many have heard that it is a little flattened at the top and bottom. But there are a few people whose job it is to try to discover more about the problems the earth's shape presents, and their study is known as 'geodesy.'

This knowledge of the world's dimensions is needed, with ever increasing accuracy, to help in the development of such projects as space rockets and guided missiles. It is not so long ago that a good average figure of the earth was enough for map making and navigation, but that is not so today.

A series of measurements under the name of a geodetic survey must be taken over large portions of the earth's surface before geodesists can begin work on their calculations, and these surveys are made with almost complete disregard for the nature of the terrain. Mountains offering near impossible resistance, burning deserts, and disease-infested jungles have been, and are still being, attacked the world over — such is the important need for geodetic surveys. Information obtained from them is pooled, and it all helps towards giving us an overall picture. The measurements take the form of a great number of points fixed in relationship to each other by instruments with the greatest precision possible, and they follow the course on the ground in the direction of the currently required geodetic link on paper.

Many such long-needed links have never been made, simply because the areas, up to the present time, have defied penetration. Greater effort has recently been put into the onslaught of some of these with the arrival of new-type instruments, vehicles, and air support, and, in some cases, of heavy equipment for the carving of access roads in advance. One such area lies to the west of the centre of Australia and comprises about 2.5 million square kilometres of desolate, waterless semi-desert, uninhabited except for the few small tribes of Aborigines.

The story of the making of the first access road through the middle of this region, for the initial purpose of a geodetic link, is told in *Too Long in the Bush*, an outback phrase applied to anybody who, after being in remote places for lengthy periods, appears to the town dweller to be just a trifle *different* . . .

1
The Happy Family

Even if the sun is too hot, people don't usually ask you to drive your vehicle into their lounge-room unless they know you. At least, not without saying hello first. But after seeing the heavy motor bike leaning against the wardrobe, it didn't seem so very unusual when this happened to me. A man was sitting on a bed covered with tools, working on a truck, and a girl of about fifteen sat on a bullock-hide chair playing a guitar. A white-haired woman swayed back and forth on a rocking-chair, knitting. This could be seen at a glance, as the house had no walls and the floor was the same as the surrounding desert, except for the spinifex. This had been scraped off and heaped on the wire netting roof, which was held up by a series of black oak posts with stock-whips and bridles hanging from nails in them. Before I could switch off the engine of my Land Rover, another woman, who had been attending to a baby in a box on a petrol drum in the sitting-room, hurried over to the set of sliprails between the road and the house. Pulling the sliprails back she beckoned to me to come in out of the sun, Land Rover and all. After steering carefully past a chest of drawers, I stopped short of a kerosene refrigerator. Before I could give any indication as to who I was, or the reason for and possible duration of my visit, they told me where my place was to be at the table and where I would be sleeping.

I had really only just dropped in after completing a reconnaissance survey for the first 160 kilometres of my new project — a road access across the geographical centre of Australia, from the Alice Springs road near the South Australian border to Carnegie cattle station 1450 kilometres away to the west.

Before I had time to explain, a girl of about eighteen with a branding iron in her hand appeared from behind the stove, and announced that they now had one black snake fewer for grandma to frighten away when she went to bed. Grandma smiled from her rocking-chair. She apparently slept in the screened-off section of the house done out in hessian. She told me she often found snakes coiled up on her bed in the cool, but it was quite all right as they went away when she rattled a treacle tin full of stones that she kept especially for this purpose. Her bed was made of flour bags stretched between log rails.

The man working on the truck in the bedroom must have decided he'd done enough mechanical work for a while, and he dropped the grease gun on his bed. I was about to tell him I came from the Rocket Range, and that he would soon be seeing some activity around his station, when he asked in a loud voice who was game enough to go for a ride with him on his motor·bike. The guitar and branding iron were immediately discarded, and Miss Guitar, leaving the pillion seat to Miss Branding Iron, took her usual place on the headlight. The man had the machine revved to full throttle and took off with a cowboy's 'Yippeee!' travelling at 30 kilometres an hour before he had passed the sink. They were doing sixty as they roared past a dressing table, with their hats, held by thongs around their necks, flying behind. After they had disappeared from sight over a sand ridge alongside the house, Grandma merely looked up and said, 'Noisy things, ain't they?'

It seemed as if I'd lived there for years, the way this family carried on. Paying me no attention at all, they made me feel more welcome than if they had laid out a red carpet.

The lady of the sliprails handed me a curved skinning knife and, pointing to a shade house, said we wanted some steak for dinner, and I'd find a bullock's leg hanging there. It was almost midday. Everyone is expected to be able to do anything in the bush, the theory being that if you don't know how, right now is the best time to learn. As I came back with the meat, it struck me that no one had even said 'Hello' yet.

The motor bike, coming in from the opposite direction, careered through the house without the slightest hesitation. As it raced past Grandma, who was sitting forward in her rocking-chair, knitting, I noticed the offside handlebar hook in her wool. When the dust cleared she was smiling, holding the two empty knitting needles, as a single strand of wool travelled at 65 kilometres an hour over the sandhill. She simply said, 'Fast, ain't they? Now what was I knitting?'

On the next circuit the riders were flagged down with a tea towel, and the simmering motor bike was returned to the wardrobe.

Bush people are always glad to see strangers, and they take it for granted you're okay or you wouldn't be out there in the first place. So during dinner I wasn't surprised when they asked casually how many weeks I would be staying with them. I could now, at last, tell them I was from Woomera, and what I was doing here. On hearing of my road project, the man asked if I was the feller he'd heard tell about, making a few new roads hereabouts, and did I have a bulldozer? He could sure use a turkey's nest dam by the mill.

I told him we did have a bulldozer, and a grader too, with a small party of five men, three trucks, and my Land Rover. I asked if they would sell us beef from time to time, because theirs was the last homestead we'd be seeing for the entire distance. We planned to establish a new weather recording station halfway over at the Rawlinson Ranges, and for this a construction party would soon be along who would be glad of any meat and water these people could let them have.

Their curiosity mounted as to the purpose of this new road, and I explained that an Australia-wide survey was under way for measuring the earth's surface; this was needed to help any large-scale project for development. When the area came anywhere near the country covered by our testing range, we gave all our assistance with access roads and a reconnaissance of the millions of square kilometres involved. Next would come the trig survey, as we called it, resulting in accurate maps. As this country was mostly unexplored, apart from an occasional expedition in the 1800s, the place was as yet unmapped.

When I told them how I would find my way, they seemed somewhat doubtful. They pointed out that it wouldn't be much good looking at the stars, because they kept moving all the time.

The Happy Family were, by now, firing questions, getting more excited at the prospect of all this activity, and planning with a gleam in their eye how the new road would help them muster cattle, for a few kilometres out anyway.

The man, at this stage, reached for a rifle hanging from a nail in a post at the end of the table, and shot a wedge-tailed eagle that had come to rest on the shade house containing the bullock's leg.

A further diversion started as the younger girl decided playfully to flick a spoonful of water across the table at her sister, who retaliated with a cupful. Quickly hanging up his rifle, the man joined in by tipping a jugful over them both; the woman, by this time, had brought a dish of water which she proceeded to empty over him. The originator now filled a bucket and, struggling over with it, poured the water on her mother. In no time water was cascading from the table, converting the floor into a lake, and everyone was rapidly being soaked.

I sat in my Rover watching this amazing family through the windscreen while they filled anything capable of holding water and saturated each other. It would evidently save washing up after dinner, which I assumed to be over. Then, as suddenly as it had started, the fight was finished, most of the things having been washed off the table. I thought that here was one of the few households where you could get bogged driving from the lounge to the kitchen by way of the dining-room.

Throughout all this Grandma was clapping and barracking, and now she called me over to ask if I could post a letter for her in the next month or so. I said I'd be glad to, and gave her an envelope she'd asked for. She then wondered if I had a piece of paper that she could write the letter on, so I gave her a pad. I heard her muttering, loud enough for me to hear, that if she had a pencil she could get started, so I handed her one from my bag. After a while she held the letter up proudly and remarked that it would be finished if only she had one of 'them stamps' to put on it. Having already anticipated her, and determined to be helpful to the bitter end, I said she would make me very pleased if she would take off my hands this one I happened to have. Before putting the finished product safely away, I was inquisitive enough to notice the real bush classic she had written as an address:

Master Tommy,
Care of his father,
Northern Territory

As long as they knew his father, I'm sure Master Tommy would receive his letter, through the efficient postal service. And, knowing the outback and its people, I'm sure that this was very likely the only information required for its safe delivery.

The family were now ready for more talk of this latest excitement coming their way. My camp consisted of a small group I'd named, originally as a joke, 'The Gunbarrel Road Construction Party,' because whenever

possible we liked to make our roads straight. It didn't matter that when we got into the sandhills a more suitable name might have been 'The Corkscrew Road Construction Party.'

I mentioned we'd be skirting the little-known Gibson Desert west of the range system 1000 kilometres from Alice Springs, and our supplies would have to be brought by our own truck from the nearest place — a return trip of well over 1600 kilometres. My present camp was 160 kilometres away, and I usually went on ahead to make a survey of the route. When finished, this road would be the only one linking east to west across that part of Central Australia.

An Aboriginal came to the homestead at this point, with a badly swollen, obviously poisoned finger, to ask in broken English for help. Before deciding on a method of treatment, we inquired if it hurt him very much. His reply was typical of the outlook the Australian Aboriginal usually has about such things: 'Him all right, but he keeps on faintin' all the time.' After a long course of hot water bathing and some blood-poisoning pills from my kit, with advice to return for more pills from time to time, he went back to his camp, only to lance it himself with a sharp mulga stick. The Aborigines, who make ideal patients, seem to be able to do things like this, which might have a much more serious effect on a white man. A little Aboriginal girl once came to me with a poisoned thumb, and I was forced to relieve it by giving her an injection through the base of her nail. She didn't move a muscle of her face or arm, and even smiled up at me and said. 'Sankyou,' as I put a lolly in her small hand afterwards.

The rest of the afternoon was taken up in discussing our new work — how we could help them and they could help us. They could let us have water in unlimited quantities from an unusual spring, only a few metres deep, which never dried up. That immediately explained the apparently careless use of water, during the recent water fight, in a country as noticeably dry as this. I intended to establish a large fuel dump at their station for the future use of the diesel plant as well as the trucks, and was assured this would be quite all right. When I asked about their own supply line, they told me they had a mail truck through now and then, and that it was due now. As this was Wednesday I asked if it was their usual mail day. They told me it was, and they would be expecting it at ten minutes past three. Just as I was thinking how fortunate they were to have such a reliable mail driver, to be able to quote to the minute when he would arrive, they added casually that if he didn't get here then, 'Well, he may not come till Saturday.'

As the evening drew near, with everyone brimming with expectations as to the future, out came the guitar again, accompanied this time by a large banjo, and this happiest of families made the desert come alive to the sound of cowboy songs and very professional yodelling. I was made to join in, although I tried to escape, having more knowledge of my own limitations than they.

That night black clouds gathered and it looked as if we were in for the father of all storms, but this only made them more pleased than ever. I thought their joy was due to the good cattle feed that would result from rain, but in this case it wasn't. It was because it would keep me with them longer. The bottom falls out of that country after a downpour, and a motor vehicle is useless. Grandma went off to bed in high spirits, chuckling and rattling her tin of stones.

Then someone noticed the absence of Miss Guitar. Her mother knew why she had slipped away, for she had admonished her just beforehand for an incorrect note she had played on the instrument, and had forced her to play it several times properly. The storm rumbled ominously, and there was still no reappearance of the girl, so they began to think better of letting her camp out in the sandhills, which had been their first intention.

Taking a kerosene lantern we trooped off into the night in the direction of the Aborigines' camp. They had not seen her, but immediately assumed control of the tracking operations. Cutting her tracks by lamplight, and sorting them out from all of ours, they followed them in a twisting pattern for over a kilometre through the sandhills. It was there they found her, asleep under a mulga tree, her tear-stained face buried in her arms.

Being the newcomer in the group, it happened that I was the only one to whom she would listen, so the others retraced their steps to the house with the aid of the Aborigines, leaving the lamp for me. I spoke of what wonderful people they were, and of how fortunate she was to be a member of such a pleasant family, who took such an interest in her. I told how I'd been camping in the bush for a long time and what a happy surprise it had been for me to have met them that morning. She had been living among Aboriginal children and in cattle camps all her life and had grown to be one of the truly genuine outdoor girls, found only in the Australian back country. It might have looked a little unusual anywhere else, people creeping about at dead of night rounding up their family, but when we arrived back at the homestead, no one referred to the incident again. A lesson had been learnt, and now all was well.

Relatively early, by city standards, everyone settled down at last. The few drops of rain had not increased as is so often the case with these desert storms, and I lay quietly thinking about the events of half a day in the lives of these newly discovered friends.

Suddenly, as if in answer to my feeling that there could never be a dull moment here, there came a loud explosion from the kitchen. The family were all up in a flash. I groped for my torch before the lamp could be lit, and we went looking for this latest disturbance — the cattleman armed with his rifle, grandma with her tin of stones. On a tea chest we found a newly made cake, lying among some shattered plastic that had been its container. The cake had warmed the plastic, and the few drops of cold rain that followed had placed such undue stress on it that it blew to pieces. We still refer to that as their 'Atomic Sponge.'

We went back to our well-earned attempts at sleep, and amazingly enough the remainder of the night passed without further entertainment. The morning brought clear, hot skies once more — the 'storm' had not even laid the dust.

It was time for me to be on my way back to camp. Assuring them I would soon return with the best turkey's nest dam-making equipment in the north-west, I asked which was the best way out. With the most solemn expression I'd seen since arriving, the man informed me: 'Just go straight on past the chest of drawers, turn left at the wardrobe, and leave the sink on your right. Don't make a sharp turn at the head of the bed and you can't miss it.' The tracks from the rocking-chair past the dressing table apparently led out only to a windmill.

The 160 kilometres to my camp were gone before I realised it, although the journey was all across country. I had so much to think about.

The Happy Family's station was on the line from my present starting point, but could be reached at this time only by a very round-about system of existing station tracks. I therefore planned to make a direct link across, thus saving 130 kilometres return for each supply trip and all subsequent trips necessary for the following weather station construction team. Incidentally, it would open up a new and shorter way for the station people, something that is always welcome. The country in between is nearly all solid mulga scrub, as I found from my reconnaissance; this explained to me why a direct road had never been made before. It is so thick that, in a number of cases, the flat tyres I collected on the way could not be changed where they happened as, owing to the heavy scrub, it was impossible to open the Land Rover doors. Even to get out of the vehicle, I had to drive on a way.

I never dreamt, at the time, that this particular section of the road would be used for the constant coming and going of tourist coaches on their way to Ayers Rock in the cooler season. Being close to the Northern Territory-South Australian border, it proved a considerably shorter cut to our 'Rock', and tourist agencies were quick to realise it. Much later, when I was returning from farther afield, I came on one such bus that had been brought to a sudden stop when the wheel had fallen off. Tourists of all ages were camping everywhere in little tents, waiting for the repairs to be carried out, and they didn't seem over happy at the delay. One woman had a broken denture, which I offered to mend. But after that I hurried away while I was still in their good books and before they found out I had anything to do with making the road.

When I returned to my camp, I found the party had the machinery serviced and were all ready to go. They asked me how the trip had gone. 'Well,' I began, 'there was this Happy Family...' Then I shrugged helplessly, giving it up almost before starting. 'You'd never believe me anyway.'

2

The Formation of the Gunbarrel Road Construction Party

Meeting near the Coober Pedy opal fields, we made the journey to our starting point together. Half the party had come from Adelaide, with the bulldozer on a huge loader, accompanied by the operator and cook; the rest of us arrived on a road we had recently made from Maralinga, near the Nullarbor Plain. This group was made up of our grader driver and his machine, a heavy equipment fitter, a handyman, and myself. We had all been preparing the bomb-testing site before this new work became necessary.

Both sections of our party had received their share of excitement before reaching our meeting place. I had put some trucks and equipment on a goods train at Woomera, and our group, as they often did, had travelled with them. On a trip such as this, meals are cooked alongside the railway line on grilling wire, which is left hanging on a mulga tree for each subsequent trip. The train's endless shunting, backing up, and banging at the sidings leave ample time to make a fire and cook a meal before reboarding. It's not unusual to be awakened at these stops by a goat noisily eating your shirt too close to your ear. And at one of these sidings I woke up just in time to see a shirt sleeve disappearing into a goat's mouth. It was here we had our unrehearsed diversion.

After we had boiled a billy and cooked some chops, a small boy of about eight wanted to sit in one of our big lorries and look at the things we had tied down to several flat-top railway carriages. Only too pleased at his interest, I took him along the train to where our equipment was supposed to be. But I couldn't even find the carriages. We ran to the other side of the train, which was now ready to go, and I couldn't believe my eyes at the scene that greeted me. All our trucks had been shunted off the main line on to the siding, and unhooked. A whistle blew as I raced along to the driver and begged him not to drive the train away until I'd seen the station master. I was told that the train, having taken on a number of water tanks, had become too heavy by law for the track. The tanks were for the people on the waterless Nullarbor Plain, so they'd decided to leave our cars behind.

I said the old hackneyed, 'But you can't do that,' to which he replied by pointing out the obvious, 'I already have,' as he waved again to the engine driver. I must have sounded convincingly urgent, however, for the station master agreed to get in touch with the train controller at Port Augusta by phone. I tried to explain the situation to the controller, but I'm sure he didn't believe me when I told him I had to make a road across Australia with this equipment. I went on to say I had arrangements made halfway to Alice Springs and these would be thrown out if they didn't hook our trucks back on the train. Before recovering from his doubt at my story, he at last arranged with the station master and engine driver, who by this time were fuming, to have the trucks recoupled.

The small boy was delighted at the havoc he'd caused as the two-hour delay gave him a longer look at our gear. We let him sit at the wheel of the largest truck as it was shunted about, and he couldn't quite understand why I was so pleased with him.

At the next siding I climbed into my Rover, on its carriage, where I had a radio transmitter installed to check on how the others were getting on with the bulldozer. No sooner had I made contact than the astounding news came over the speaker that they would be delayed a long time before reaching the meeting place. Trying to avoid a cyclist, they had crashed the whole 30 tonnes of the low loader and tractor into a hotel near Adelaide. They couldn't attempt to remove the prime mover, as it was the only thing now holding up the buiding. Meanwhile, a second loader was on its way for the transfer of the tractor, leaving the first to prop up the hotel. The driver told the manager that he wasn't really supposed to drop into hotels while on duty — it seemed that this 'drive-in' was the first in Adelaide.

As I walked back along the train to relate this latest turn of events to the others, I met the handyman, who said he wanted a few words with me. He had slowly realised just where we were going, and wanted to know if it would put our arrangements out very much if he stayed behind. He explained that he felt he was far too young to die. Although this would leave me short of a driver, I was really very pleased he had told me of his feelings at this stage instead of waiting until we reached a point of no return, so I relieved him of his job there and then and told him we would manage.

At last we reached the Nullarbor Plain, so we again unhooked the carriages, and proceeded to unload our equipment. Travelling with us were a number of men bound for the Maralinga construction camps, and as they disembarked from the train they looked around mournfully. All they saw was a flat, bare, simmering horizon which so depressed them that, mumbling something about how you could 'see an awful lot of nothing,' they tried to get straight back on the train. I overheard one say, 'Well, at least you can see when the boss is coming.'

To the clicking of every official camera in the area, we at last moved away from Maralinga on our way to meet the others. One vehicle, for want of a driver, was bolted, with its front wheels removed, to a fitting we had just welded to the rear of the grader.

The first night out it rained so heavily and unexpectedly that one member estimated he wrung 100 litres of water out of his pillow and blankets next morning. Whenever it rains, or even looks like rain, in Central Australia, the centipedes, accompanied by the scorpions, come out of hiding, and it was a very tired group which got under way that day, through lack of sleep searching for them. I found them in my boots after carrying out a routine check before putting them on.

I was beginning to think that this project could only improve with age. There's always a bright side, however, because if everything is running well, then the only change that can occur is one for the worse. In this case, all we could look forward to was a rosy future, even though at the time it was difficult to convince everyone of this.

As unbelievable as it at first appeared, we all met at the arranged place near Coober Pedy, and the Gunbarrel Road Construction Party came into being. It eventuated that the grader driver and cook stayed with me for the next eight years; the bulldozer driver's little daughter made up his mind for him after six. We had obtained the services of a new handyman, and he was to provide us with many episodes of unscheduled entertainment in the years to follow.

The one who was to be the long range supply driver had been with me off and on for nine years already in many very remote and difficult situations, so I was sure of his continued faithful services; coming originally from Ireland he had a suitable approach to any problem likely to arise. If he didn't want to go anywhere, he would use such Irishisms as, 'You can include me out.' The cook had been a former shearer's cook, and had lived in the bush all his life; he had an exceptionally calm and quiet temperament, and a good measure of bush humour in his make-up. Because of the long periods he spent alone on his machine, the grader

24

driver was always called 'Grader Garbo.' He had been operating a road grader for many years on the country roads of South Australia, and had gained valuable knowledge of the mechanical side of his job. The main heavy equipment fitter was recruited for this job because of his specialised experience in the many technical details surrounding the smooth operation and repairing of earth-moving plant. He came on loan from another department, and got us out of many holdups caused by mechanical trouble.

For those people who have a reason, as we had, for entering or passing through Aboriginal reserves, it is necessary by law to have a medical examination first. We only learnt this, however, when we were on our way, so we had to arrange it before going on. A radio call to Woomera set the organisation in motion for a doctor to be flown the 400 kilometres out to us. We were at a local station watching the cowboys breaking in some wild horses when the plane appeared and circled over the horse yards, much to the disturbance of the already quivering animals, one of which injured a rider against the rail. I told him how lucky he was that the plane had brought a doctor, but as we pulled him out quickly from under the low bottom rail, he made no effort to conceal the fact that he was entirely unconvinced.

Our dog managed to ferret out a large sand goanna during the ensuing examination, which was conducted at our camp — in a tent open at both ends. Just as the doctor adjusted his stethoscope, dog and goanna headed for the tent, the goanna leading the way at a terrific rate through the awning, between the medical officer and the unfortunate horse-breaker, with the dog a metre behind. The black bag went flying, and it looked for a while as if the trembling doctor was about to direct the receiving end of the stethoscope against himself. After the animals had gone he retrieved his bag and, shutting it with a snap, confirmed shakily that we were all fit to go anywhere, and that he would take care of the paper work on his return to Woomera. He added, as he hustled back to the plane, that he wouldn't pass himself for the job.

Now, at last, it seemed we could travel together as a complete unit to where our unusual project was to start. It was comparative civilisation on the Alice Springs road to the border. Some travellers on this road might hesitate at the use of the word civilisation, but to us it could just as well have been Broadway.

By the time we had pulled all the plant off the road to camp that night, I had managed to kill two snakes, and had them tied to a rail on the Rover for everyone to see. I noticed that no one slept on the ground after seeing them, but opened their swag rolls along the seats of the bulldozer and grader as high up as possible.

There were three trucks: one full of bulk rations, one for the transport of fuel and water and all the oils and greases needed for the machinery, and the third was intended for use as a supply line for everything. We then had two Land Rovers, one fitted out as a mobile workshop carrying oxy-welding equipment, vice, and tools, and the other I'd had especially made up as a survey wagon. To mention a few of the items on it — a theodolite and tripod with stopwatches and calculation books for astronomical fixations, a radio transceiver also capable of receiving time signals needed for star observations, axe, shovel, mechanical spares and tools, a comprehensive outfit for emergency dental work and first aid, rifle, revolver, and hair clippers. One becomes quite good at packing in the bush, whether loading a vehicle or pack camel. The modifications on this survey wagon were the result of experience gained after many years of what is known as bushbashing, or pushing a vehicle through scrub. As most of the trips lasted for five months twice a year much was learnt of the vehicle's performance, and improvements were carried out after each expedition.

I'd had the road grader since it was new, to prepare various testing sites after a survey nine years before, and it was still in use with the same party. Having graded over 6500 kilometres of our subsequent new roads, much of this several times during the construction as well as later, it could be estimated conservatively that this machine has graded about 50 000 kilometres of road. The tractor, which had bulldozed down the hotel, was one of many hired from another department for our use. This often had to be unloaded in order to pull the rest of the plant through sandy creek beds, and then reloaded on its float. A small refrigerator trailer and water-tank carrier completed the convoy, which had a 1600-kilometre trip to do before even starting on the work in hand.

We considered it more of a privilege than a job of work, to have been given the opportunity of doing something which had not as yet been attempted.

As we came to one section of the main road with heavy scrub on either side, we saw it was becoming boggy. Then around a curve, blocking the way, was one of the largest trucks I'd ever seen stuck down to its bumper bar in the mud. It was at least a metre deep, and so was its trailer with its load of a second lighter lorry. The rain we had encountered at the centipede camp must have been widespread. Where the timber is thickest, there is generally a depression any water will lodge in after rain, and the resulting intensity of growth makes it impossible to by-pass an obstruction such as this. There was not a soul in sight. So, starting the bulldozer and driving it off the float once more, we attached a logging-winch cable to the stranded mountain of a vehicle and pulled it, and its trailer, out bodily.

Once we had it moving we towed it well clear of the mud to a rise high and dry off the road, leaving it parked neatly in a stony clearing.

This left a crater in the main road, which we repaired by bulldozing in dry dirt and stones from the rise. After compacting it with the dozer and grading it smooth, this turned out to be one of the best parts of the main road, allowing our own convoy to press on as if nothing had happened. The driver of this outfit, I heard later, had seen at a glance what a hopeless plight he had got himself into, so he walked 65 kilometres to the next homestead caught their mail truck to the railway a further 160 kilometres away, and went to his boss and resigned. The owner of the transport had been surprised to see his driver arrive in a taxi, but he was even more surprised when informed of the whereabouts of the truck. 'Twelve hundred kilometres away clean out of sight in a bog.' I often wondered just what this owner must have thought when, on going to salvage his property, he found it waiting alongside the road with no sign of a bog in sight.

That night, as we settled down for the evening on an open stony plain, I thought that nothing more could possibly happen to anyone on one trip. How wrong I was! At midnight, with everything quiet and our fire flickering its last, headlights appeared on the starlit skyline. As they neared the camp, a car slowed to a stop. I was fully awake by now, and, as I was nearest the road, a man carrying a torch approached me. He told me they were tourists on their way to the Northern Territory and hadn't seen a stick of wood for a great distance where they could stop and camp. They wondered if they could boil a billy of water on our fire, which we had made with some sticks we carried with us. Telling him they were very welcome, I asked him to bring his passengers over and make use of the table and lamp. As I stirred up the fire he brought his wife and baby over. I thought as it was late they might like to camp here, so mentioned it as I handed them our tin of tea leaves. They accepted, and he set about erecting a small tent while his wife prepared their meal.

Everything went smoothly until the baby stirred, reminding them that it too was hungry. Encouraged by our friendly manner, the woman ventured to ask a question which had probably been in her mind since she first sighted our fire. Could she possibly bath her baby? Assuming they had a tub and the sort of things necessary for such an operation, I assured her we could supply water, that it wasn't too late, and that it would be a perfect opportunity. I asked if there was anything I could do to help. The baby looked pretty clean to me, but as we weren't very good judges, I just followed instructions while her husband finished preparing the tent for what was left of the night. The washing up over, I put on another billy to supply more hot water.

It seemed she didn't have a tub, as she wanted to know if we had anything that could be used. I offered her a mixing bowl, not wanting to appear at a loss, and realising it was the most presentable item among our utensils. Out of politeness, I'm sure she would have used the camp oven, but I knew nobody bathed babies in camp ovens. She seemed pleased, but when I brought it out from the ration truck it was smaller than I had imagined. In fact it didn't look quite as large as the baby. Apologising for our lack of baby-bathing equipment, and explaining that we did not need it very often, I was relieved to hear her say what a lovely dish it was, and just right. Here we were, at past midnight, in the open plains, getting a bath ready for a baby — a bird's eye view of the scene might have appeared just a little odd!

She now declared the water to be ready, after first testing it with her elbow, and asked if I would hold the infant while she prepared the bowl. Up until now I'd been trying my best, but here was something different. I must have been holding the baby like a theodolite, because she assured me it wouldn't break. Then came the actual bathing. As I feared, the baby wouldn't quite fit in the bowl, so I suggested putting one end in at a time. I held the baby while she used the cotton wool and little sticks with knobs on the ends — I was glad she carried *something* with her. We could have had a go at making even those, I supposed, as I watched, fascinated. Then it was time to end for end it, but after that it was still dry in the middle. I took the practical approach to this problem by

pointing out that it could be overcome if I were to put a bit of a bend in the baby to help it to fit. This worked half its diameter, an outside bend coping with the remainder.

Throughout all this the baby didn't murmur, but as I put it down on a coloured rug it looked up at me with an expression that clearly said, 'Thank heaven that's over.' The husband came over as his wife dusted and rolled up their child, and announced that all was ready for them to turn in. I felt relief next morning when I saw the baby still breathing and gurgling; it must have been stronger than I'd imagined. The family set off again, after an early breakfast, before everyone had got up. Our handyman, who had slept late, said he dreamt he'd heard a baby crying during the night.

We caused great excitement when at last we rolled into the homestead planned to be our starting point. The children were immediately all over everything, and watched wide-eyed the process of unloading the big bulldozer for the last time. From here it was on its own, and the float received a well-earned servicing for its return to Adelaide free of the weight on its back.

Introductions and explanations were made over afternoon tea. The station people found it hard to believe that the normally quiet atmosphere of their routine was to be changed, but at the same time they were pleased enough. It would be easier for them to reach parts of their own property now only accessible on horseback.

The next day saw the last of the float, and work was begun on the maintenance of the plant in readiness for our project. It seemed odd that, before starting even, much work of this kind was needed, and I wondered what it would be like at the finish. It was during these operations that I set out on the reconnaissance for the first section, and found the Happy Family.

On my return, and as a goodwill gesture for the help we'd received, we used the bulldozer to make a truck-loading pit, and a small swimming pool in a dry creek-bed for the children. If it ever rained some water might collect in it, and the overflow from a windmill could help. They might get a swim in it one day, but as we were told it had rained an average of only 50 millimetres a year for eleven years, we were doubtful.

Our actual work on the project started the next day, bulldozing right outside the homestead, while the station owner's wife photographed the historic event with her small home-movie camera. We were to see the film later, after spending an afternoon helping to mend the projector.

The making of the first road across Central Australia had begun.

3
An Introduction to Central Australia

Until our project, there had never been any road access in the area bounded by the Nullarbor Plain in the south, the latitude of Broome and Halls Creek 1400 kilometres north, the road bisecting Australia through Alice Springs, and the longitude of 122 degrees in the vicinity of Broome, southerly to Carnegie cattle station, the most eastern and remote homestead in central Western Australia.

Due to this complete absence of roads, and of surface water, this area of more than 1630 square kilometres had only been entered by a handful of hardy explorers. In the early part of this century surveyor Canning and his party located his remarkable stock route, and later a few venturesome missionaries and stockmen settled around the fringes.

Just how iron-willed these men must have been can be realised only by someone who has had to battle with this country over a long period of time. A short trip cannot give very much indication of the underlying thoughts and feelings that surround camps and expeditions, for these don't develop until prolonged hardship has been endured. Such things as the memory of one vivid sunset, seen from a place where no white man has ever been, is enough to keep an explorer going long after all regard for personal comfort has been abandoned. It is the anticipation of discovery, possibly more than the discovery itself, that is the strong factor governing these men, and encouraging them to continue despite inhospitable surroundings.

Much has been written about the fight for survival of the Aboriginal tribes of Central Australia, but here again without personal contact with the problems involved the magnitude of their fight cannot be fully appreciated. To read of heat, hunger, and thirst while sitting in a cool house, alongside a well-stocked pantry, and within reach of a water tap that never runs dry, cannot possibly bring more than a sympathetic comment. But if the reader has experienced such things himself, he can understand how value out of all proportion can be placed on the seemingly worthless. For example, to the white man, a metre length of fencing wire, to hand at the right time and place, can assume importance in the extreme; a rusty axe head is a treasure to the Aboriginal. This general approach to everything comes to bushmen both black and white, and is in the basic characteristics of the explorer.

The country of Central Australia can be divided into four types: sand ridges covered with thick mulga scrub, sand ridges among mountain ranges, sand ridges covered with spinifex, and bare sand ridges.

Bordering the northern edge of the Nullarbor Plain are the sand ridges covered with mulga. These extend for 800 kilometres east to west without a break, and the belt is 300 kilometres wide. The ridges are parallel, often only 50 metres apart, and a single ridge can be 150 kilometres long. They average 12 metres in height, and their southern face is the steeper. Travelling from north to south is almost feasible, therefore, whereas in most instances the reverse is impossible except on foot. The mulga trees are up to 4 metres high, casting about 20 per cent shade, and are extremely old for their size, being hardy enough to survive each five-month-long scorching summer.

During a drought in the cattle country, where mulga is often found, stock can live on the herbage. Here and there are small patches, not more than about a kilometre across, of she-oak, indicating the sure presence of a limestone ground surface in that area, which in turn means higher country. This region is also relieved by occasional salt lakes, varying in size from very small to many kilometres in diameter. Very close to these, the regular pattern of the sand ridges is disturbed; they are converted into confused mountains of sand which are very often quite bare and move about with the wind. The lakes are mostly bottomless mud with a thin coating of white salt, and must be avoided at all costs. I was hopelessly bogged for a week at a time during my early contacts with them, as they look so invitingly smooth after months of pushing over sandhills and through dense mulga.

Claypans on which heavy aircraft can land without previous preparation of any kind are also to be found, and can be driven over without danger. Although they can be distinguished by their red colour, in some cases it pays to check before venturing on to them. When water is found by drilling near these claypans and salt lakes, it is invariably undrinkable

Top: Four of the original Gunbarrel Road Construction Party—Eric Graefling, Len Beadell, Doug Stoneham, and Paul Christensen—with the famous machine that covered over 50 000 kilometres as it graded their new roads. *Bottom:* The Gunbarrel boys moved their camp daily to the head of the new road during eight years of construction

and often as briny as sea water, even when struck at a depth of 15 metres. There is a perfect example of colloidal suspension of clay in any rain water which collects on their surface, and which adds another wafer-thin floor when it has evaporated, explaining the way in which these pans are originally formed. It will not clear or settle when the water is left in a container for weeks, but in an emergency a sprinkling of white ashes from a fire will make it usable. A collecting hole must be dug under the water, as it is rarely more than 25 millimetres deep, and this will fill by draining a large area. I once came upon a dry claypan after dark, and camped on it at one end. It was a clear starry night, but next morning I woke to find myself surrounded by water. I was amazed until it occurred to me that a slight breeze must have come up in the night and eased the remaining water, which was apparently still on the far end of the claypan, along to my end, which shows how exactly level these claypans are. On a salt lake, however, rain will seep in, rendering the surface more treacherous than ever. I have heard that farther east a complete camel wagon slowly went out of sight in one.

Saltbush and bluebush seem to accompany mulga as a ground herbage, while spinifex keeps nearer mallee.

This country gave me the most valuable experience for vehicle modification. It was here that, during more than five years, research for a suitable vehicle was automatically carried out in conjunction with my work. Each year new weaknesses became evident, and our ever helpful but harassed workshops at headquarters managed to cope with my latest discoveries and suggestions.

The northern edge of this most heart-breaking section of Australia is reasonably well defined. The 'sand ridge among mountain range' type takes over and the mulga gives way to a greater variety of plants. Also the intensity of both sand ridges and general foliage eases, and spinifex predominates.

Spinifex is a vegetation closely resembling darning needles, growing in spherical clumps from several centimetres to 2 metres in diameter. These spheres are separate from each other, leaving quite bare, clean, sandy patches in between. The distance between each plant varies with different types of spinifex — of which many are found — there being ample walking space between the largest clusters, whereas the smaller they are the closer they are together. It was often referred to by the early explorers as the 'Deadly trioda,' using a portion of its botanical name, as the fetlocks of horses and camels became raw and bleeding as they brushed through it. In the mid-year season long, straw-like shoots with ears of grain, like a prairie of cultivated wheat, emerge from the clusters. Stock thrives on this and horses take on a healthy glister after feeding on

One cut with the bulldozer blade on open plains was sufficient to allow the grader to follow and to widen the road to its finished width it for a period. These heads don't last long, but in a good year the growth is above eye-level; nothing can be seen beyond the bonnet of a vehicle when driving through it, and for direction total reliance must be placed on a compass. Within minutes, the husks clog radiator cores, even though a fine screen is used, and make it necessary to clean them out many times an hour. I thought I had a wonderful idea, after a particularly inconvenient day of this, but my hopes were dulled by the fitter next day when he informed me that 'blow back' fans had already been invented.

Spinifex, however green it looks, will ignite in seconds, owing to the presence in it of a resinous gum, quickly becoming a raging inferno giving off dense clouds of black smoke and intense heat. The fury in each cluster is short-lived, but it is enough to light the next one, and so on; with a wind behind it, the fire can continue on out of sight. Small lizards are always to be seen darting from clump to clump, and Aborigines secure them for food by burning off great areas to drive them out. The presence and location of a tribe are often indicated by volumes of black smoke wafting skyward, visible for great distances. The gum is separated from the spinifex by a method developed by the Aborigines, and used for moulding their spear throwers or woomera handles, or patching holes in wooden dishes. While the gum is still pliable as a knob on the woomera handles, they can insert in it a sharp chip of stone which is used as a chisel after the whole thing has hardened. Spinifex is really a blessing in disguise. It breaks springs in winter, boils radiators in summer, reduces you to one big ache at the end of a day's drive over it, and pierces your ankles as you walks through it. But without the deadly trioda, which covers all of Central Australia, we would quickly have the infinitely worse condition of a bare and desolate sandy desert, blown about at will by the equinoctial gales.

In place of the reduced quantity of mulga, this section of country has park-like regions of straight-trunked desert oaks which have their only foliage at the top, about 6 metres up, and provide full shade. The trunks, averaging 30 centimetres in diameter, have rough black bark and are, as everything has to be in this country, tough. Resembling cork, and easily cut with a pocket knife, the bark of the corkwood trees that grow in the desert-oak areas burns to a clean, fine white ash. The presence of a sugary substance among the foliage is indicated to the Aboriginal children by small ants, and they chew it as a sweet. Bloodwoods add to the variety, and these heal quickly when chopped, with the bleeding and hardening of the red gum that oozes out. Then come what are possibly the most beautiful of all the gums, the well-known ghost gums — a dream come true for the artist or the colour photographer. In some seasons of the year they produce a snow-white, chalk-like powder, which leaves on the smooth

34

bark a thin film covering even the smallest branch. This will come off to the touch, and the contrast with the healthy bright green of the leaves is then shown at its striking best. As well as in creek beds, they flourish in the most unlikely places, such as high on a steep, rocky slope of a mountain.

This country sounds like a paradise when the wild peach trees are then described with their fruit, which can be made into a pie or eaten as it is. But don't be misled. The fruit of the quandong trees, as they are called, is the size of a large marble with a seed, which is used in the game of checkers, almost as big. It ripens to a bright red in the late spring, and a grove of such trees looks like a cultivated orchard.

The mountain range system occupies the eastern half of this 300 kilometre wide region, and terminates abruptly with the western end of the Rawlinson Range, where the Gibson Desert takes over. Giles, who in 1874 was the first to explore the area, named the Gibson Desert after the first white man to lose his life there, and it is probably some of the most inhospitable country of the outback.

Gibson was a member of Giles' party of four, the others being Tietkens and Andrews. They were all camped at a base near a rock waterhole at the newly named Rawlinson Range, and were waiting for rain before attempting a trip farther to the west. When no change in the weather came for a long time, Giles thought he would try anyway. Against his better judgment, he left his usual mainstay of the party, Tietkens, in the camp when Gibson persuaded Giles to allow him to go instead. They got about 100 kilometres, left a small supply of water and dried horse meat in a mulga tree, and sent loose two pack horses to find their own way back to base along the tracks. After struggling on another 100 kilometres westerly, in intense heat, it became obvious, after the horse Gibson was riding collapsed from thirst, that to continue was out of the question. So they turned back, and the two desperate men spelled each other by alternately riding and walking. In a bid to speed up the return, and considering himself to be possessed of the greater endurance of the two, Giles sent Gibson riding on ahead to base, to get Tietkens to return for him. Meanwhile he endeavoured to shorten the distance on foot. Gibson was to use part of the horse meat and water left in the tree, leaving the remainder for Giles if he could reach it before help came.

My impression of this arrangement is that it was a misguided self-sacrifice on the part of Giles. He often mentions in his diary that Gibson was unreliable because of his inexperience, and in such a situation, it might be thought he would have kept this in mind and made a rescue surer for both by going himself. The task of following tracks freshly made, without becoming lost, seemed easy enough but that was the last anyone saw of Gibson. The first two horses sent back to base had wandered away from their own tracks, which is unusual for horses, but they were probably crazed with thirst. These second tracks were the ones Gibson followed, in error. Giles realised this after finally struggling to the junction of the two, on an examination of the tracks, and he knew then that help would not be coming. With the water container on his back, holding the meagre supply left after Gibson had used it, Giles now had to almost crawl the rest of the way to base if he were to survive and begin looking for Gibson. He was to do it by drawing to the utmost on his nearly spent reserves.

After the day it took for him to be able to move again, he and Tietkens went in search of Gibson. Reaching the wrong set of tracks and pursuing them, they found that he must have caught sight of a range of hills, and branched off once again towards them, thinking them to be the Rawlinsons, but in effect he would have been travelling in almost the opposite direction away from the base. Gibson, although he had the only compass left, could not have checked with it first, and, being now in the grip of panic, terror, and thirst for a certainty, had wandered to a horrible death in the sandhills. His would-be rescuers followed him to a point beyond which there would surely be no returning, and were forced back to base once more, hoping that a merciful death would quickly claim him, and so put him out of the agony they were themselves experiencing. It must have been with a heavy heart that Giles made the note in his diary that this desolate region west of the Rawlinsons was now to be known as the Gibson Desert.

As near as I can ascertain, my final location for the road we were about to make, and which now exists, passes the spot where the search for Gibson was ultimately abandoned. I had reason later to know exactly how he must have felt in his last hours of consciousness.

For want of a better name, somebody called the remainder of our area to the north the Great Sandy Desert, as it is composed in the main of the 'sand ridges covered with spinifex' type of country. This region is almost completely devoid of trees, leaving the wider valleys between the ridges quite open and making a route parallel to them comparatively easy to negotiate. But a course set across them, say to the north-north-east, would be virtually impossible with anything short of a camel or an aeroplane, as it would be fraught with thousands of sand-ridge crossings.

The climatic conditions in this country can easily be classified. From November to March it is searingly hot and dry; April, May, June, and July have ideal temperatures but it is dry; August and September are dry with seemingly never-ending winds, and it appears to be fairly dry in October. It might be a little unjust to say it is all that dry, because for some years we have had up to 50 millimetres of rain. After a cycle of about twelve years, 150 millimetres can be expected. But clear skies will be seen for most of the year. To quote one small boy's answer to an examination question, 'The climate of Central Australia in summer is such that its inhabitants have to live elsewhere.'

The unpleasantness of even a slight contact with a blanket has forced me to get up around midnight and try to cool down with a wet cloth, and even then the temperature has been over 40°C. I know I wished I were elsewhere.

In the winter month of July, on the other hand, the water in the tank taps freezes solid, and where it lies protected from the sun in deep boot tracks, white frost can be seen until mid-morning. The days, however, probably could not be improved on anywhere.

By far the most disturbing period of the whole year follows the winter, with a succession of gales, making camping out in the open most disconcerting. Our cook is obliged to hold down the billy lids and pots with rocks of varying sizes, and in some areas he carries a collection of them. Some days he only needs to use his 50-kilometre per hour model, while on others he has to struggle over to the small stove with his 90-kilometre pot-lid rocks. The winds come laden with sand or fine dust, and often our canvas awning is torn and then ripped to shreds with us perhaps still inside, holding one hand over our eyes, the other covering a mug of tea. The winds can take one completely unawares and once, while making some survey cakes, a particularly unpleasant gale hit us. Afterwards it seemed we had discovered a novel way of making double-sided sandpaper. When the gales hit during the night, we almost have to dig ourselves out next morning from the sand and dirt heaped on our beds, only to find the awning flattened with everything swept from the table and broken. We find the bread-tin lids and frying-pans by determining the direction of the wind and driving on a reverse compass bearing through the bush for anything up to a kilometre.

I once saw a duststorm coming while alone on a reconnaissance survey in an open vehicle. Whereas a piece of paper would have fallen vertically if dropped just before the storm struck, I don't think an anvil would have touched ground a moment later. I was suddenly in the midst of the most violent outback storm I had ever encountered. The sun was obliterated by a dense fog of red dirt and, as midday turned to night in the space of a minute, I pressed a towel over my face in order to breathe. After four hours I began to wonder when it was going to ease as I huddled down under the windscreen. I was still wondering the same thing two days later. Hungry and grimy, I decided that there must be easier ways of earning a living. I shall never forget the relief I experienced when the storm eventually stopped. At last I could eat something, and have a drink.

These experiences have all happened at around the same time of year, so we look forward to having September behind us, even though temperatures around 50°C are on the way. We then wish it were cold again, as do all humans, who are difficult to keep satisfied.

As a rule, rabbits are few and far between and sometimes we don't see even one for years. During very severe droughts near areas where they are

more common, however, I have seen them climb to the topmost branches of a mulga tree to eat the herbage there. At first glance, we thought we'd found a koala farm.

Although there are a few kangaroos in this country, they are not often found, and a year's work can be done without more than half a dozen being seen.

Dingo tracks cover our freshly made road each morning in most areas, but we rarely see the animal. And, although we have often noticed wild camel tracks superimposed upon tracks made by us the previous evening, we have only seen one camel in this part of the country. I had been flashing a mirror to the bulldozer driver 3 kilometres away to give him his next direction, when I casually looked behind me. A long neck protruded from a small bush, and a pair of eyes with a supercilious expression in them peered down over a long nose at me. The start I received must have shortened my life by six months. No visible body or legs; just a bush with a neck.

Before this we were not very sure of the exact construction of a camel's foot, and once, after finding fresh pad marks the size of a dinner plate over our new road made only an hour before, we decided to track down and photograph their maker. In half an hour's time the tracks seemed to be getting fainter and then they disappeared altogether, so we just had to walk back, unsuccessful. When later I studied the tracks of 'the neck,' I discovered that we'd been tracking our previous one the wrong way, and so the quarry and its pursuers had drawn farther apart every minute.

With the training they get in this country, these animals seem to be able to exist without water for considerable periods — some even indefinitely. We've found the odd kangaroo in places it has taken us weeks to reach in vehicles, and where there has only been a horizon of dry sandhills. Even knowing how kangaroos can travel great distances, we never fail to marvel that they survive.

Wedge-tailed eagles, with wingspans of 2 metres, which occasionally hover over us hoping one of us might drop, have an advantage over the earthbound, and don't draw undue comment. But the small finches have more of a task to cover the great distances to water, and the frail grey birds, 40 millimetres long, are present in their thousands at any unusual seepage. There is one bird-call very familiar throughout Central Australia, sending out the word 'is' in morse code continually. A visiting scientist from England asked me what the bird was called. Not really knowing, I told him 'the *is* bird.' I forgot the incident, but he must have been thinking about it for days because he asked me later what was the reason for its odd name. Another bird practises the tonic sol-fa for hours beginning with the high note, continuing for the next two, and finishing with the fifth. It would drive a musically minded listener to an early grave, waiting in vain to hear that fourth note.

Emu tracks are also around but, as is the case with many birds, we rarely see the emu itself. I did see one once, however, in thick scrub, after firing a flare pistol in lieu of the mirror flash on the bulldozer. It suddenly sprang up in a flurry of feathers and raced off into the bush as if pursued by demons. I went to where it had been sitting and found seven still warm eggs. Not having the heart to disturb them, I put a bend in the road especially to by-pass the nest. This is known as Emu Egg Bend, but from an inspection of the eggs next morning I could have saved myself the trouble. They were still there, but had not been revisited by the mother and were white with frost and just as cold. Another time when an emu track was clearly visible in the dried mud of a claypan, I was asked by a team from England what had made it; after telling them, the site for the first atomic tests in Australia was given the name of Emu Field.

We had better luck with another mother bird and her nest of eggs. They had all been in a small bush complete with the little bird still sitting, but when the noise of the bulldozer grew louder she became frightened and flew away. Her particular selection for a home was in a sand saddle narrow enough for only the road, so we carefully dug up the whole bush, nest and all, and replanted it halfway up the sandhill. As we passed along the road next day, we noticed, to our delight and satisfaction at our house removal system, that the mother was chirping from her nest as if nothing had happened.

At different times varieties of plagues arrive and flourish in the most desolate places. A loop worm plague was one of these, the worms coming in tens of millions and covering everything. When walking, or whatever name could be given to their progress, they resembled the Greek capital letter Omega, and showed how they received their name. They appeared in shovelfuls on the windscreen of the Rover, even after a relatively short journey of 'bush bashing,' giving me an ideal arena on which to study their characteristics. From 6 millimetres long and as thin as a pin, they increase in size to the thickness of a 25-millimetre-long nail. A cluster of four little pads at each end forms what legs they have, and while one cluster holds on to any surface, the other waves about in search of a landing ground the length of the worm distant. Then the following end attaches itself against and behind the front one, thus forcing the middle into a loop, before the first part sets out once again. They must be unable to see because they are unafraid of any obstacle placed in their path, and merely use it for their next landing ground. With one end anchored, and searching with the other, they fight each other violently if contact is made with a neighbour in a similar stance, which is frequent in their numbers, and wave about in fury striking their opponent with all the force at their command. I watched for hours in the hope of seeing two join up in a reef knot.

Another type of invasion comes in the form of hairy caterpillars, all a little over 25 millimetres long. They crawl along, head touching tail, in winding lines up to ten metres long, and it becomes obvious that only their leader has the compass. When we have taken one out of the middle and replaced it quickly with the leader, the last half of the line follows the leader as it diverges from the rest on a course of its own, refusing to have another in front of it. The front of the original line is left to mill around in confusion not knowing where to go. Again, if one is rudely removed from the middle of the column and not replaced at all, the rear portion will stop as if someone had pulled the communication cord, which is in fact the case. They leave behind them, as they march along the sand, a silken-like thread of the same material with which they ultimately build their home. This is built in the form of a pear-shaped, silver-webbed bag, hanging from a tree branch, and in it they will hibernate, all huddled up together. The bag is only 10 centimetres long by about 5 centimetres in diameter, and the whole line enters it. We used to wonder what would happen if the one in the centre sneezed. Another experiment we tried was to guide the leader around to the tail of the line to form a circle. They did not, however, go around forever in the same spot as we thought they would, because, as we discovered, the caterpillar leader has a mind of its own.

No description of the back country of Australia could ever be complete without reference to the flies. They cannot be called a plague, because plagues go away, but when millions of things come and stay, then life just gets lonely without them. Sitting in my Rover one day, plotting on a map where our latest length of road came while awaiting the arrival of the bulldozer, I suddenly realised that my personal cloud of flies, which had been with me all along, was slowly growing in intensity. As I was vaguely wondering why, a cough caused me to jump and drop the protractor. An Aboriginal had crept silently up to my window, bringing his own cloud along, and this had joined mine. It was rather hot that day so I got out of the vehicle to talk with him and also to give our flies more room. I forgot to put on my hat, but didn't miss it as I stood in the shade thrown by the double cloud of flies. I still wonder if the Aboriginal retained his original lot or departed with a mixture.

Termites, or white ants, make their presence known in a very big way for such small creatures. Wood is their favourite main course, but the great variety of their diet shows them to be the least particular of all the inhabitants of our bush. They settle down to an entrée of leather, followed by masonite and lead with canvas on the side, and as if that didn't mildly surprise their waiter, they finish up by devouring a generous helping of concrete. It appears to the layman observer that they have an extremely potent fluid which they use for systematically demolishing man-made structures, and as mortar for carrying out huge construction projects of their own. Their better-known achievements are the blocks of flats rising out of the dry ground to well over skyscraper proportions in comparison to the size of their engineers — anything up to 5 metres high and 3 metres through. The larger of these are solid enough to stop a bulldozer in its tracks, and the smaller ones will resist the attack of a heavy truck.

Another colony prefers to live in a built-up area closely resembling a collection of playing cards stuck on their ends in the sand; the 'cards' are about a metre high, a metre wide, and only a few centimetres thick. The most wonderful feature of these is the direction of the centre line passing through each one, not only all exactly parallel but placed precisely along their respective local meridians.

When seen from the east or west the settlement takes on the appearance of a continuous wall of hard clay, but the whole structure seems to vanish when viewed end on. Just how they accurately determine their meridian in the first place remains one of our unsolved mysteries. My own theory is that because the hottest period of the day is noon when the sun is north, in order to be least exposed to the sun's rays at that time the thinnest edges point that way. Had they put them at right angles the maximum blast of the sun's heat would be absorbed all day long. I wondered if only one surveyor was commissioned for the entire project, or if each magnetic anthill, as they are called, had one of its own, but this point may have been cleared up by the human experts who study them. As the hills are metres apart, the separate surveys certainly checked if the latter was the case, which is probably more likely.

Another type of dwelling evolved by these termites is in beds under the ground. To make these they start at the surface and work down, gradually solidifying the sand to an extremely compact mass the consistency of iron, and of spherical proportions a metre in diameter. These are by far our greatest worry in making a road surface in this country, as a bulldozer blade can only lift them out intact, leaving a large crater that has to be filled in with softer material. Trucks sink deeper in these spots, and make a permanent depression unless worked on again later; if, however, the ant-bed is left in, it withstands traffic wear for ever, and the immediate surroundings become softer and sink down instead. Along some stretches of our roads there may be great distances where the beds are only a matter of a metre apart, and the ones we have been able to smooth out have taken an enormous amount of work with a ripper. We were obliged to do the work, in these instances, for the good of the truck travelling back and forth with our supplies on a future project farther out.

A piece of three-ply wood I once left for a few days was converted into a piece of two-ply, the middle ply being completely replaced by termites. I saw another example of their work in an outback bush residence I visited. The roof seemed rather low — you had to bend over almost double in one place to move about — and I remarked to the old bushman owner how inconvenient it must be for him. He explained his serious problem to me as he sat on a box covered with a chaff bag. 'It's them white ants,' he said slowly, studying the dirt floor. 'As they chew the bottoms orf me posts, me roof gets lower and lower.'

This, then, is the country over which our little party of half a dozen has laid a network of more than 6500 kilometres of road.

The atomic project of Maralinga which had come into existence in 1954 before the start of the road-making operations had urgent need of a series of meteorological reports before the actual bomb trials could commence. This was purely for safety reasons relating to the radio-active fallout and the direction in which it would be transported by winds and upper air currents, and no atomic device was to be triggered until the weather was favourable. One main source of these readings would need to come from a geographical location uninhabited and completely isolated from any previous access.

A general area about 600 kilometres south-west of Alice Springs was decided upon and an expedition was arranged to select an exact spot, after which the first commitment for the Gunbarrel Road Construction Party would be to link it by road to the nearest established access. This was a point on the Stuart Highway between Adelaide and Alice Springs just south of the small store and cattle station homestead of Kulgera.

Before setting off across country in four-wheel-drive vehicles, an air reconnaissance was organised to fly over the Rawlinson Range area being, by plot, situated roughly in the desirable locality for the future meteorological station. A Bristol freighter was landed on a cleared spinifex plain near the north-west corner of South Australia for the use of the small ground party on the eve of their overland trip.

4
A Christmas Expedition

The aeroplane we had for the job was one that needed petrol to make it go. It was astonishing how quickly it took on the appearance of a neat pile of scrap metal when it came to the night before the reconnaissance flight and the mail truck had not arrived with the petrol for it. The plane had been able to carry only enough fuel for the trip to the airfield and back, so the success of the survey flight now depended completely on the local mailman.

After dark we sat around wondering what had gone wrong with his truck, which I knew to be composed of more number eight fencing wire than the original vehicle. It had no doors or windscreen, and the mud-guards were made from oil drums held together by wires joined over the top of the engine, a huge diesel, which, as there were no side plates, was in full view, and the enormous radiator was protected by the 15-centimetre bore casing bumper bar. Still, I had quite a respect for it; it had kept us supplied with fuel for our last 160 kilometres of road making. But now I began to wonder, as did the others. We had been very definite, when we first asked him to do the job, about when the flight was to take place, and that it was most important for petrol to be delivered to the airfield on time.

It was now decided that the aircraft would have to return in the morning, using what fuel it had left, and we would carry on overland. I felt the flight could have helped me in the following year's work, but at the same time, especially in the heat of summer, I remembered I was not a very good airman. It was, nevertheless, a disappointed lot of men who lay down to sleep after loading our old bulldozer's pilot motor and the personal belongings of my party for the return trip.

Before dawn next morning a faint sound penetrated our subconscious, and woke us; once awake we couldn't think what had caused it. Some minutes later we heard a more definite sound and our pilots wondered who could be flying another search plane so soon. Just then, in the first light of dawn, someone noticed a small spiral of dust, and into binocular view chugged a huge load of petrol drums, with the mail truck underneath.

Our great silver aircraft immediately lost its scrap-heap appearance — we had never really thought it looked ugly anyway. As the old diesel shuddered to a stop without the use of brakes, the mailman informed us he'd been bogged in the sand and had been forced to leave his trailer with the rest of the petrol. But everything was all right because an old Aboriginal driver was coming along in an escort vehicle and they would go for it as soon as they'd unloaded. I took the party on a tour of inspection of the truck, and they wondered what magic kept it going — even without a load and trailer. We were up to the wire and bore casing when the mailman apologetically pointed out that it didn't look much, 'but she's a good old bus.' He added, in case they'd missed the fact, that lately it seemed to be falling to bits.

A motor-driven pump was already at work pumping the petrol into the plane, so that, together with what there was for the return trip, we now had sufficient for the survey. The party's ultimate journey back to civilisation thus depended on the subsequent salvaging of the sand-bogged trailer, but after this episode they had confidence that in due course it would arrive. The Aboriginal escort then came into sight, carrying out his duties to the bitter end, and without a word began checking over his vehicle. Our conversation was periodically interrupted while time out was taken to read the sums on the tyre gauge he held up for inspection; the old Aboriginal would resume his pumping if the stick wasn't out far enough.

By the time all was ready for the take-off, the sun was out in all its force and the aluminium plane was like an oven. I already felt off colour as we climbed aboard, only to sit wringing wet for half an hour until something was attended to in the cockpit. After take-off I went up to the front in order to have a better vantage point, and secured the navigator's map. What seemed like hours later, but was really much less, there slowly took shape on the northern skyline a hazy blue line of hills — the Rawlinson Range, and our destination. I began to wish the mail truck had stayed bogged; I was not feeling at all steady, and my heart dropped as I thought we must be much closer. The pilot was a rather large man and beads of perspiration were rolling from his face, so I made sure I concentrated only on the map and the country. He was in high spirits, of course, because the mission was once more under way, but I'm afraid I couldn't share his elation.

Flying low for a better study of the ground, the plane was thrown about by the heat thermals and air pockets until we reached the Rawlinsons, where I gritted my teeth and tried to take more of an interest. I had to keep thinking of our future ground work. On the way I had identified a natural pass through a bad bottleneck of sandhills and rocky mountain ranges, so I made a special note of it on the map. This was the only obvious way through a difficult section halfway up, and I knew that wherever else the road went I would put it through here. It proved to be an extremely valuable piece of information and well worth the whole effort, but that was the only help the flight gave me.

After a closer look at the proposed site, involving circling and banking, shuddering and surging up and down, an extensive examination of the Rawlinson Range from the air was made probably for the first time in history. Then, as the pilot mopped his face and neck, he asked me what I'd like to see next to help in our future work. My first thought was, 'Are you kidding?' as I secured the navigator's protractor and read off a straight line bearing to the airfield. I informed him that this course would help me most in the work to come as it might keep me alive long enough to do it.

Not wishing to appear distrustful, and before giving way to delirium, I glanced furtively at the compass to ensure it read the homeward bearing. We must have landed back at the airfield because as the doors were being opened I was out of that machine before the catches were in place. I'm not sure what happened in the next hour or so, but the trailer had apparently arrived because the plane was being refuelled, and the rest of my party said something about seeing me later. I very much doubted if I'd ever see anyone again, as the large pilot once again had the plane in the air. He must have had the stamina of an ox, for I couldn't have lived through another flight. It took me four days to recover as it was.

At last there seemed nothing more to hold us up, so we set off with our four Land Rovers and six men. Usually I like to look over the straight-line course first, and put in the deviations later if that proves impracticable, and as I felt I could use this trip for the additional purpose of the future road reconnaissance, everyone was only too agreeable to follow along.

All went reasonably well for the first day, although I'd already decided a considerably more detailed survey would be necessary later owing to the rocky nature of the country. The Rovers' radiators were heating to a varying degree depending on their position in the line, the first collecting most of the spinifex husks, the second some of what were left, and so on. Mine was already in a bad way before starting, even though we had first blown out the core with our truck compressor, but as it took in the bulk of the husks it was now boiling furiously in spite of the protecting screens. That night one of the members helped by hooking out the rubbish with a length of soft copper wire, as no compressor was available.

Everyone was glad to be under way at last after all the preparations, and we were still able to laugh and joke at this stage. Thinking of the various competitions for 'Miss Australia' and 'Miss Orange Blossom Festival,' I often thought I should have a 'Mr Expedition' ribbon made, which could be presented to the one who remained the most jolly throughout. The winner would have to have greeted everyone in the party cheerfully every morning, and never have become visibly upset under stress.

Nobody had to be reminded that water was as precious as liquid gold in these areas, after someone timidly mentioned a moist-rag wash.

Next day we reached a hopelessly confused belt of sandhills surrounding a rocky jump-up named Mount Gosse after the man who first visited and named Ayers Rock. Engines were revved to screaming pitch to negotiate the saddles in the sandhills, and they boiled and spluttered in soaring temperatures of 50°C, as we travelled on tyres deflated to their limit. I was just thinking that here was one area definitely to be avoided when someone who was under a vehicle digging it out of a hummock called out that according to the air photos this was a sandy area. We couldn't help agreeing with the photos.

Soon my Rover stopped, and refused to go even after the 'atomizer' treatment. This involved squirting a small mouthful of water over strategic petrol lines in order to relieve a vapour lock when the engine would not respond to the starter; I found this would usually clear it. But now evidently something else was in trouble. It had stopped in an open area, halfway up a steep sand ridge, where the sun was unbearable and the metal parts were quite impossible to touch, even without the red-hot exhaust pipe adding to the Celsius. I found the spark plugs had been cooked as black as coal but they appeared to be still working, and after searching for several hours, the trouble was located in the condenser. It resembled a knocked over honey jar with something like melted wax coming from its end; the engine fired at last when the condenser was replaced with a spare, allowing us to have a second run at the sandhill and carry on.

Even now I was just as pleased not to have had the benefit of air support as we did on a previous expedition, which incidentally resulted in the selection of the testing ground now known as Maralinga. On that trip, an aeroplane had been made available to us to drop supplies of fresh food, mail, petrol, and water periodically to our various camps among the

Top: There were no traffic problems when the party slept on the newly made Gunbarrel Highway.
Bottom: This mountain devil had laid its eggs only ten minutes before

sandhills. They would come down in the form of 'storepedos' — cardboard cylinders with supply parachutes attached — all except the mail, which came down on a free fall.

One day we had summoned the plane to our transmitted latitude and longitude position in the difficult endless horizon of sandhill country for the purpose of dropping some necessary supplies. Talking to the air-crew by means of the radio as the plane circled overhead, we were delighted to hear that they had thought to collect some mail for us before taking off, and would make a low run to drop it out. Sure enough, as the plane came towards us at little over sandhill height, a small container with a length of white rag tied to it emerged from the cockpit and spiralled down into the scrub. It fell a hundred metres away, and as we picked it up we found the letters were rolled into a spent signal-flare cartridge-case with the rag tied through holes cut in the cardboard. I untied the white streamer and withdrew what turned out to be a single letter for me, which I opened, thinking of the marvels of modern civilisation, and of what an efficient postman we had. It was certainly an unusual way to receive mail in such a wilderness of desolate isolation. My elation, however, was shortlived. I unfolded the cold informal page and read in large, stark, and black lettering, words as inhospitable as the surrounding country:

FINAL NOTICE — TAXATION DEPARTMENT

It appears that for some reason I had not received their other letters — possibly the last three postmen had perished — and that I owed them the balance of seven shillings and four pence from my last return. It brought home to me clearly that 'crime doesn't pay,' and that you just can't escape from the long arm of the law. I had visions of being thrown straight into a debtors' prison, if I survived my present surroundings, to rot miserably on bread and water, which was at least more than I had here.

When I did eventually return to civilisation, I took the letter, complete with the cartridge case and rag, into the deputy commissioner who had signed it, put them all on his polished desk, and told him the story. I found he was quite human after all.

Dark came upon us mercifully once more, and the expert with the copper wire again operated on the radiator, as everyone else had flat tyres to mend and vehicle wounds to lick. We were making an impression on the distance now, as seen from the 'morale astrofix' I observed.

In due course, the Rawlinsons could be seen occasionally from the top of a sandhill. There was much room for improvement in the straight-line course I had been trying, but this could not be known until it had been investigated. I would have to find the 'pass' later, perhaps on the return journey. As I had been using up everyone's spare condensers, they were

Top: This red bluff scenery of the Rawlinson Range helped the author decide on the location of the Giles Meteorological Station, 6 kilometres distant. *Bottom:* The newly built Giles Meteorological Station

becoming a little scarce, but luckily the last one held out. I once tried letting out some of the bottled-up hot air from around the engine by removing the bonnet cover. This quickly proved hazardous when the flying sticks, which collected in the enclosure like a crow's nest, caught fire. At the sight of flames appearing from the engine in my line of vision, I was roused into swifter action than I felt like and, with no water to spare, shovelled sand over the whole thing at a great rate, as the distributor cap already resembled a quartpot billycan on a cooking fire. Grateful that the wiring had not been burnt beyond repair, I replaced the bonnet immediately and resigned myself once more to vapour locks.

As it happened, we followed the range too closely when it was eventually reached, and the drivers did an excellent job negotiating the steep rocky gutters coming from it. They were all still in the running for the 'Mr Expedition' ribbon, and that helped considerably.

I had been aware of a small trickle of water coming from the water pump for some time and it was becoming more of a flow at each stop, the radiator requiring an increasing quantity of water which we could barely afford. When I mentioned it that night as we mended our flat tyres, it settled the topic of conversation for the evening. It was impossible to return with our limited water supply and the heat as it was, unless something could be done. The native welfare member of the expedition came to light with a seal he had carried for a long time together with an impeller, which looked as if they belonged inside a water pump.

An impeller is a cast-iron wheel with fins attached for spinning the water and sending it on its cooling mission around the engine block. It seemed that a hydraulic press was needed to install these pieces, always provided the worn-out pump could first be taken apart. Placing the Rover in a dry creek bed alongside a large tree with a low fork in its trunk, the unusual operation to restore a water pump in the bush was attempted. There was nothing to be lost if it proved a failure, as the vehicle could not be driven back anyway, but on the other hand it just might work. I made a mental note that from now on a complete water pump would forever be part of my equipment.

This was going to take days, so the rest of the party went exploring on foot and noticed some small birds that kept to the one area. The geologist announced that he was about to perform his first official duties as hydrologist for the party by discovering water. He dug a hole in a depression of the dry creek bed frequented by the birds, and it soon became moist; then some actual water seeped into the bottom. After that each took turns at enlarging the hole until basinfuls of water were being thrown around with careless abandon. Tins were filled and, even though the water was brackish, our little expedition took on an altogether brighter complexion. This was the same creek bed in which Giles, more than eighty years earlier, had watered his twenty horses from what he had described as being 'a half-mile long lake.'

Meanwhile I had unscrewed the unserviceable pump and dismantled it as far as possible. It was obvious the old impeller was holding back the offending seal inside and was there to stay, having been forced in the factory on to the shaft by tons of effort from a press. On examining the new impeller I saw that the hole for the shaft was machined through a thick collar of cast iron, as thick as the length of a small drill I had among my tools. There was nothing else for it but to sit in the sand and start drilling holes in the collar in an effort to break it away from the shaft. I sat there with the little handdrill for nearly two days, being very careful not to break the only drill in the camp, and by then I had six holes through the thick collar across its diameter. It now remained to try a chisel and hammer in the hope that all this effort would finally break away the collar. Quite a lot depended on my success, and as the tension built up no one could watch the climax. Placing the chisel along the line of holes, I tried a tentative tap with the hammer; to my delight that was all it needed. The old impeller fell apart revealing through the rust the wornout seal.

A hydraulic press was now needed, and this is where the fork in the tree came into the proceedings. Laying the water pump shaft on the ground alongside a 7-tonne jack, which we always carry with us, with the new impeller covering the vital seal now in place alongside the shaft, and a ball hammer alongside the impeller to concentrate the pressure in the right spot at the collar, the overall length could be measured. This was marked in pencil in the tree fork, and with the razor sharp survey axe I managed to chop out my press. There was just enough lettering left on the jack to inform its user that when it was to be operated in a horizontal position the arrow had to be pointing upwards. Silently thanking the makers for their foresight, I set up all this apparatus in the press, checking the straight line of the axis with a stretched-out length of grass.

Now came the final test of applying the strain with the jack to see whether the days of effort were to give any results. Once again everyone deserted the scene as they admitted they just couldn't bear to watch, but, to my relief, with every action of the jack the new impeller began to slide into place on the shaft. The strain must have been terrific on the tree as well as on me, but we both survived and soon the water pump was as new. Eight large official departmental envelopes, cut with care and oiled, served as the gasket to reinstall the unit on to the engine, and we were mobile once again. This pump was to last for the drive back not only to civilisation but right to our workshops in Adelaide, where some unfortunate mechanic would be confronted with the puzzle of his career.

The pinpointing of the meteorological station could now continue with renewed supplies of water, and morale at a high level. A hard flat-topped rise became an obvious, unanimous choice for all concerned, only 6.5 kilometres from our Forked Tree Service Station where repairs are carried out while you wait, if you bring your own bed. The Rawlinsons would not obstruct low-flying weather balloons in windy flights, the prospect was good for the future boring programme to supply the site with water, and the interests of the Aborigines were satisfied.

We camped on the site that night, and three stones were placed one on top of another to mark the birth of the Giles Meteorological Station, appropriately named after the first white man to have been in the area. These three small stones were an insignificant start to what now appears on all new maps of Australia, and is to be seen daily on our television screens in its place among the weather information charts.

But we still had to get ourselves out of these temperatures of 50°C and cover the 250 kilometres back through the bush over a different route. Knowing that a star position would be needed for the report to the bureau, and a latitude and longitude would also help me in the new year, I set about observing the stars and finishing the calculations before lying down for the night.

We set off next morning with doubts about ever being home in time for Christmas, now only a week away. On this part of the trip I discarded the straight-line route completely in favour of the 'pass,' using the return trip to try to locate it. The replenished water tins kept up with the boiling of the radiators caused by the husks, but the water pump on my vehicle held out and helped to conserve our supplies. Thick scrub in places and spinifex kept the pace down to almost a walking speed, and flat tyres came one after the other. A constant thought was that the last spare condenser was already in use, so we tried to keep down the heat of our engine by frequent stops to replace the water that had boiled away. The expert also made greater use of his bent copper wire husk remover.

The same lion-shaped mountain first seen from the air, which I knew to be an indication of the pass, gradually became visible from sand and stone rises, so we made for it feeling very pleased at our progress. But just as we reached it and found it to be up to all our expectations, the rear axle on my vehicle snapped, causing our new-found elation to be short-lived. With the tyres deflated even more than usual, the front wheels managed to pull the vehicle along for a few more kilometres until a fresh belt of sandhills began and it became obvious it would be impossible to continue. Now we were through the pass and more than halfway back, so we decided to rob another vehicle of its axle and leave it in the bush for recovery by our road party when we reached this area later with the construction. Two of the remaining three vehicles had only one driver each, and so the occupants of the robbed Rover split up and travelled in those.

The broken stub from the axle had become jammed in the differential, and its removal presented a further problem. This was solved by using a leg from a billy tripod and a jack handle. The leg was heated in a fire, which greatly helped to raise the normal day temperature, and hammered into a flattish, curved shape on a bumper bar. It was then hacksawed off a fraction longer than the jack handle which, being tubular, was slipped over it. When this prehistoric 'instrument' was in place in the axle housing against the broken stub, and the opposite good one removed, a sharp blow with a heavy hammer was enough to dislodge the stub, firing it out of the other side like a rifle bullet. The jack handle had supported the thin, billy tripod leg in practice as well as in theory. A nasty accident was narrowly averted when someone, who was about to bend down to look in the opposite side to see how it was going, had his attention diverted a second before the steel flew past his legs. Mechanics do have other less exciting ways of coping with these situations, but we weren't feeling our brightest just then.

As we rushed on, leaving the Rover to the tender mercies of the bush but hoping to find it again some day, I somehow felt guilty of robbing a vehicle that would have been perfectly capable of making the journey back. Unfortunately, my Rover needed an overhaul for the new year's work, and carried instruments still wanted on this trip. A good opening for a speech to the transport officer at headquarters would be, I thought, a casual, 'Oh, there you are. Now there's something we feel you should know...'

It took only a day to reach the airfield, where another plane had been organised to land and take the party away. I made a wide circuit of the aircraft, trying not even to look at it as the others eagerly climbed aboard. I'm sure they were all thinking the same as I was: that it would be a long time before they would again be members of a Christmas expedition in Central Australia. Although it would be difficult to judge with such a good group, I mentally pinned the 'Mr Expedition' ribbon on the hydrologist.

Not long afterwards I learnt, with great regret, that our expert with the bent copper wire had been killed in a traffic accident. I always think of him every time I clean husks from radiator cores.

Even before the plane had taken off, the Aboriginal affairs member and I had started our 1500-kilometre overland drive south, where we arrived after all just in time for Christmas. I tried not to think about making a road to the three stones through the country we had just penetrated.

As I handed my Rover in to the workshops in Adelaide, I mentioned to the mechanics that there were a few things that probably needed looking into, including the water pump.

Thousands of kilometres of detailed survey trips were needed to plan a route for the road which would have to accommodate heavy trucks carrying building materials and men to construct the station. This would consist of a meteorological office, balloon-filling room, barracks, power house for domestic current and to operate the radio-sonde tracking radar, and a kitchen. The link would be 600 kilometres long passing through the Musgrave, Mann, and Tompkinson ranges into Western Australia, then north to the Petermann Range area and west to the site near the Rawlinson Range.

All based on astronomical fixes, the little party eventually arrived with the first brand new road ever to be made west of the Alice Springs Highway in those latitudes, at the spot which is now well known as the Giles Meteorological Station.

Then came the operation of continuing on the access a further 800 kilometres west through the waterless Gibson Desert to the nearest existing road at Carnegie cattle station homestead. This was selected by virtue of the fact it was the most easterly in that area of outback Western Australia. However, first a series of solo expeditions had to be carried out in completely unknown desert country to decide on the best route . . .

5
An Unshared Nightmare

The country over which our next 320 kilometres of road was to cross was completely unknown to me, and the time came all too quickly to begin my reconnaissance of it. For the trig survey that was to follow, hills were needed, or high ground at intervals of anything from 15 to 50 kilometres, so for a start it seemed that the road should stay with the Rawlinson Range as long as possible after leaving Giles, before swinging southward to skirt the Gibson Desert.

We had returned to Giles stocked with rations and equipment, including as many spare parts as practicable, and had begun the most important work of servicing the machinery. It was early in the year and the heat was almost unbearable, with the sun beating down from early morning to late evening at temperatures around 43°C. The temperature on the surface of the ground was in the vicinity of 65°C, not unusual for this time of the year; we wondered how plant and insect life could carry on in that inferno, especially with the complete absence of water for many months at a stretch.

Despite these conditions, however, the survey trip had still to be done, and I repacked my Land Rover in a way different from that for normal work. Any item that came under the 'might come in handy' category was discarded for those in the 'will come in handy' one. The big problem was how to carry enough petrol on one vehicle to get through. In this instance the first place where I could expect to get supplies of fuel was an Aboriginal mission, and I hoped I could borrow some there for my journey back, on the assurance that it would be returned when we had the road through.

With two 55-litre oil drums, rolled in an old bed mattress and tied with wire on to the roof, and the 160 litres the two tanks carried, I could travel nearly 500 kilometres at the rate of 18 kilometres to every 10 litres; I felt quite safe, as the mission was roughly 320 kilometres away. But on thinking it over, I realized I might be forced to make quite substantial deviations around sandhill belts and to hill-tops to scan the horizon for distant high ground in order that maximum use could be made of the road by veering near to the crests. The future trig survey stations would be occupying the highest points in the surrounding country and would have to be visited on a number of occasions by the parties who would be following later. So perhaps it would be wise to tie on two more 18-litre tins. Sheer weight was coming into consideration by now and I hadn't got past the fuel supply as yet. The centre of gravity of the vehicle, with all the weight on the specially reinforced roof, had been raised considerably, making it a hazardous operation to drive side-on to a sandhill or rocky outcrop, as is often necessary, without the risk of overturning. But it had to be carried, so up went the extra two tins.

Next came the water supply, a heavy, bulky item requiring a weighty container; I had nothing whatever to lose if I didn't carry it — apart from my life. I had arranged for the water tin, holding 70 litres, to be placed in the tray of the Rover alongside the spare fuel tank, padded around on all sides with soft felt. I hoped that this would see me through as the vehicle was already weighed down beyond its normal load with 385 litres of liquid now, including 9 litres of oil, as well as the radio transmitter, six spare tubes and two tyres, engine spares and tools, instruments and books for star fixes, and a small swag roll for sleeping. There was still the small matter of food, but in that kind of heat meals hold no attraction at all and only enough for emergencies is carried. A rifle is part of the standard load always, but it is virtually impossible to rely on it for food in this harsh, deserted country, especially in summer. Even over a lengthy period of camping there is little chance of shooting any game, for months go by without a living thing being seen.

A few tins of meat, some flour, jam, and cheese completed the load, and there was nothing left to do but set off. I planned to leave first thing in the morning.

During the night I thought about an expedition I had made in the winter when I had broken a front axle and, owing to the longer detours off-course made necessary by the loss of the four-wheel drive feature, had almost run out of petrol. The nature of the sandhills had forced me to stop in the centre of a circle 500 kilometres in diameter, surrounded by an area of thick scrub and high sandhills. I remembered how I had lived in that spot for three weeks until a party in three Land Rovers had answered my radio call for assistance. The first thing I had done, even before making the call, was to observe the stars for a latitude and longitude position to discover exactly where I was, because the battery would not have lasted long with almost no petrol left with which to recharge it. As it was during the winter the water lasted, with care, and my food position was such that when it was eaten, that was that. The operators at the receiving end of the transmission had repeated in detail my position and were fully aware that without outside help I couldn't get out of this predicament.

As the days went on into weeks, I had some misgivings about placing too much reliance on the radio; it was now too late to attempt to walk out, something that is usually most unwise to consider. Then, in the middle of a radio talk as to how their salvage arrangements were progressing, when I was not wanting to appear too eager, the battery died away. This meant leaving it overnight, and attempting to start the engine by hand cranking, and using what little fuel I had left, to try to bring enough life back into the battery to make a further radio contact. Before obliging, the engine waited until my small reserve of strength had diminished and my complete reliance on this transmitter as my only means of survival was brought home very clearly to me.

I had not seen a living thing since setting out nearly a month before, and I was becoming steadily weaker as the last of my few rations disappeared. I had been in the habit of taking short walks hoping to find something to shoot, but there was never anything, except one dingo that could barely get itself away from where I almost trod on it before even noticing it.

By this time I was confined to the small limits of my camp, with the radio in temporary order, but no more petrol left for recharging the battery should it fade again. It was then I was informed that the resuce party was on its way and, with a series of pistol flares fired at night, and after a most difficult trip, the rescuers came into sight over a sandhill. I had heard the sound of their motors and had made up the camp fire so that I could give them a cup of coffee when they got in, provided they supplied the sugar and tinned milk, and of course the coffee. Their first words were, 'Excuse us, but do you know of anyone around here who needs help?'

This trip planned for the morning was, I hoped, to be mechanically possible, but I knew the weather would be hopeless. My thoughts turned to another spare tin that could perhaps be added to the already overloaded roof of petrol containers. So, hoping it would not be a case of 'the last straw,' I got up, filled it, and tied it on. I had cause later to feel pleased with myself for making use of previous experiences.

After an early breakfast I left the camp and headed west towards the Gibson Desert, with the temperatures already showing over 40°C on the maximum and minimum thermometer screwed to the panel in the cabin of my vehicle. The windows were tightly closed as a protection against the flicking dry mulga sticks, but that increased the oven-like atmosphere of the cabin. The duralium roof, by now hot enough to fry an egg, was a persistent reminder of what was to come. After an hour the speedo indicated that I had now covered the great distance of 9.5 kilometres, not unusual in this country, but I felt no joy about it other than being pleased to be actually on my way. Coming to grips with this country and then getting on with the task is, I always find, far better than making decisions and preparations before-hand. Something forgotten could mean disaster for the trip and myself, and lying awake the night before thinking about it is considerably more disturbing than setting out next morning.

There are many small things to occupy one's mind during the early stages of such a trip: after about 50 kilometres some petrol can be transferred from the roof to the lower tanks to relieve the weight higher up — a goal to strive for. It may take all day, but it provides a better thought than the several hundred kilometres to be travelled in these conditions.

Somebody once asked me incredulously how trips like this were possible at all, and weren't the chances of getting through very remote? I had pointed to a quandong tree several hundred metres away and said that it would indeed be unlikely if I couldn't reach it. Once there, I continued, I might have a fair chance of reaching the next one, and simply by not thinking of the distance to some far off destination as a whole, it did seem a little more feasible after all. That approach, I know, has been the means of seeing me through, and helped in some situations that at first appeared to be impossible. You are reminded of the old proverb about constant dripping wearing away a stone.

By noon the heat in the closed cabin registered something well in excess of 53°C; the instrument gradations ceased at that figure, and the indicator was lying on its side in the glass bulb at the top. All thoughts of food disappeared in favour of the eternal longing for water, but I knew from experience that the longer a drink could be postponed, the better I would be. Then, as the labouring vehicle crawled its way over the hummocks of sand, the familiar feel of the steering wheel pulling to one side told me of my first flat tyre for the trip.

In a great majority of cases it is the near front tyre that runs into trouble and this had happened now — there was a large mulga stake protruding from it. To prevent the stake from penetrating the opposite wall of the tube it is wise to stop immediately, and without even looking I reached for the jack and steel jack plate and began the operation. The jack plate was needed to stop the base of the jack sinking into the sand. The sun was unbearable and the scrub offered no shade at all, but it was almost a relief to be temporarily out of that inferno of a cabin. Although the tools

58

were under the vehicle, they were soon too hot to handle, as the ground temperature was even worse than that inside the cabin.

After one of the spare wheels was in place and the tools were put away, I had to make a big effort to lift the wheel with the flat tyre on it into the vacant rack, for it had been made hot almost to the point of burning by long, slow contact with the fiery sand. Covered in spinifex dust clinging to soaking sweat, and trying to ease the burns from the tyre, I sat on my heels in the small shade cast by the Rover, and thirst finally took over. Sipping the now almost boiling water from a tin mug equally as hot, I thought how much some water from a water bag would be appreciated, but I knew I wouldn't dare use one where water must be conserved.

This was not getting me anywhere, so, relucantly climbing into the red-hot cabin, I pushed on. The petrol lines alongside the sizzling engine had been left for so long that the fuel began to boil, causing air locks in the system, and no sooner had I set off than the engine faltered, stopped, and refused to restart. The only remedy for this is to wet the lines. I had found by trial and error just where the least water would do the most good, and I sprayed water from my mouth on those parts. It seemed a most unfortunate waste of water, but without this treatment I knew only too well I would stay right where I was. Nursing a reddish burn on my chest caused by an unlucky contact with the mudguard, I tried the engine. It fired and I was on my way. Grudgingly taking a doctor's advice, I was wearing a hat on this trip, and I think I would have perished there and then without it.

The sun had shone through the windscreen all the afternoon, and as it dipped below the western horizon I decided to stop — a tyre had to be mended, and the day's course had to be plotted on an almost blank map. An astronomical position was not needed as yet, for the Rawlinsons were still in full view to the north, and as I switched off the motor I noted with satisfaction that I had covered 72 kilometres. Usually at the end of such a day, a sort of deflation reaction sets in, and only the thought of the tyre and the plotting made me get out of the cabin instead of falling asleep over the steering wheel.

As I went round to the back of the Rover to get the spare wheel, I saw a movement on the ground among the spinifex, and for the next few seconds I did a square dance with a spinifex snake as it sprang about like an animated length of steel wire. At last it darted off leaving me breathless and shakily fumbling as I unscrewed the catches on the spare wheel. The jobs finished, the call of the camp sheet was stronger than that of food, which I couldn't face anyway, so I lay down on the ground and was soon asleep. To save the petrol that would have been used up by the engine pump, four hundred and fifty pumps by hand had to be put in the tyre and this together with the day's activity made me forget to check if that snake had been accompanied by any of its relatives.

The sun was up about five next morning and with it came the flies, which could never be accused of sleeping in. I poured some precious water into the radiator, after stiffly getting to my feet and rolling the swag in the one action, siphoned what petrol I could into the tanks, and started off once more. The going was almost pleasant at this time of day despite the rough ride and before I knew it I had gone 8 kilometres. During the morning I came to the western end of the Rawlinsons and the start of the Gibson Desert, which from a rise appeared to be an area of scrub-covered sandhills, red as far as the eye could see. It was certainly a desolate-looking region shimmering with the heat mirage and I decided to turn south towards some low ranges I could barely make out from my vantage-point. A sea of sandhills was all I had observed to the south from previous rises and it looked as if the going would become more difficult from now on.

As I changed my course towards the hills my thoughts were very much with Gibson who had done the same thing, only he had mistaken these hills for the Rawlinson Range. I was within a radius of perhaps 15 kilometres of where he had ultimately lost his life, and I wondered what remains were left after the years of weathering. There should be a compass, revolver, and the metal parts of a horse's harness buried under the sand drifts, but even with the information about the tragedy extracted from Giles's diary they would be impossible to find.

I was incredibly thirsty and had not been able to eat for two days, but I did have some water and I knew where I was going or, to be more precise, knew where I was. Nearing the small rocky range after battling through a belt of very high sandhills, I found myself in a forest of dead mulga trees through which I was forced to struggle in order to reach the higher ground. From there I wanted to take a brief note of the geological formations and types of rock.

I was constantly on the lookout for fossils or any gold that might be lying around, as I climbed with prismatic compass and binoculars to the highest point. This was for the most important purpose of scanning the horizons to the west and south and of locating further high ground or hills for the trigs. I also hoped to discover some relief in the terrain. When I reached the top, I was so dry I couldn't move my lips and my heart sank as I surveyed the endless sandhills and mulga right to the skyline. But a small glimmer of hope appeared in the form of what looked like open spinifex, away to the south-west.

The glass not only magnifies the object but also the mirage, and it is never very certain that what is seen is actually there unless the scrutiny is done in the late afternoon or early morning when conditions have settled. But this, although it seemed too good to be true, did look real, so after taking a careful compass bearing, I began the climb back down to the vehicle and a drink of water with renewed strength.

This open country was still a long way off and it would take a lot of effort to reach it, but it was a goal I knew would keep me going. After trudging over the last stretch to the Rover and having a drink of the hot water, I took off my hobnailed boots and emptied out the stones and sticks that always collect around my otherwise bare feet. I noticed that the iron nails in my boots had loosened with the intense heat and the steel heels had fallen off.

I tried not to see the Rover dismally drooping down on one wheel, but at last I forced myself to replace the flat tyre. It was good that it had gone down while I was away because it'd had time to cool and was now easy to handle; the sooner I set it right, the sooner I could be on my way.

It was almost impossible to keep to the observed bearing because the sandhills were worse than ever, some requiring a dozen attempts before they were negotiated, and others defying crossing altogether. Water had to be sprayed frequently on to the fuel lines due to the added heat caused by these desperate attempts, and the engine often died just when success was in sight. It was becoming almost hopeless, but I couldn't retrace my tracks as on many of the crossings the vehicle had slid down the far side in a small avalanche of sand; and the distant goal of open spinifex kept coming to the rescue.

During one enforced spell I opened the transmitter box and found to my dismay that in the intense heat of the cabin some plastic parts on the instrument panel had withered to half their size and dropped out of their sockets. The packing around other dials had melted, causing the glass covering to drop on to the needles so that they couldn't be tuned, and I began to wonder what havoc would be found behind the instrument panel and if the transmitter could still operate at all. I decided not even to try until it was needed.

I was feeling weak from lack of food, but still unable to eat, and all my actions were now becoming automatic. If only the heat would ease for a while — but the indicator in the thermometer remained in a horizontal position. I was fully aware, however, that this was going to get worse. Another tyre went down that afternoon and, after fixing it with the second spare, the engine began missing to such an extent that it had no power left. This was not surprising, as I had been pushing it to its limit until dark each day. As I was inspecting the coughing and spluttering motor in the gloom, a shower of sparks revealed the cause as the current shorted along a cracked plug. Pleased that it was such a minor repair, after imagining much worse, I promised myself something to eat that night, but my thirst was one of almost complete dehydration and could not be quenched. I knew if I survived it would take many days for me to return to normal.

Having plotted the position of the supposed spinifex patch, and knowing I was probably well off course in the mountains of sand, I decided to observe the stars and obtain a fresh bearing, so between spells at hand pumping the tyres I set up my theodolite. I couldn't stand up to it for long at a time, but with the observing eventually done, and the tyres away in their racks ready for the next day, I was able to start the calculations involved. Although the speedo indicated I had travelled 40 kilometres that day, the astrofix showed that I had moved only 25 kilometres as the crow flies, from my last night's camp. My first meal since leaving Giles consisted of a small tin of meat and a mug of water, after which I lay down and was again quickly asleep.

When I opened my eyes next morning I saw without even having to move my head the dismal sight of a tyre that had gradually gone down overnight. I quickly shut out the sight, but when the flies and early sun forced me to get up I found it was not the dream I'd hoped and, after changing it for one mended in between star observations the night before, I resolved to make the most of the early, slightly cooler conditions. A small drink of water served as breakfast.

After filling the radiator, as usual, I began to flog the unfortunate vehicle over sandhill after sandhill, using the new direction. Every few hours, I transferred more fuel from the roof and was beginning to feel quite pleased at having brought the extra tins. The first hint of relief came that afternoon when I noticed traces of ironstone gravel showing through the sand in the depressions; this had meant open spinifex flats so many times in the past that I was now reasonably certain that what I had seen from the rocky range was in fact open country.

Considerably cheered by this, I pressed on as fast as the rough ground would allow, to discover that the country was surely becoming progressively harder. Topping the last rise I saw rolling out in front the gently undulating gravel slopes of the open spinifex. Now, as well as being able to breathe freely, I could, after deciding on one from a plot ascertained by last night's latitude and longitude, at last choose a course I could stay with. It would have taken more than the second flat tyre for the day to dampen my spirits as I looked behind me, in the heat-hazed distance, at the outline of the rocky range from where I had first seen this opening, and at the shimmering jumble of red sandhills separating us. I knew I would never see that range again from a point any closer than where I was. I also knew that this was where the road would be, if I could succeed in getting myself out in one piece, and that a great deal of detailed survey would have to be done to discover a way to reach here from Giles other than the way I had just traversed.

By the end of the afternoon I had moved 60 kilometres south, and except for the incessant heat things began to take on a brighter appearance. The open rises were separated in the depressions by narrow belts of the thickest mulga I had ever seen. For centuries the rain had washed the seeds into the valleys, and each succeeding downpour had added nourishment. The result now, as I battered my way through one after the other of these barriers, was a tangled mass of growth that gave the bodywork of the vehicle, even protected as it was, a terrific beating. Before plunging into each one, the following bare rise could be seen over the treetops, but it was always obliterated during the time it took to get through. The undergrowth often became so thick that I was forced to hack a way through, and a flat tyre resulted on an average of every second belt. After about 100 kilometres the ends of the tyre levers looked as if they had been silver plated, and I thought ruefully of how the bulldozer would make short work of this later on. Although the temperature was still around 48°C, the windows had now only to be closed when going through the scrub and this made the cabin a little more bearable.

I got my third flat tyre for the day after coming out of a hundred-metre wall of scrub, far enough away to be unable to return to the shade of a tree and not near enough to the next. This necessitated mending the whole three on a completely barren flat with no protection at all from the blistering sun. I was sure I wouldn't be able to move if I became thirstier. The sips of hot water from the tank barely helped now, but somehow I felt a measure of contentment at being clear of those treacherous sandhills.

All I'd had to eat in three days was a tin of meat, and by nightfall the violent ache across my eyes and a feverish feeling of weakness prevented me from being able to stand up unaided; after pulling up for the night I fell asleep over the steering wheel. When I woke just before midnight, the temperature had dropped to 38°C. I had some cheese and a drink of water, offered grateful thanks that all the tyres had been mended, and fell asleep again, this time on the gravel.

Travelling conditions improved next day, but the radiator was using more water than I could afford, due to the spinifex husks in the core, and I was beginning to have doubts about how long the water would last. I spent a lot of time with the bent copper wire cleaning out the radiator but it was becoming worse. The vehicle was still mobile, however, although two more plug covers had cracked and the fan belt showed deep fissures; but the vapour locks could be dealt with as long as the water lasted.

Turning on the tap that afternoon, I found to my dismay that only a small trickle came out, and soon only a few drops. This happened when the engine was in need of a water cure from a vapour lock and would not start without treatment. I had to jack up the front of the vehicle in order to send what water was left towards the tap, a thing I had often done before by driving the vehicle up a slope. By this means enough came out to cool the pipe. The position was now becoming desperate and I resolved to travel as far as possible after dark with the aid of the stars, a resolution which had soon to be broken after the Rover became entangled in a huge outcrop of rocks, forcing me to camp. It was a very troubled sleep that claimed me that night, and caused me to be up and ready well before dawn next morning.

At first light I found I had run into a region of rocky hills, and as there was no way of by-passing it I was forced to go ahead. The trip had now become an all-out effort to get out alive. I was on the last tank of petrol, with practically no water, and the heat beginning to play tricks. As the vehicle laboured over the boulders towards the water-worn gutters in the folds of the hill, I was increasingly aware of some freshly made marks in the red clay between the rocks that could have been cut by trickling water. At this stage the vehicle was straddling a narrow water-worn gully where one slip would have put one pair of wheels into the gutter for good, so I couldn't relax for a moment.

It was not until I had cleared the worst part that I was able to examine the story written in the ground of a quite recent fall of rain. Determined to follow this evidence to its conclusion, even if it meant going on foot, I managed to persuade the vehicle to clear the last of the rocks and allow me to follow the logical course of the water. It was at the extreme point of a sharp angle, where the creek bed almost doubled back on itself a quarter of a mile further on, that I eventually came upon one of the most valuable finds I had ever made. The evidence of water had been strong, but it was not until I discovered this pool of water, which was half a metre in diameter and a few centimetres deep, that I dared allow myself to grow too elated.

I had been tempted to cut across the sharp corner instead of following the creek bed around, but previous experiences again came to the rescue. I have usually found that water mills about at the bends, cutting a hole for itself, and the sharper the bend, the larger the hole. It was fortunate that I did investigate this bend, for it turned out that there was not another drop of water throughout the length of the watercourse, which ended up by spreading out on to a large flat. I felt sure that some unseen hand had guided me to this place. Stumbling into the rocks in the dead of night, and successfully negotiating that roughest of rocky descents, I had found water.

I wanted very much to photograph the area, but first I went to the pool and, dropping to my knees among the wild dog tracks that surrounded it, drank more than I knew I should in my present state. It was an unlimited supply of the coolest water I'd had in four days of near furnace heat. Only after that long, long drink did I manage to hold a camera still enough for a picture that would recapture this moment. I filled the tank with what I could scoop from the pool before shovelling the hole deeper; then I waited for the enlarged amount of water to settle, and carried on. It took dozens of trips at half a litre at a time to fill the tank, but while there was water I was determined not to leave until this was done.

The next operation was to top up the almost dry battery, then fill the radiator, wash out that grimy sticky cabin, and have my first wash since pulling out from Giles. Reluctantly I drove away from the miniature oasis, in one way hoping that I would never have to see it again. Making camp early enough to mend the flat tyres of the day and eat another tin of meat, I slept deeply and more contentedly than I had the previous night.

I awoke in a happier frame of mind that worked wonders with the question of the rapidly dwindling fuel supplies, but all the same I decided to carry out a sun observation at midday to check my position and decide on a fresh bearing to my estimated site for the mission. According to my calculations, I was within 32 kilometres of where I had guessed the mission to be, and as the sandhills were left behind and the going improving all the

time I had high hopes of making it — provided it was where I thought it was.

As I drove to the top of a rise, a small mountain range came into view with flat country covered by dense mulga scrub sweeping away to the western horizon. Making now for the foothills of the range as the only possible site for a settlement of any kind, I came upon footprints, and when I saw wheeltracks I knew this nightmare was over.

Some Aborigines ran out of the bush towards my Rover. I recognised one of them, whom I had seen at the Rawlinson Range, and it was obvious they knew me as they grabbed at familiar objects on the vehicle. It was difficult to know which of us was the more surprised and pleased. Pointing towards the bush, with their lips extended and their eyebrows raised as is their way, they told me where their mission was located. Less than a kilometre away, it consisted of several stone buildings and a tin shed.

The speedometer showed that my deviations totalled more than 160 kilometres, as I had travelled more than 480 kilometres from my camp against the 320 kilometres plotted. I also noted grimly that within sight of my destination I had just 27 litres of fuel left.

I shall never forget the yelling Aborigines who gave me an enthusiastic welcome, crowding and jostling for positions so close to the vehicle that it was impossible for me to open the door for quite some time. There were at least a hundred of them, some calling my name, which they had learnt from our friends from the Rawlinsons, and the uproar continued until several white men, with a look of amazement on their faces, pushed their way through the mob.

I managed to get out of the Rover to shake hands with them, answering their anticipated question as to where on this earth I had just come from. I realised that this was going to take some time so I began by telling them that my camp was back in Yulia Country, giving the Aboriginal name for the Rawlinsons area. My voice was almost a croak to start with, as I hadn't said anything for nearly a week. They made what was to me rather an obvious statement, after I had briefly outlined the route I had taken, that they had never before had any visitors from that direction.

When they noticed my involuntary swaying they were roused out of their immediate surprise and asked me to go in and have a meal before answering questions. Although it was my first meal for several days, I was grateful for the small service held first to give thanks for the guidance that resulted in my ultimate safe arrival, which I concluded with a silent but most sincere Amen.

The result of that reconnaissance provided sufficient knowledge of the intervening country between Giles and Warburton Aboriginal Mission to be able to negotiate it with a bulldozer and road grader for the best access to future survey marks selected on the way.

Warburton was already connected by track and road to Leonora, 750 kilometres away to the south-west, and after completing the link from Giles a route would be then open from Alice Springs to Perth south-westerly across Australia for the first time in history.

After the Gunbarrel party completed this, a further expedition was necessarily undertaken from a selected point on that road near the mission to determine the course the following surveys would take with an eye to unobstructed lines of sight between high country or hills. The direction would therefore be governed by what topography was discovered in the remaining 500 kilometres of yet another unexplored section of the southern Gibson Desert generally due west to the Carnegie homestead.

This was the first crossing ever attempted from east to west in those latitudes and on its successful breakthrough, Australia had been traversed throughout its centre also for the first time from the Alice Springs highway to the Western Australian road system, a distance of 1500 kilometres, by motor vehicle.

Returning to the Gunbarrel camp the task now waiting to begin was the construction of the last leg of the actual road itself . . .

6
All Over
Bar the Barbeque

W hen we reassembled at the camp, where the equipment was standing
in readiness with the stores of fuel and rations, we were all glad
to be resuming a job that had become of personal interest to each one of
us. The attempt to continue the road across the last 480 kilometres was
up to us.

The machinery was urged into life by the pilot motors, protesting after
their enforced rest, and started immediately on the slow trip along the
road up to the 65-kilometres turn off, while the rest of the camp equipment
was packed on to the trucks. By the morning of the following day the
heavy bulldozer had lumbered its way to our new starting point and
manoeuvred itself into position facing west, at right angles to the existing
road. Roaring, and with its blade down, it came towards my sun-flashing
mirror like a bull in a Spanish arena, leaving the start of the new road
behind it. The grader followed in hot pursuit, leaving the trucks and the
rest of the equipment waiting on the 'old' road until they had something to
drive on. We were on the job once again.

As we were fresh after the spell from this familiar routine, the kilometres
seemed to fall behind rapidly and a fortnight later we found ourselves 100
kilometres on the way. The supply truck had returned to Giles for water,
fresh rations, and more fuel, and everything was going well. On machinery
maintenance days and in the late afternoons I could go on with the detailed
surveys ahead without loss of time during the day; I was greatly helped by
the map we had made on the previous expedition.

It was one Wednesday night when the supply truck failed to arrive back at camp as scheduled that something first went wrong. We were not worried when it was not in the next morning or even that night, as it often required that amount of time to clean water from petrol lines or mend several flat tyres. But when two more days of waiting in vain had elapsed, with no radio message from the driver, I loaded my Rover with petrol and set off after tea in search of him. Being prepared for anything up to a 500-kilometre trip, I was pleasantly surprised to see a pair of headlights appear in the distance before midnight. He had at least rounded the corner to start after us along the new road, but I soon discovered that the lights were stationary. Drawing nearer I noticed the driver sitting on top of the cabin of his vehicle calmly awaiting my arrival. He had spent nearly four days there looking hopefully in our direction. His radio transmitter was out of order, preventing him from sending a signal telling of his plight. He had enough water and food on his truck to last him for months but, as he said, it just could become monotonous after he had finished reading all the labels on the tins.

The engine, he explained, had refused to move after he heard a violent knock. It was locked solid, with some broken part inside jamming the entire works. He also told me that gradually, as the fresh meat turned bad, he had thrown it well away from his bedroom in the back of the truck. The road was still new and soft, so that towing with the smaller vehicle was out of the question. We loaded my Rover with some of the rations that we were short of in the camp, and I set off once again in the early hours of the morning, having arranged to have the grader back next day to do the towing. The fitter would then diagnose the trouble, and we would be able to send a radio signal to H.Q. for the necessary replacements.

In the morning the camp received the news almost with delight as at last something had happened to break the monotony of routine. Everyone sounded as if they would have been quite disappointed had it been anything less exciting. The grader was soon on its way back with all the steel tow ropes we had, and the fitter had started planning how to cope with the new problem. He was already convinced, from the description of the trouble, that it would probably mean a whole new engine, and everyone was in high spirits except the cook, who bemoaned the loss of the fresh meat. But there were still plenty of tins.

We carried on with the road construction as though nothing had happened while the grader was away on its mission of mercy, and that night we were all back together in camp once more. Eventually the truck had to be towed for more than a month, while each section of the road received its final grade; the fitter had found the engine to be quiet irreparable in the field. One of the component parts was sticking out of the side of the block, making it look very untidy indeed. A message had been sent off at once and other signals were sent back and forth across Australia for a new engine to be sent to us as soon as possible. A local contractor with several trucks was commissioned to collect it from a government depot 1300 kilometres away and cart it up to the mission, where we would meet him and transfer the load from one truck to the other. This all sounded most satisfactory, but the contractor's vehicle broke down 1100 kilometres from us and he needed time to repair and recruit his other vehicle to finish his part of the job. Meanwhile we just continued making the road and doing our best with what rations we had, towing and using the water sparingly, while awaiting further signals on developments.

About this time the fitter started carrying a huge log on his truck; it hung from the side by wires and rope. We didn't want to appear curious, so it took a month to discover that it was to become the cross member for a bush crane we would have to devise for handling such weights as the broken engine and the new one. He was carrying it until needed, for such logs were rare in this country.

One day we decided to try our hand at mending the radio, which had failed when it was most needed and meant the loss of the fresh food. Using the good set in my Rover, we summoned the expert at H.Q. who had designed this type to be at his microphone and tell us what to do, as radio is still as much a mystery to us as it is to the Aborigines. Choosing a time when reception was best we began the operation by removing the unserviceable radio from its box. The expert had a similar model in front of him and the lengthy step-by-step procedure began. The parts were examined under instruction and replaced; we had told him how we could receive on it but not transmit. Certain valves were replaced from our box of spares, half clockwise turns given to screws and plugs, and connections checked. After each stage, a short conversation was necessary on the other microphone before proceeding.

Hours later, after what must surely have been the most unusual radio repair job ever, the whole thing was put back together and installed in its box. Switches were thrown and, after a warming-up period, word was sent over the good set that all was ready for a test. Nothing happened, of course. We could hear the expert calling in vain, but finally had to answer him on the other unit. We all concluded it was a laboratory job and too complicated to cope with in the field. That same night, however, I dreamt of the solution while I slept.

We had already checked on the tension of the microphone lead connection — it was the first thing the expert had said to do. But what if the soldered knobs inside the coupling had worn down, with the terrific vibration, to a point when they would never meet no matter how tight the collar was screwed? Leaping out of my swag immediately, I looked in the light from a torch, and sure enough there was hardly any solder left at each contact. Heating a soldering iron right then, at three in the morning, I placed a sizeable blob on the two knobs and tried the reaction of a whistle through the microphone on the meter. It jumped nearly an inch.

When the H.Q. should have started work next day we called them up and had quite a conversation with the expert before mentioning that the unserviceable set of the day before was being used. He sounded as if he thought we should come out of the bush for a spell when I told him the answer had come from a dream.

Eventually word came that the replacement engine was due at the mission soon. The fitter untied his log, as his truck was to be used to fetch the engine, while we prepared for the job. We were by now a third of the way across, and were camping almost in what small shade was being cast by my own personal mountain.

A great hole was first dug out with the bulldozer, deep enough to take the complete truck, which was then towed into it. The grader was positioned on one side of the hole, the thousand-gallon water tank trailer on the other, and the log dragged up to lie across each. This was now vertically over the engine to be removed, which was attached to the log by a chain hoist. After everything joining the engine to the truck had been unscrewed, the strain was applied and the engine came free.

Now the bulldozer had to drag the engineless truck up out of the hole, and replace it with the fitter's truck which had arrived in camp with the new unit. The broken engine was lowered on to it and the chain hoist transferred to the new engine, which had been uncrated and was ready. The dozer pulled the vehicle now carrying the useless engine up out of the steep ramp of the hole, and back came the truck without its engine. It was like playing a game of draughts. As usual, something on the replacement was different and did not quite fit, but that was overcome by the use of the oxy-cutting equipment. We could already picture the mechanics at H.Q. wondering, 'What butcher last had a go at this?' But we knew they would have done the same had they been with us.

After another period of joining up petrol lines and cables and adjusting the clutch, the finished product was dragged out of the hole by the dozer for what we hoped was the last time. I thought a bulldozer was a necessary extra to any mechanic's kit after this. The engine started once more on the supply truck and off it went for a road test drive. Our camp was again in possession of a third truck complete with a radio transceiver.

There was no time to sit and look at it, however, as it was on its way immediately to Giles for much-needed rations and fuel, taking with it the broken engine to be sent away — as far away from us as the plane that brought the rations could take it.

Things began to settle down as we pushed on with the road once again, and the kilometres fell behind now that the stores were arriving on time. With the constant moving of the camp, the cook continued his now perfected method of knocking back the dough for the bread with his elbow as he drove, with the basin balanced on a flour bag in the warmth at the rear of the engine in his cabin. It would be ready for placing in the bread tins for its final proving when he arrived at the new camp clearing. Everyone, it seemed, could sense the goal was at last within sight, and their spirits were kept up by the usual bulletins received when they repeatedly asked how far there was to go now.

There was still much hard work to be done negotiating the large salt lake areas and threading through the sandhill patches, but by far the worst part was over. The weather was becoming hotter, and the flies made meal times unpleasant, but these things were overshadowed by thoughts of the final victory now so near at hand. The old expedition map was still invaluable as was obvious from the appearance of one I had been using: it was now in separate squares of paper, having worn away at each fold. But I treated it with as much care as possible, for it contained all the information relating to the exact location of the finished road, with all its deviations and astronomically fixed points, which I had been adding after each day's construction had been done. It was to be used later to transfer the result on to a future publication of a map of that area.

So as the signal pistol flares and mirror flashes were sent, the amazing machinery kept bashing down the scrub, never failing under the watchful eye of the fitter. The plant operators finished each day covered with sweat and red dust, but still they kept on coming. The cook and cherry picker had been having a long, hard, and monotonous job, but they also knew that soon it would all be over. The supply driver and his truck now had a 1600-kilometre trip for stores, but they kept on with the job. It was here and at times such as these that the members of the party were tried and tested to the limit both physically and mentally, and it proved that the care taken when we had chosen them was indeed warranted.

We eventually reached a point where I decided to drive right on to the Carnegie homestead to survey the last 80 kilometres in the one go. We wanted to make the last part look as neat on the ground as it would on the maps, and as we had come more than 1300 kilometres, the last link seemed as small as if we were there already. So after observing a star latitude and longitude at the head of the road, and taking into account the one observed at the homestead at the end of the reconnaissance, I set off on the calculated bearing to make a detour of the last huge salt lake.

As I crossed a small stony tableland within 30 kilometres of our destination, I realised I was in the Rubberneck country again, where I soon cut our expedition wheel-tracks, which would lead to the station roads. Arriving at the homestead I found them all ready to go on a picnic, as it was Sunday, and I had to accompany them to hear all their news and tell them mine. I gathered that an Aboriginal needed two teeth out, and that my Aboriginal women patients were well. The cooling system on their meat house wanted fixing, the piebald mare had thrown another rider, and no rain had fallen. I could only tell them our road across Australia was nearly through, and a bit of a noise was coming from the gearbox of the bulldozer.

On the way to the waterhole that was to be the picnic ground, they had planned to rope and brand a few cleanskins that had been yarded. I was handed a raw-hide lasso and told to try my hand at it from the saddle of a wild-eyed horse complete with bronco gear. This gear is extra equipment for the horse to use to help it in its fight with the struggles of the mickeys after they have been lassoed. My lack of skill meant that I got only one compared to the dozen roped by the Aboriginal stockman alongside.

Leaving the station that afternoon to return to my camp for a rest, I followed my wheeltracks made that morning. With a few variations these would lead me back to the head of the road and as it would be well after dark before I could be anywhere near, I would have to follow them carefully. Without them in the dark bush there would be no hope of finding so small a target as the end of the road. It was dark when I reached the stony tableland, where I found the tracks almost completely invisible. This meant walking ahead with a torch in ever increasing arcs, while leaving the headlights switched on at the vehicle. As soon as I discovered where a stone had been moved or a piece of salt bush had been freshly broken off, I would then leave the torch alight on the ground, aim it towards the headlights, and walk back to bring the Rover up to it. Sometimes it would be a kilometre before I located the tracks, and this performance was repeated for a distance of some 15 kilometres, until I was once again in the scrub where the tracks showed clearly. It was nearly five o'clock in the morning when I eventually arrived at the camp, with certain symptoms reminding me of my cowboy work in the saddle.

But the day's events for me were not yet over, even though I was ready to drop into my swag. Bending to move a small plywood box from my bed, I became aware in the gloom that there was something on top of it, so I reached quickly for the torch. There, slowly uncoiling itself from its night's sleep, was a snake, which obviously did not like being disturbed at that late, or rather early, hour. It began moving off as I, by now fully awake, watched and gingerly checked the rest of my blankets for any of its relatives. At last I could sleep for what was left of the night.

The route now being clear of sandhills and the reconnaissance finished, we reached the station track without further incident one afternoon as it was time to stop work. I explained that we had only 15 kilometres to go to the house so we all turned in for the night with a very contented feeling.

But no sooner had we moved off to our swags than we heard the sound of an engine approaching. The astounding thing was that it was coming from the direction of the road that we had just made. We wondered who at this early stage could possibly know of the existence of the new road, and as we got up we saw the headlights of two vehicles. They turned out to contain two young men — with a vehicle each — on a holiday trip, who had been told at Giles that we should be almost over to the west with the new road by the time they caught up to us. The news of our progress had been given to Giles by the supply driver on each of his trips. As the young men were well equipped with transceiver and stores, they decided to give the new road a try.

So it was that the first outside users of our new road pulled up at our camp saying they thought they would never catch up with us. They had come almost 1400 kilometres. Their engines were running cooler with the night travelling, which explained why they were still mobile at that hour. They had also been taking notice of our aluminium sign plates on the trees and knew according to their speedo readings that they must be near to us during that night. It was an extraordinary coincidence of timing, and after a shower they decided to carry on the 15 kilometres to the homestead in the cool.

There seemed to be never a dull moment lately. Months after this, a magazine was sent to me by post, which contained an article they had written about their trip.

Two days later the bulldozer was within sight of the station buildings, including the warm meat house and the main road leading off to the west and further civilisation. We had already arranged just where to come out on to this road for the convenience of all concerned, and the thought crossed my mind that if everything were to break down suddenly we could finish off the road with a shovel.

The station occupants were all out to see the finish as we stopped the dozer with five metres to go, and to photograph what was to us an historic event. Then, with a wild cheer from the Aborigines and cowboys and a sigh of relief from us, the dozer blade closed the gap with the main road, the grader rounded the section off, and the first access road across Central Australia was through.

The lady of the house was quite pleased to know that she now had neighbours on either side of her at last, but agreed that 1400 kilometres was probably a bit too far to go to borrow a cup of sugar. The cattleman began to acquaint the surrounding stations with the news and the invitation to come along over for a barbecue to mark the event. Our machinery was placed in a prearranged spot out of the way, and the Aboriginal had his teeth extracted. After all, some of the surrounding station people lived only 500 kilometres away. We asked whether, as our life was one long barbecue, perhaps we could go inside and have ours on the table.

More than half the return journey to Adelaide 2700 kilometres away, was to be back along our own new road, and as once again the year was nearly over we prepared for the trip. Packing what equipment needed renewing, and refuelling the vehicles, we were ready to go the morning after the barbecue, which we had outside anyway, feeling that we had all been 'too long in the bush.'

It was several years later that the Western Australian survey teams brought out their latest revised maps covering the area of the road and I was shown a finished set of those published. There, sure enough, extending from map to map throughout its length in their State, was our road, with the addition of a name printed along it at intervals. With the approval of the Western Australian Government departments concerned, it was to be named after the party who had endured so much to construct it, and it now appears on maps, to be known for all time as the Gunbarrel Highway.

The establishment of a rocket range was decided upon in Britain as the second World War came to an end, and being a project at that time primarily for defence, a British Army General was directed to initiate the proceedings. Upon arrival in Australia, one of the more likely locations, he naturally contacted the Australian Army Survey Corps for help. A year had elapsed since the cessation of hostilities, but there were wartime members still in uniform awaiting discharge.

Several of these were approached and for such an exciting prospect, the discharge machinery was readily waived and this meant the first on-site work was carried out by them. Nothing whatsoever had been done up to that time, not even the location of the actual range head, as surveyors usually precede any operation of this nature to prepare the way for construction.

Everything that has been done since early 1947, such as the aerial bombing trials in the early 1950s, the atomic programme in the mid-1950s, the satellite launching rockets, and the unprecedented work of exploring and opening up 2.5 million square kilometres of the remaining unknown of Central and Western Australia, was initiated entirely by this survey work and its allied projects . . .

78

7
Before We
Called It Woomera

It would be quite justifiable to say that this whole operation stemmed from the inception of the Woomera Rocket Range and the need for large-scale surveys for the tracking instrumentation involved. That, coupled with the requirements for the atomic ranges, provided the reasons for opening up vast, untouched areas of Central and Western Australia. The first inkling that such a range was being thought of came to me in a casual remark made by the then Director of the Australian Army Survey Corps, Colonel Fitzgerald, as we leant against a mantelpiece over an old fireplace in the Melbourne Observatory buildings.

I had just driven in after accompanying a scientific expedition with a combination of experts in various fields from the CSIRO in Canberra, which had spent almost a year in the Alligator River country of the Northern Territory's Arnhem Land. I had gone along in 1946 in response to a request to the army for someone to carry out astronomical observations for the small expedition, so that their scientific discoveries and results could be recorded in map form.

While I was yarning to the Colonel about the year's work, he mentioned that the Corps had just been approached by a small team of Englishmen who had asked if it would be possible for us to send somebody over to South Australia to start 'some sort of a rocket range — er — or something.' Apparently towards the close of the second World War, it became necessary to develop and test missiles of various types. Six scientists in England were selected to look into the prospect of locating a suitable site somewhere in the British Empire large enough to conduct the trials as

the projectiles were developed. We both knew that this or any other similar undertaking in remote areas would involve an enormous number of star observations and associated calculations for pinpointing positions and bearings on the surface of the earth, and I seemed to be a reasonable sort of choice. Of course this was quite apart from the fact that members of the Corps were obtaining their discharges from the army at a great rate after service in a long war, and there weren't many left to choose from. So when I was asked if I would be willing to remain in the army for another year, it was a turning point in my life which was to govern the next quarter of a century.

The colonel went on to tell me, after I'd agreed to waive my discharge rights for another year, that when I got to Adelaide I was to contact an English general there who was in charge of the team, and find out what it was all about.

His name was General Evetts, and he was later knighted for his work and became General Sir John Evetts. British army officers of that rank were people I hadn't had very much to do with. Before leaving Melbourne

Top: The nearest 'other' dentist was 1500 kilometres away in Alice Springs, and so the author extracted one of Scotty's teeth. *Bottom:* Scotty survived to grade the new airstrip at the Giles Meteorological Station

our own director realised this and sent me off to Victoria Barracks to obtain a more conventional Australian army uniform. It replaced my shorts worn under a battle-dress jacket held together by a standard Japanese army issue belt I'd acquired in one of their camps in the jungle near Wewak in New Guinea. The fact that the original owner had no more use for it would have made it seem otherwise a waste.

The regimental sergeant-major at the barracks couldn't believe his eyes when I ambled into the guard post in my regalia, including a huge pair of hobnailed boots and army-type 'half-hose' pulled up. The expanse of bare ankle between the two had, I decided, to be covered up, which I accomplished by wrapping a canvas gaiter around each leg. I didn't have a slouch hat, the one I had been issued with having been trampled by a buffalo in Arnhem Land during the year, but the first thing the astounded R.S.M. spluttered about was the belt. I pointed out I had to wear it to hold my watch and penknife pouches, as after all I'd just got in from the bush. In the C.O.'s office, where he had hustled me quickly to prevent as many soldiers as possible from seeing me, I was shown a despatch which had been sent in advance as a warning. It read that our unit would be grateful if they could re-outfit a bushranger who would arrive on their doorstep shortly wearing a hunting knife on his belt. They added that I was in fact a soldier in the same army but any resemblance was purely coincidental.

In no time I was sitting on the C.O.'s glass-topped desk, sketching crocodiles and Aborigines with whom I had very recently been in contact, on his blotting pad, and generally giving him and the poor R.S.M., still rigidly standing to attention, a travel talk about the much-publicised scientific expedition into the remote parts of the Alligator and Wildman river country. After several hours, during which other officers had gathered to form a sizeable audience, even the R.S.M. thawed and the C.O. seemed reluctant to send me off to the quartermaster to get into a more conventional costume. He almost apologised by pointing out that it was the army after all, and the military police did have a thankless job to do.

When I returned to the observatory I was shown a second reply despatch stating that the bushranger had been taken care of and pointing out that the job of endeavouring to tame him was now up to them. A footnote from the C.O. of one of the strictest and most regimented barracks in Australia mentioned that they had a job on their hands which he secretly hoped they wouldn't accomplish. I deduced from this that he was human after all.

Armed with my new hat complete with shiny chin-strap and puggaree, a matching uniform, boots laced up in a parallel pattern as against my crisscross method, socks with feet in them, and regulation webbing belt,

Top: Two pools from a recent downpour saved the author's life on a lone expedition in the Gibson Desert. *Bottom:* Jackie Forbes had the heaviest foot on the accelerator at the Warburton Mission

I set off for Adelaide to start 'some sort of a rocket range or something.' The slight bulges in the service-dress jacket were made by the watch and penknife pouches still attached to the Japanese belt, but now worn underneath and out of sight.

I was met in Adelaide by a green-and-yellow camouflaged army jeep from Keswick Barracks and transported through the city to the South Australian counterpart of the grey rock establishment with which I had so recently been entangled in Victoria. I could feel that sense of trepidation, as though they were wondering just what to expect, having been forewarned of my arrival. This eased when they saw I was, if only temporarily, normal in outward appearance anyway. They confided they had been expecting Ned Kelly in person at least and in fact I had to reveal the bulge in my jacket to convince them it was not really made by a holstered revolver.

Major Lindsay Lockwood from our Survey Corps was already installed in the barracks to coordinate these activities and we got together immediately, much to the relief of the C.O., glad to have me off his hands. I thought that if this kept up, I would be getting a complex.

The visit to interview the British general came next, and on the way through the main streets of Adelaide in a canvas-topped army jeep given to me for the purpose, I was stopped in a line of heavy traffic by a policeman. There were cars everywhere and while waiting for him to sort out the crush, I casually glanced around behind me after hearing a peculiar noise. There, occupying the rear compartment, was the head of a horse, winkers and all, regarding me balefully with tired, big, brown eyes, as a globule of white foam dripped from the end of the bit in his mouth on to the back seat. On looking further I noticed he was still harnessed to a cart which had not stopped as soon as I did, leaving the unfortunate horse with no alternative but to thread his head through the vertical opening in the canvas hood. By then the man from the force was waving us on, but we all had to pool our resources to extricate the head while at the same time leaving the ears which had sprung upright after the squeeze, still attached to the head.

I was sure that this could only happen to me and I couldn't wait to get back to the bush where I seemed to belong.

Eventually, with the jeep parked, probably illegally, outside the general's hotel, I was waiting for him in the lobby after the receptionist had called him. The tall, ramrod-straight officer with the toothbrush moustache approached, and I made myself known to him. He was slightly built and although he wore glasses, a monocle would have looked quite in place, I thought. He started straight in with the observation that they would need quite a large area for his rocket range, 'eh what?' After I

told him I knew of 2.5 million square kilometres of virtually unexplored sandhills and spinifex country in Central and Western Australia, he exclaimed, 'By Jove, that's much more than we've got in Gloucester!' The birth of the rocket range was on the way there and then, although at the time I thought it was only going to be a one-night fireworks display akin to the Guy Fawkes exhibition, and didn't dream it would develop into a 'village' of 7000 people.

Later, after several air reconnaissance flights, an area 160 kilometres north-west of Port Augusta seemed to be roomy enough for development. Also an extensive flood in 1946, caused by a twenty-five-year cycle of torrential rains, had filled several usually dust-dry lakes to the brim. The country with a normal annual rainfall of 120 to 150 millimetres was deluged, leaving the few sheep station homesteads either on islands surrounded by horizons of rainwater, or partly submerged with the waves swirling half a metre deep around their pianos, as I was soon to find out.

The sight of these freshwater lakes complete with swans and ducks made the area look like a veritable paradise; the water could be used to start our project immediately. I was told that the distance from the nearest town, Port Augusta, would be sufficient to allow any stray, off-course missiles to be destroyed in mid-air by radio before endangering any civilisation. Also, only half a dozen stations lay between there and the Indian Ocean nearly 2400 kilometres to the north-west, and even these stopped within the first 300 kilometres. It was a perfect geographical location and an intensive survey of the area was first on the programme.

General Evetts' party consisted of a scientist, an engineer who had come to write reports of the progress to relay back to the British Government, and several other experts in the fields of rocketry and electronics.

In the jeep again, which I discovered had been left unmolested by parking inspectors, I drove back to the barracks to make a start on the stores of survey and camping equipment we would need. Other members of our first little survey party numbering about six in all were made available and the onslaught on the facilities of Keswick Barracks began. High on the list came poles and discs for the trig survey beacons as they were the first stage in laying down a triangulation network over the entire area, and I spent quite a time in the workshops to see they were made to our requirements — probably too much time for the peace of mind of the sheet-metal workers and other army tradesmen.

Vehicles needed modifying to cope with the job in hand. Racks to carry water and petrol and a truck to transport the bulk of our equipment gave the motor transport boys plenty to do as we planned what we needed. At this stage four jeeps and one 3-tonne truck comprised our whole outfit.

An extraordinary coincidence occurred on another visit to Adelaide to select some items for star observation which were not usually to be found in army stores. I stopped again in heavy traffic, heard a noise behind me, turned around, and said to no one in particular 'Here we go again.' The open back window of my jeep seemed to hold some sort of morbid fascination for horses, I thought, as I pushed one ear after the other back out through the hole, followed closely by the winkers.

Knowing just what amount of work lay ahead, we were as anxious as General Evetts and his party to get on with it. In a relatively short time we drove our five vehicles, loaded with trig poles, theodolites, and porridge, out of the gates of the barracks bound for a site as yet unknown in detail, 480 kilometres distant. We were on our way at last.

While at Port Augusta the party seemed to have some vague idea that this was to be their last sight of civilisation for some time to come, and indicated they would like to stay overnight and continue in the morning. It was late afternoon so I set out alone to drive the slow 3-tonne truck until dark, after arranging for them to follow in the four jeeps the next day. At that stage there was only one road in the direction we were going: just well-used wheel-tracks through the saltbush and mulga, which had originally been made and used in the latter part of the last century by a horse team and coach. This travelled about 300 kilometres to Kingoonya, now a siding on the main east-west railway, bringing mail and passengers to the various sheep stations on the way which were then in their early stages of development. The horse team was changed halfway at a place named Phillip Ponds which was where we were bound for, as it was quite centrally situated near the fresh lakes and only 10 kilometres from the railway siding at Pimba. The teams were watered on the way at underground concrete tanks covered by roofing iron and placed in positions where they could best be filled by the scant rainwater which would trickle down the natural folds in the topography. The roofs were also used as catchment to channel water into the tank. A horse trough and pump completed these watering stops and made it possible for the Royal Mail to get through.

After I drove the truck slowly out of Port Augusta, it was to be ten months before I saw another glimpse of a settlement. As I cleared the last few houses in a kilometre or so, the saltbush took over. It was all I would see for nearly a year. I noticed black clouds building up in the sky followed by a few spots of rain which made me glad I had decided to head off when I did. The lighter jeeps could pull each other out of bogs but the heavy army blitz truck was another story, so I endeavoured to get as far as possible before camping.

After 80 kilometres the wheeltracks passed a lonely grave with a marble headstone, surrounded by a broken fence. Here some early traveller had been laid to rest. By then the rain was pouring down so I didn't climb out to read the inscription. A couple of hundred metres beyond that, the headlights picked out a stony patch off the road on a slightly raised level and as it had been black night for several hours already, I decided to stop and camp. With the truck on the higher ground, it wouldn't sink into a bog during the rest of the night at least, and I could survey the situation in daylight to see if it were safe to drive down on to the track or if I should wait until things dried out. There was ample room under the vehicle out of the rain so I rolled out my swag between the back wheels and lay down.

The night was inky black, broken by forks of lightning. The rain poured down incessantly and kept me awake lying there on the stones for at least an hour, overtired as I was. Then around midnight. I suddenly heard an engine revving back along the road in the direction of the grave. It kept up for half an hour as though someone was trying to extract a motor car from a bog but getting in deeper with every wheel-spinning revolution of his engine. I thought about the lonely headstone, glowing white with each flash of lightning, the only witness to this episode being enacted close by at midnight, and it all sounded quite eerie. I could not do much with the lorry and had no idea, but for the sound and direction, how far away he was. Apart from sitting up and probing the blackness from under the truck for his lights, I stayed where I was, determining to help him when morning came. Eventually the sounds stopped and, as I hadn't been able to see any evidence of headlights through the rain-soaked mulga scrub, I finally went to sleep after the bruise I'd collected on my forehead, by hitting it on the steel tail-shaft when I sat up, had stopped throbbing.

Next morning the rain had gone but the country was a sea of red mud, so I began walking back between the twin rivulets of water forming in the wheeltracks in search of my as yet unseen midnight neighbour. I reached the gravestone and kept on for a kilometre but not a sign or trace of a bogged vehicle or fresh mud tracks could I see. A little further on I emerged from the mulga patch to see the old tracks stretching away across open saltbush flats but still not a suggestion of anything else.

As I plodded back in my mud-clogged boots, I relived the happenings of that night and the sure feeling I had had of finding a lone bushman in trouble within very easy walking distance of my gloomy camp. I could ask the boys when I saw them later if they had seen anything on their way to me in the jeeps, but right then, as I dragged my boots one after the other through the mud past the tombstone gleaming in the morning sunlight, I felt a sense of weirdness I wanted to explain away. When the rest of the party eventually turned up, none of them had seen a thing since leaving Port Augusta. The final answer to it all has never been found.

When I tried to press on, I discovered that although the wheeltracks were miniature creeks, they had been compacted enough over the years to be able to support my truck. Still thinking about the unexplained drama, I sloshed the tyre-slackened truck away from the scene. Every time I have driven past the spot in the succeeding quarter of a century I can't help but bring to mind the ghostly unaccountable noises by the old white tombstone in the bush. The stone is still there today as good as ever but is rarely seen by travellers owing to the subsequent relocation of the main road to Woomera, bypassing the spot several hundred metres away.

By mid-afternoon the faster jeeps had all caught up to my lumbering wagon and we pulled up for something to eat. The area was so bare that someone remarked that 'you could see a bull ant for ten miles in any direction.' According to the only map we could find of the area we had about 30 kilometres to go to reach Phillip Ponds. We planned to have the jeeps continue on to give the cook time to settle in before nightfall and get something on for tea, while I would grind on slowly behind.

We were making for an old stone outstation which had been used originally as a coach-house about seventy years before. Later it was occupied by old Joe Stanford and his family who moved about that country working for various stations as the jobs came to hand. It had been empty for the previous ten years, and we planned to use it for survey instrument storage, and for calculations and plotting of fieldwork. We would also use one room for meals at the odd times when we returned to this base from temporary survey camps in a radius of about 80 kilometres.

The outstation belonged to the Arcoona sheep station which spread for nearly 4000 square kilometres over the area to be studied for future testing of rockets. We had contacted the owners and discovered that a stone and cement rainwater tank lay underground next to the building and was still full of water from the previous year's floods. There was also a stove and from the appearance of the surrounding country, we would need to carry the wood for it quite a distance.

Eventually the pattern of the country changed, and from the crest of a hill I looked over the intervening small watercourse to see the roof of the old stone coach-house. Smoke was already coming from the chimney, indicating that Joe Fitzgerald, our first cook, was getting on with his job. The sight of it made me remember that apart from the piece of bread and jam I'd had when we all met recently, I hadn't eaten anything since leaving Port Augusta the previous afternoon.

Quite eagerly I headed the blitz down the stony incline and started out along the flat at the bottom to cover the last 300 metres to my future home. No sooner had the truck progressed a few metres along the flat, than I was shaken by the sound of a loud explosion at the rear. Just as I was thinking that it was a bit soon for the rocket trials to be taking place, the truck dropped down at the offside back corner and I knew the big tyre had collapsed. Within a couple of minutes' walk of the destination, I was forced to unload the jack and tools and begin to repair the first of a long line of mishaps which beset this project.

The boys noticed that the truck seemed a long time in closing the remaining distance to 'the Ponds' as we ever after referred to this camp, so they jumped into a jeep and came over. I could hear their laughter a hundred metres away before they reached me.

After putting up a couple of tents outside the house on the stony, quartzite saltbush flat, we felt at last that this huge programme was really under way. The date was Wednesday 12 March 1947.

Before an operation of the size of Woomera can be planned, many detailed topographical contour maps must be produced and these rely on a triangulation network covering the whole field of operation. This is known as a trig or geodetic survey and is dependent for its origin as to position on the earth's surface and its initial azimuth or direction upon astronomical observations, if it is in country which had never been visited by any accurate surveys before.

The site for the range head and future settlement was just such an area, although a triangulation had been carried out over parts of the country involved by surveyor Brooks in 1875. A new origin for the present surveys was needed and the first actual work on the site consisted of a week of star observations and their calculations after which the framework of trig survey suited to the new project could be planned.

Contour maps were needed to plan a village site, airport, interim short rocket ranges, and of course the main launching pads for the forthcoming trials. A pilotless jet airstrip, bomb ballistic and anti-aircraft ranges, and the long-range satellite vehicles launching zones were all planned with the use of this first set of topographical maps, although at the time of the first trig survey no such developments could possibly be imagined.

Periodically the British General and his small party would visit the lone survey camp to enable him to report to Britain on the progress being made, and a place name which is in common use today was decided upon to cover the entire project ...

88

8
The Project is Christened

During this time the wheels of the army had been turning and now, in May, they pointed to Lindsay Lockwood. He was to be posted to direct a school of army survey in another State and would be replaced by Wally Relf, a Survey Corps major who had been installed, the last I saw of him, in the observatory buildings in Melbourne, where I had first talked with the Colonel Director about going to start some sort of a rocket range. At that time there was no thought of Wally joining us, but now with Lindsay going, someone was needed to coordinate the proceedings so that we could concentrate full time on the actual fieldwork.

Lindsay and Wally drove up to our camp together for the former's last trip then, amid more farewells, they left for Adelaide where Wally would generally be stationed, allowing easier liaison with the Englishmen. As they disappeared over the hill in the direction of Port Augusta I didn't realise it would be fifteen years before I again set eyes on Lindsay Lockwood. I was driving from Adelaide to Melbourne at the time in pouring rain when I happened to notice a theodolite covered with a water-proof bag set up under a tree, and a pair of figures huddled under a canvas camp-sheet next to it. I stopped at the sight of the instrument and called out to ask if there was anything I could do, as there was no other vehicle in sight, when who should stand up and hurry over but Lindsay. He was soaked as he climbed into my car and explained that his own vehicle wouldn't be returning for him for several more hours. What a yarn we had sitting there out of the rain, catching up on the previous fifteen years' news. He was out of the army by then but I was still completely occupied with the project we had started together so many years before on Pearson's Hill.

That was the last time I saw him alive, because ten years later, just a quarter of a century after farewelling him on that morning at the Ponds, he died of a shocking illness in Sydney.

So it was Wally's turn to gather instructions from General Evetts and his team to pass on to me for carrying out on the site, and he would be making occasional trips up when it became necessary.

These comings and goings couldn't be allowed to interfere with our work, and no sooner had their dust subsided than I was off with the instruments across the saltbush flats to continue the vast survey programme which had so far merely scratched the surface.

Two nights later, after Lindsay's departure, I felt I just could not work on that plan another night without a spell, so I reported to my swag of blankets in the tent at a reasonably early hour and in minutes was sound asleep. Then what seemed like an instant later, but actually was just before midnight, I felt myself being shaken and an urgent voice penetrated the fog of sleep, pleading with me to wake up. There never seemed to be a dull moment here, night or day, I thought, as I sat up on my canvas sheet.

It was Ozzie, Max, and old George complete with torches, and at a glance I knew something serious was wrong. George stood to the rear holding his forearm while Ozzie made the explanations.

They had all decided to take George out for a night's spell from the kitchen to shoot rabbits, and during the process their headlights had picked up the white-reflecting eyes of a fox, which they promptly proceeded to chase. On the side mudguards of the jeeps, we'd had the workshops at Keswick Barracks install a pair of threaded bolts to take a bracket clamp for carrying emergency water and petrol cans. These were adjacent to the back seat where George had been sitting, rifle in hands, ready for a shot if and when the fox condescended to stop. A rough jolting ride it had turned out to be.

Travelling at speed over one large bump on the paddock gave their jeep a violent lurch, sending George into the air still clutching the rifle. It was quite painless until he returned heavily to his seat a split second later. Even that part had been all right but not so with the underside of his forearm which had become impaled to the depth of nearly 3 centimetres on one of the vertical, threaded bolts. It was not only a deep hole but it trailed off into a jagged gash as his arm freed itself, and now here he stood in my tent with the blood oozing down over his hand on to the ground alongside my swag.

If you have ever had the experience of waking from a deep sleep to be

immediately confronted by such a gory spectacle, I'm sure you would never forget it, as I haven't from that day to this. From George's tone I gathered he was more than concerned about it, as were we all, so after quickly washing it with warm water and bandaging it, I readily agreed to them heading off then and there to Port Augusta for a doctor's help. It was less than 200 kilometres away and they should make it before daylight, so the jeep was refuelled and off they went. At least we had done our best under the circumstances and I only hoped George could be with us again as soon as possible. I lay down again after their red tail-light became obliterated in the dust cloud behind them as they raced off, and had quite a job to return to sleep. The last thing I remembered thinking about was: 'Back to the elastic porridge.'

Actually, a few stitches and a week of proper care from Dr John Thompson, Port Augusta's only doctor at the time, were all that George needed before he could return to us, much to our delight, as we were running low on the scrambled eggs and Yorkshire pudding mixture. The next time Wally came up through the Port he collected George and delivered him safe and sound to his kitchen. I hitched our telephone-box pack to Arcoona station's party wire to Pimba and asked Michael if a sheep could be ready to collect, as we were soon to be reunited with our cook, and I was told I could have it the next morning.

I pulled up at the homestead, and while we were talking alongside the jeep, I felt a tugging at my hair from behind and turned to be confronted by a pet kangaroo which had hopped up on to the bonnet. The first thing that seemed to fascinate him was my short hair which, although a different colour from grass, could stand a nibble or two for a taste.

After tea, and the scones we referred to as survey cakes, I drove off with the killed and dressed sheep wrapped up in a canvas sheet to keep the flies at bay until we could install the pieces in our own kerosene refrigerator box. At this stage we used to collect the meat ready to break up and use straight away but later on we graduated to choosing our own from a flock in a sheep yard, and taking it home alive to combat the blowflies. I was taught to first discover the condition of the animal by feeling the stub of its cut-off tail and if this was soft and full, then the meat should be better than if it came off a sheep with a hard bony stub. The number of teeth and their respective lengths had a lot to do with meat quality and in no time we were selecting fatty-tailed, 'two tooth — rising four' wethers like veterans. It required a separate course to learn the correct way of killing and bleeding, skinning and butchering, and this became a weekly task which always seemed to fall to me.

The Department of the Army couldn't seem to leave us alone; although we were out of sight, we were certainly not out of mind, and Ivan was the next to go. His discharge from the army had fallen due and he made his exit from this country on Wally's return trip. As he climbed on to the jeep we were all sorry to see him go; the last word we heard him say as he pulled out, muttered in an undertone with bowed head, was 'remorse.'

With so many months of constant work behind us we decided to go for a picnic, and we thought we'd drive to the Andamooka opal fields, a return trip of 240 kilometres, as we'd already entertained several travellers bound for them. They had said that if ever we made the trip we must look them up, or rather down, for in those days people there lived underground in holes. Max, John, and I headed off north to call into Arcoona first where Michael showed us how to get there by a map he scratched in the mud with a stick. Andamooka certainly was a unique place with a very sparse population, none of whom could be seen above ground. Caves had been chiselled out of the slopes to form rooms and after peering in quite a few into the blackness, a contrast with the glare of the sun, we eventually located some of our friends. John eagerly opened the conversation with 'Here we are; where do we dig?'

Dick Clarke had been riding on the train to Perth and happened to get talking with the mail contractor at Pimba. Interrupting his train journey he accompanied the truck to the fields and never left. He is still there thirty years later, and a sure port of call on our hundreds of subsequent visits. Doug Adams and his mother had also passed through the Ponds and were temporarily installed in a dugout but had plans to build the first house above ground in the area. This he gradually did, with pine logs and mud packing, complete with a verandah which accommodated all the passengers I brought there for many years.

Right now we had to see down an opal hole and were soon lowered on a windlass rope 12 metres into the earth through a hole about a metre square. Being used to wide open spaces I found it a most disturbing experience, and once on the bottom I chanced to look up to see a tiny rectangle of sky. I was particularly distressed when the next one was on his way down, cutting off any hope of my escape; and a feeling almost of panic proportions swept over me. This phobia was obviously what had driven me away from cities and enclosures to live and work in country in which 'you could see a bull-ant for ten miles.' When the others were down, our interest overrode everything else, and we were soon gouging away at the walls by the beam of a carbide lamp, but of course with no results.

These fields were reputed to have been discovered by accident after a bout of horseplay at a sheep musterers' dinner camp. One station hand had tossed a quartzite gibber at a battered quartpot billy of tea owned by old Sam Brooks from Andamooka Station. His immediate reaction was to throw the stone back, but as it scored a direct hit some tea had splashed over it, washing away the dust. It revealed a glassy coating which reflected the most wonderful colours from the sun that was beating down on it. Noticing the pretty reds, greens, and yellows glistening in his hand, old Sam had decided against retaliating and put it in his saddlebag to show to people back at the main station 40 kilometres away.

This stone was identified as an opal floater or gibber which had once been submerged with its opal coating, but over countless thousands of years had become exposed to the open. Subsequent weathering had allowed it to be washed down the slope, and so by searching uphill, the strata in which it had been embedded for millions of years could be discovered. It caused great excitement at the station and a return trip had taken place immediately, successful enough to locate not only other such floaters but their original home as well.

The story went that this secret was kept for over a year, and the station hands virtually became partners in the diggings which were carried out as part of the station work. Then one day, while on a spell in Port Augusta, one of the members in the plot, under the loosening effect of what he'd been sipping, had opened his mouth too wide and the cat was out of the bag.

Within weeks, dozens of prospectors had converged on the area, borne by anything from old trucks to camels, and the opal fever grew as more and more sites were uncovered. This was early in the 1930s as far as I could gather. Although the sheer remoteness of the place in those days had prevented a boom rush, the hunt was really on and growing.

Much to our delight, we soon discovered that old Sam Brooks of the quartpot billy days was still camping in a semi-dugout on a near-by rise, so it wasn't long after we surfaced from that narrow, deep hole, that we all set off to interview him in person. A typical weather-beaten old bushman with the brightest twinkling blue eyes I'd seen came out to meet us. His quiet but jolly wife and family followed him and in return for the foregoing history straight from the horse's mouth, we filled them in on our activities, of which they were already vaguely aware.

The sun was nudging the western skyline by now, telling us it was past the time when we should begin the long return journey to our camp. As we drove away we knew we'd be back again and again but we couldn't visualise then that this extraordinary little place would mushroom into a thriving settlement including motels, garages, and the inevitable places for entertainment. We also didn't know that one of old Sam Brooks' wonderful little daughters would be cruelly murdered, or that a prize opal of record proportions and lustre would be dug from one of these holes and presented in a world-publicised ceremony to Queen Elizabeth II.

Our 'picnic' over, with a renewed effort we pressed on with the work once more. Midday dinner on the plains had become a ritual of stopping near a patch of ground covered more with saltbush and bluebush than gibbers, pulling out handfuls by the roots, and making a fire. An old bent billy with water out of the can went on next, hanging from a tripod which I'd made from heavy-gauge fencing wire, while pieces of George's bread were toasted. The tripod ensured the billy would never fall over and put out our tiny fire which was able to burn freely under it. After the toast was placed on a flat stone, a slab of cheese was anchored on top by a smearing of plum jam. Unconventional though it was, the whole effect was relished by us all, and a tin mug of weak tea and sugar finished it off. We had to use plum jam as this was the best 'carrying' jam, for when the open tin was upended as we drove over the rough surface, it would remain unspilt. Apricot jam, on the other hand, would coat the inside of the tuckerbox with a liberal thickness of the sweet gluey mass, leaving its tin quite empty. As a change from toast, about every month we heated an open tin of stew, stirring it periodically with a twig of salt-bush. This replaced the cheese and jam as a good cold weather substitute. The countryside was soon scattered with little mounds of buried, burnt-out tins alongside small piles of white saltbush ash.

One day Harold, Ozzie, and Mick went out in two jeeps to carry on with the programme of levelling. At the end of the day the three of them returned in only one vehicle. Mick reported that his vehicle had stopped for good, refusing to go at all after they had done everything possible to the dead engine. It was 50 kilometres away standing alone on the tableland with no fear of parking violations, so he and I set off with tow rope and the usual coil of fencing wire to get it. From 15 kilometres away we could see it, so we drove towards it in a dead-straight line. Soon we were looking under the bonnet before starting the long tow. A high-tension lead wire from the coil to the distributor cap looked a bit the worse for wear at a sharp bend so we pulled it off. Cutting the same length off a piece of heavy wire, we bent it to fit and merely dropped each end into the open sockets. After that, one touch of the starter button was all that was needed to hear the engine burst into life. There were no brakes and all in all, the thing mightn't have passed a test of road-worthiness but as there weren't any roads it was driven home as good as new. The same job done in the city would have been quite expensive.

A new and rather exciting requirement and one I was eager to carry out, eventually came over the telegraph. Taking into account the relative position of the Development Area and airfield site, I had to discover a point from which rockets could be fired: this was really what the whole project was about. Although the spot first decided on had to be amended later to cope with a smaller interim range which became necessary, the operation made me feel we were really getting down to it at last.

I drove 20 kilometres west to one of Brooks' old trig rises, named Ashton Hill. By inspection of our own maps which had been taking shape, I went 6.5 kilometres due north to a particularly expansive flat area and proceeded to build a rock cairn there, fixing its position on the surface by angles to our other trig stations. Then I telegraphed a signal that it was ready for perusal by the British rocket scientists who were gradually arriving in Adelaide.

This cairn, after subsequent inspection by many selected visitors, was photographed officially and I was soon to see a reproduction of it in a well-known Australian periodical. The caption read to the effect that here was the very site on which the launching pads for the firing of the future missiles from this new range would be built.

For a long time I had been trying to think of an appropriate name for this project to use on plans and communications, instead of vaguely referring to a rocket range site in Australia, but I'd constantly rejected my ideas because of their clumsiness or unsuitability. It had to be short and easy to pronounce; preferably one word to save time and space in the countless reports, and at the same time synonymous with the purpose of the project. So it was that with a visit by General Evetts and Major Wynne-Williams a name came to light. Being polite English gentlemen they had acquired a glossary of Aboriginal words and their equivalent meanings, and they indicated that it would be a nice gesture to think in these terms, as the Aborigines were the first inhabitants of the country after all.

Running their fingers down the pages the word 'spear launcher' stood out, stimulating their imagination. An excited exclamation followed, 'By Jove! These Aborigines are launching spears and we are about to be launching rockets. I say, but wouldn't it be polite to refer to this place by the name for their apparatus for a similar function, and christen it "Woomera" for the time being?' It was instantly agreed that the Aborigines would certainly be pleased with the choice, and so, temporarily, it began to appear on signals and maps until a permanent name could be found. Twenty-five years later it is still being called the Woomera Rocket Range and it seems that this name will finally stick with it.

The fact that there were no Aborigines to be seen didn't make any difference. The name was certain to become a reality after the postal department cast a metal stamp using the word as a postmark, because they are expensive and they didn't want to waste this first one.

At the time the description of a woomera was asked for and we explained it as a throwing-stick which had the effect of lengthening its user's arm by about 60 centimetres, thus increasing the leverage and force with

Top: Siesta time in the camp at the Warburton Mission. *Bottom:* An 'outpatient' taking an antidote pill for blood poisoning after the author had amputated a mangled toe

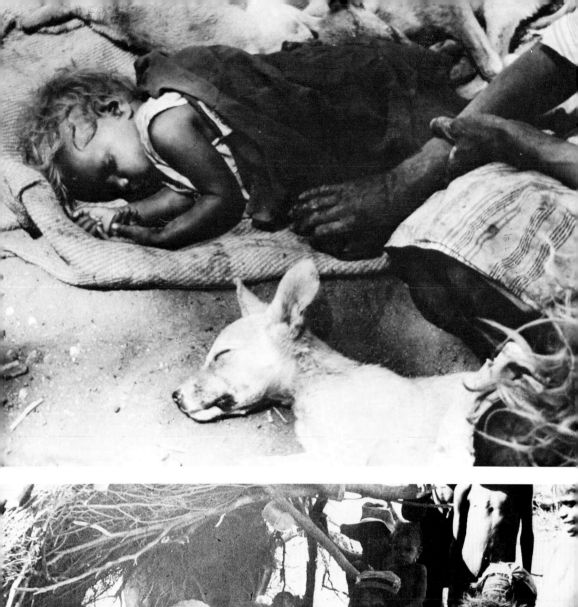

which the spear could be launched. A small barb at the rear of the stick engaged in a hole in the trailing end of the shaft, which disconnected at the instant it was ready for flight.

This title fitted in perfectly with the features we thought such a name should have, and at last Major Wynne-Williams could shorten his cables to England dealing with the progress of this enormous job of national importance. Instead of the usual 'some sort of a rocket range in Australia,' it appeared merely as 'Woomera.'

Top: Aluminium sign plates of various styles were erected in a number of ways at intervals on the new roads to provide information for future travellers. *Bottom:* Woomera, a village on the saltbush and gibber plains, grew to larger proportions than first imagined by the author

A great deal of work must necessarily be done in a gigantic development of any kind for which not much outward evidence is apparent. Years of thought and field work is undertaken by a great many people in all phases of the operation to achieve an ultimate result — and the task at Woomera was certainly no exception.

Comparatively small-scale expeditions into the unknown country had to be organised. The first 300 kilometres of the proposed centre line of fire from the launcher was inhabited by only a handful of sheep stations and their owners, managers, and hands, so the first tentative reconnaissance trips were beyond the last habitation in that north-westerly direction. To cover the first 500 kilometres with instrumentation to track the initial behaviour of the rockets after firing needed years of exploration and map making in previously untouched country, and this in turn presented great problems in supplying food, fuel, and water and necessitated camping constantly for almost a year at a time in all weathers. Medical difficulties arose occasionally as would be expected over such long terms in the bush and these had to be coped with as seemed practical at the time.

So it was that very little could be actually seen for the first two or three years of the beginnings of the rocket range in the field. A knowledge had to be gained of the vast area concerned, more detailed than ever needed before, and the surface had just been scratched after the initial twelve months had elapsed. A start had nevertheless been made on work that was to occupy a quarter of a century of the author's life . . .

98

9
The End
of the Beginning

As if to make quite sure we weren't too long without entertainment, we were involved in another exciting drama just one day after returning to Eba, while we were still working out the results of the star observations we'd taken.

I was sitting at George's kitchen table poring over open nautical almanacs and books of mathematical tables, deeply engrossed in the sums. Suddenly Bob Crombie's eight-year-old son, Barry, burst in to break the news coming over their Flying Doctor transceiver. A civilian Dakota aircraft, full of passengers from Alice Springs bound for Adelaide, was in trouble. One engine, although not actually on fire, had registered alarm readings on the instrument panel before coughing to a grinding halt. Right now the engine was smoking hot, and with its propellers feathered the stricken aeroplane was limping over the saltbush plains east of Coober Pedy about 150 kilometres north of Eba, on its one remaining engine. All twin-engined aircraft are built to be able to fly on only one motor, but with the intense heat of the mid-November desert causing considerable turbulence, it would be much safer to have both working at once.

As we rushed up to the homestead, the radioed messages indicated that the plane was gradually losing height and we knew it would soon be over a belt of heavy mulga scrub which would make any sort of forced landing impossible. Of course they were desperately trying to make the distance to the airstrip at Eba which was normally a routine stop; it was a calculated risk to attempt the mulga belt leaving behind the last hope of landing on an open gibber plain.

We assured them over the transceiver that we were standing by with our jeeps in the event of any last-minute ditching operation, and requested constant information as to their location. Their radio operator was well aware that if they reached our strip we would be on hand at the landing. The minutes dragged by and reports of the scenery below the plane were enough for us to know almost exactly where they were all the time, as we had covered every centimetre of that country in the course of our survey work. A mention of a sheoak patch or an angle in a fence line were enough to allow us to plot their positions. If any failure in their radio occurred or if they made a sudden announcement that they were coming down, we could head off accurately across country to where we last heard from them.

The burning heat of the country at that time of year made any sort of travelling an ordeal at best, and it must have been an explosive atmosphere on board because we were tensed-up just listening to their reports, but the longer they kept coming, the closer they would be to us, and eventually it seemed as if they would actually reach the strip. As we listened, their navigator broke in with the news to the radio operator that Mount Eba homestead was then actually in sight. Leaving someone at the transceiver, we burst outside and in a matter of a minute, the drone of an aeroplane engine wafted over the quiet mulga trees to us. Tumbling into our jeeps we streaked over to the airfield as the Dakota came into sight. With its undercarriage already down it made a direct approach, disregarding the usual circling inspection of the wind-sock and a glance over the dirt runway for stray horses or sheep. They had obviously had enough excitement and were eager to bring the adventure to a close as quickly as possible.

The wing tips exaggerated the effect of the hot ground thermals as the plane was lifted and dropped by them, and appeared anything but level or steady, but at least it was coming down here and not over a sea of hard mulga trees. One set of propellers was labouring gallantly while the port set was quite stationary. Within the next minute the lucky aeroplane was settled on the wonderful, solid ground, shimmering like a huge silver jelly in the mirage.

We were right there by the door as it opened and the sweating passengers spilled out with various expressions of relief. One young man, more light-hearted and obviously the comedian of the group, knelt down on his hands and knees in full view of everyone and kissed the hot dirt with a flourish as though he were facing Mecca.

Much exuberant bantering followed in the wake of the subsiding tension, as the passengers gradually lost their former petrified appearance. Someone even remarked brightly that we now had enough people for a cricket match. We ferried them all over to the homestead with their belongings, as they were certainly not going to re-enter that particular machine, and Flo prepared the usual scones and gallons of tea to cope with them all. In their city clothing they looked quite out of place in these parts, but at least they were all alive.

Radio messages were already being sent to the airline concerned in Adelaide and another plane was being prepared to leave on the following morning, bound for Eba. The overnight delay was due to the time taken in arranging for a replacement engine and aircraft fitters to be on board, and the same plane would of course take on all the passengers to resume their journey.

Mount Eba somehow looked different for the rest of the day as clean-looking people in polished shoes and lipstick wandered about, looking over an outback sheep station probably for the first and last time in their lives. One man, obviously a botanist, spent his time collecting specimens of saltbush and a large variety of herbage that we didn't even know existed. Their evening meal was already being prepared by George, and whatever it was, I knew they were in for a treat.

Shearers' quarters, homestead verandahs, and woolshed were to be their bedrooms with priority given to women-folk, who would sleep at the house. After tea in the cool of the long twilight the idea of the cricket match was put into effect. Barry and Robert's bats were brought out and the men challenged our survey camp to play. Nobody won, as the botanist was more intent on examining specimens while fielding than chasing the ball, but once, as he was looking hard at a small leaf structure, a haymaker swipe at the ball by Ozzie connected, sending it streaking towards his face. Just in time he saw it and, dropping the leaf, raised his hands to protect himself; the hurtling missile landed in his open palms 2 centimetres from his nose and Ozzie was out for a duck. Afterwards at tea we remarked on what a spectacular catch it was, only to receive his nonchalant reply: 'After all that's what I was there for.'

At dawn the second plane appeared and a tubular scaffold brought for the purpose was assembled, soon to have the replacement engine dangling from its strong, endless chain hoist. The small wheels at the feet of the framework, which were designed for sealed hardstandings at city airports, just sank into the red dust and refused to roll the heavy load out of the doorway. Anticipating this, I already had my jeep and tow rope waiting and we towed it clear of the plane, while the spare seats on board were anchored to their usual mounts. The passengers had all been ferried over with their belongings and were bunched around watching the proceedings. In a matter of minutes they were installed with seat belts firmly adjusted as the pilots were driven back to their aircraft from Flo Crombie's traymobile of scones and tea at the house. With engines roaring, the plane, which although small by normal airline standards still looked huge to us out here in the bush, slewed around, pelting us with dust and ironstone gravel, to face the open flat.

They buzzed us after take-off, level with the tops of the mulgas, and straightened out in the direction of Adelaide, leaving the original pilots and fitters to restore the crippled craft. Apparently for psychological reasons, pilots aren't supposed to see what goes on in the mechanical operation of repairing or replacing parts, so we willingly volunteered our help to the fitters. With the engine swinging below, I towed the makeshift structure across the saltbush, gouging deep ruts in the dirt, and finally deposited the new machine on the ground under the wing, leaving the crane free to take on the useless motor when it was detached. The weight was taken and the maze of wires and tubes was unscrewed, finishing up with the removal of the main holding bolts which allowed the heavy machine to swing freely. We towed the whole apparatus around to the door in the fuselage and manoeuvred it inside, working the chains to place the engine where it would be firmly strapped to the floor for its return down south.

The laborious operation continued by attaching the new one to the crane, and dragging it into place alongside the gaping hole in the wing left by the other engine. Bolts were replaced after much microscopic adjustment of the hoist, and the task of joining up the multitude of loose ends began.

By early afternoon the whole concern once more resembled an aeroplane and the pilots were collected to take it for a test flight in which we were invited to participate. As we screamed along the strip to the critical moment of take-off, I kept thinking of those few flimsy bolts holding that huge, thundering motor in place, and realised why the pilots themselves don't usually have anything to do with the mechanical side of flying. After crawling over the outback like snails in our comparatively slow jeeps, the speed of take-off seemed supersonic to us and soon we were circling over the homestead and woolshed as the pilots lined up for a landing, satisfied that it all worked once more.

They stayed long enough for the mobile scaffolding to be taken apart and loaded, after which, by now our firm friends, they lit out for Adelaide as if nothing had happened. Apart from joining up a thousand wires and tubes in the right places, there was really nothing to putting a new engine in an aeroplane and we felt we were learning something every day. After all, you never know when you'll be called upon to put an engine in an aeroplane.

Soon after this slight interruption the astronomical calculations were finished, and I was free to head off the following day for another star fix

160 kilometres away in the sandhills west of Dick Rankin's Ingomar homestead. It was a perfect night for the observations, which kept me going into the early hours of the morning, leaving a few hours to sleep in my swag before driving back. This was the last necessary position for our map and had to be done before we could all leave Eba and return to the Purple Downs woolshed area. Word had come to us that some special series of large-scale maps were needed around the Woomera locality as work progressed, to enable detailed planning of the various future bombing and short missile ranges which were now coming into the picture.

This meant that we would shift camp to be more central to our new scene of operations, while we extended our original trig survey to cover the enlarged area with a network of accurate points from which we could produce the new maps. 'Yandandaree Special' and 'Pimba Special' were the first two required, and the Purple Downs woolshed was willingly made available by Norman Greenfield as it was unoccupied between the annual shearing seasons.

Before pulling out from Eba I had to mend the tyre of my jeep which had deflated in one second as I neared the camp on the main road after the last star observation. It had taken a little time to stop from a speed of 80 kilometres an hour, and the flat tyre made the slowing-down process quite exciting as it slewed the jeep back and forth across the road over the loose dust and gravel. My inspection revealed an exact disc cut out of the tube, .303 inches in diameter, and the brass case of the heavy rifle cartridge was still embedded halfway through the canvas and rubber tread. How these things penetrate the thick tyre cover has always been a mystery, as it would be quite impossible to hammer the thin brass shell through, even if we tried all day.

Knowing we'd all be back eventually, we slowly drove out of Mount Eba Station. I was sure the one who would be missed most would be George, by now the established station cook. At Kingoonya there was a hitch in the journey while Harold brought Doreen up to date with all the latest news, and the people in the siding wanted us to play cricket. They had heard of the plane passengers' match of course, and it had given them something to plan for ever since. I struggled on slowly to East Well with the old 3-tonne blitz truck and spent the night with Joe and his family, cutting their hair and rehearsing our progress.

The others caught up next morning and we all drove sadly through Woomera which by now had mushroomed with shacks and tents; the atmosphere of the area as we had known it earlier in the year had gone forever. Everyone there had heard of us 'hillbillies from the sticks,' and already we seemed to have become a legend as curious newcomers gathered around our tired old vehicles from the bush.

We carried on past the Ponds for we preferred to camp at our old bog hole at Paradise Well rather than in the metropolis, leaving only 42 kilometres to go to reach the Purple woolshed. By the following midday we were installed there with several tents erected outside because the shearers' quarters made us feel too cooped up, and George had a fire going in the bread-baking oven built into the rockwork in the kitchen shed.

It was only then that we discovered the disappearance of a .22 rifle from Mick's jeep and a thorough search for it proved fruitless. This was a very serious matter for it belonged to the army, and Wally had to cover himself by submitting a report written by Mick to Keswick which might even save him a court-martial. The rifle had definitely been in his jeep as far as Kingoonya and that was the last anyone had seen of it. During the cricket match someone must have decided it was too attractive to leave lying about, and we agreed they wouldn't have taken it if they hadn't wanted it for some good reason. Wally asked Mick to give his written statement a title, and in due course it was delivered to the military police at headquarters. They read it out just as Mick had written it: 'About the rifle that was supposed to be in the truck . . .'

The first task was to establish a new network of trig stations which could be connected to our main chain covering Woomera, and this work began immediately. New points were located and more of Brooks' old stations were discovered, and eventually the actual theodolite work could start with the observations of hundreds of angles between the beacons.

The Purple Downs children weren't idle for any weekend afterwards for many months to come as I collected them to help in finding the original old sites, saving the more interesting and mysterious ones for Saturdays and Sundays when they were free from correspondence school work.

Weeks of concentrated work followed, preparing and sighting trig beacons, observing angles at first light in the mornings and just before dusk. This avoided the incessant mirage and heat shimmer which made it absolutely impossible to work with a theodolite at other times. Metal vanes, 60 centimetres in diameter, which would normally be seen through the telescope as a steady pinhead-sized black dot on the highest part of an undulation on the skyline, would during the day appear to melt into the boiling, liquid haze on the horizon which obliterated the whole undulation itself.

This more often than not meant sleeping on the spot, alongside a tripod erected in readiness for the attachment of the instrument as soon as the eastern sky showed signs of the approaching new day. A relatively short period of time was available before the sun again transformed the country into a swimming liquid. Battery-operated lights with precisely-shaped

reflectors were the ideal answer for the reading of all these angles after dark, but this involved a second party on a distant trig station to man them, a thing which we didn't always have.

Woomera now had the privilege of the company of a small band of those wonderful men from the Salvation Army who are always present at such places, and one day we received word that they even had a film showing scheduled. A large, white canvas tent fly was erected by a willing group of workers on a slope near our old escarpment and a projector was set up on a camp table, operated by a diesel generator placed far enough away so that it wouldn't blot out the sound effects with its noise.

We drove to the escarpment as we planned to be reading some angles at Pearson's Hill on the morning after the big night at the 'theatre.' By the time we got there it was already dark. Allowing the jeep to gradually roll down behind the assembled group, consisting of the entire population of Woomera at the time, we were the only ones sitting down on seats with back rests as we didn't even have to get out of our vehicle. Johnny and I couldn't believe that we were really at a drive-in cinema on this tableland. Throughout the film I could merely glance up and over the screen to watch the passage of the stars, for once not having to use them for an astrofix.

At the close of this historic evening we hurriedly backed the jeep away from the patrons and lit out across the open plains to camp at Pearson's Hill.

The pace of this work kept up at full speed despite the intense heat of the approaching summer months (it was now December), and constant high winds and dust storms battered our little camp by the woolshed. We rarely slept at the same spot two nights running but lay down wherever we happened to be at nightfall, on sandhills, gibber plains, and in occasional patches of mulga scrub. At last I could sleep throughout the desert nights without the never-ending need for star observations which had made me a slave to the heavens for so long. Those requirements would surely return and I would tackle them without reluctance, but at the same time the novelty of a full night's rest was as good as a holiday.

Christmas was approaching and a few weeks' cessation of work was imminent, so I planned to bring the surveys up to a point from which I could continue in the new year, and with this goal in mind I felt I must not waste a single minute. A fortnight short of Christmas Day we all packed up our few meagre belongings, the instruments, and the field books which in themselves were more valuable than everything else put together, and leaving the tents where they were in readiness for our return, we farewelled our Purple Downs friends and slowly moved off towards Woomera.

We straggled into Port Augusta that night and at the expense of Wally Relf, slept for almost the first time that year under a roof and in a regular bed, without the need for a canvas-covered swag roll.

Such a year couldn't have so easy a conclusion, I thought, as I drove the old 3-tonne truck out of the Port next morning. My theory proved correct as I started the drive over Horrocks Pass in the southern Flinders Ranges on our way back to Keswick. Halfway up the long, steep incline my engine literally exploded as the pulley wheel with its snapped stub of shaft flew off from the generator, to be pulled in by the fan belt and smashed through the radiator core. It was the last straw for our faithful old truck and I was able to allow it to roll back by gravity to a spot where I could turn it around, pointing once more back to Port Augusta 25 kilometres away. This was more like it, trouble to the end. I was almost relieved as I let the big vehicle roll down to the bottom of the pass where one of our jeeps could tow it back for help. The same trouble happening a week before would have meant coping with it ourselves, where the only help available was to be found at the end of our own arms.

This, then, brought to a close the first year in the development of what has often been referred to as the best testing range in the world, and the start of a project of such importance and magnitude that it was to flourish for well over a quarter of a century. It has been the life employment of many thousands of people and their families, and the scene of the joy and tragedies which accompany any community. Woomera is the birthplace of hundreds of Australians, and the final resting place of the many whose lives have come to their conclusion out there on the gibber and saltbush plains that we first knew merely as 'the Ponds.' People have begun lifelong partnerships, marrying in the churches, and 'Woomeraites' have become friends of the strongest kind, living as they did and still do in their unique town, safely clear of the approach funnel to the aerodrome which helped to govern the very location in the first place, so long before.

It has led directly to the opening up, for the first time, of the remaining 2.5 million square kilometres of virtually unexplored and unknown country in Central and Western Australia, and countless thousands of people have already benefited in various ways by the use of our 6500-kilometre network of roads covering it.

I have been constantly grateful for the incredible good fortune which ultimately steered me to that mantelpiece in Melbourne where I was asked to go over and start 'some sort of rocket range — or something.'

About the time the missile range had begun functioning as a launcher of rockets of a variety of types, a further development of a different kind came into the picture. While it had no connection whatsoever to the proceedings at Woomera, it could be greatly helped by the facilities available there and in fact would rely heavily upon it to get under way.

This was to be the culmination of years of work in the laboratories in England and was directed at testing atomic bombs developed by the British scientists. The first British atomic trial was to be held off the north-west coast of Australia but a further series of explosions was to take place on a mainland. Where in the Empire could be found a better place than Australia, with its enormous tracts of uninhabited and desolate country?

Much liaison was already taking place with the Woomera activities and it was almost only to be expected that a bomb site could be located with the experience gained in the remote expeditions for the rocket range. Also, with the help of those versed by now in coping with the local conditions, a new team would be unnecessary and actually undesirable as it would have to begin all over again from scratch.

The missiles were streaking off into the sky daily and a survey team had been imported to handle the detailed surveys required for recovery and newly developed instrumentation around the range head, so the way was clear. A bomb site was needed and would be handled immediately upon request.

10
Wanted: One Bomb Site

The huge polished desk was impressive enough on its own with its thick glass top and clean white blotting pad. You could judge its weight by the way it sank into the carpet covering the floor of the enormous office which had the blinds drawn and was so quiet you could have heard a pin drop on the desk; it would have been lost altogether if it had fallen on the carpet. The sweep hand on the silent electric clock was the only thing moving here in an atmosphere which would normally frighten the life out of anyone like me, sitting as I was in a low leather armchair before the desk with the expressionless faces of the several men present turned towards me. I'd had many pleasant encounters with most of them in the past concerning the early requirements for surveys at our rocket range at Woomera.

The day before I had been putting the finishing touches to their latest project of a new jet bombing range when I had been summoned to H.Q. of the Long Range Weapons Establishment, as it was then called, at Salisbury by an uninformative teleprinter message from the Chief Superintendent. It had merely stated that I was to come down on the old Bristol Freighter courier aircraft to see him in his office this morning, and, with the 'theirs not to reason why' approach, I left what pegs I had established for instrumentation buildings on the bombing range to the care of the Department of Works and flew down to Adelaide.

The present Chief Superintendent, Harry Pritchard, was a very easy-to-get-on-with Englishman, from Cambridge. He had once given me a globe of the world from his office to help us with some spherical trigonometrical problems we had encountered at Woomera. This was in fact his office but now he sat in another leather armchair on one side of the desk leaving the one on the other side to Frank O'Grady, the Chief Engineer. Frank was the proud owner of quite a sense of humour as was shown by the way he once pleaded with me to go and put on some old clothes so the rest of the establishment could get on with their work. I'd arrived on the job one day for the first time dressed in a suit instead of khaki shorts and hobnailed boots, a fact which temporarily seemed to upset the normal smooth running of the place. He'd had great fun in showing everyone a letter he had received one day addressed to 'The Chief *Mechanical* Engineer,' pointing out that he had not seen a spanner since he'd tightened up a nut and bolt on his own pram.

Here again though, he sat with the others, watching me in such a way that made me glance involuntarily down at my wrists to ensure the handcuffs which the police sergeant at Woomera had been recently demonstrating weren't in fact still there. I remembered only too clearly how he'd been showing me the way in which his latest bracelets worked by literally throwing them at a prisoner's arm to make one half of the circle spin around and ratchet into place, and how I had been sweating as he elaborately searched for the key he'd somehow mislaid.

There were others present in their soft understuffed leather chairs but the one sitting at the desk who seemed to be in charge of the situation was unknown to me. This morning was the first time I had ever seen him. He had his elbows planted firmly apart on the blotter with his strong-looking fingers interlaced lightly supporting his chin, and from the sleeves of his black coat emerged thick wrists covered with a mat of black hair. His swarthy heavy-jowled face was topped by a shiny brown forehead which extended all the way from his bushy black eyebrows over to the back of his neck, which in turn came from a stalwart pair of shoulders. He wasn't completely bald over the ears but the eyebrows quite made up for it, overshadowing as they did the beady black eyes which were at present fixed unwaveringly on me. I was beginning to wonder, not unnaturally, what on earth could be the matter as I searched the faces for some signs of explanation or even friendliness. But as I looked I detected signs of preoccupation, not, after all, directed wholly at me, which served to soften the atmosphere of the firing squad to a less harsh one of interrogation. Just as I had arrived at this conclusion Mr Eyebrows started to talk in a low, weighty manner. He had actually been introduced to me when I entered the office as Bill Worth, one of the chief security officers for the Commonwealth of Australia and he had already known as much about me as I did myself. 'You are about to be acquainted with certain facts,' he began. 'which at present are known in this headquarters to no one

outside this room. Furthermore,' he continued with the emphasis of one used to authority, 'that is the way it will be remaining.' I thought if someone didn't get on with it soon I'd fall completely under the spell of those hypnotic eyes. But at last it came. And it was certainly a suitably fitting climax to such a build up of atmosphere. In an even quieter tone as though the walls had sprouted ears, he concluded, '*It has been decided to detonate an atomic bomb in Australia.*'

This was something bigger than I had ever dreamed of. I partly guessed the rest — about being assigned to search for a site — before actually hearing it. From the way he was speaking and the serious tone of voice I gathered he was warning me that there was only a very limited number of people who would have to be interviewed if the project became known. Having made this point clear the Eyebrows left it now with the chief superintendent.

Alan Butement, the Chief Scientist who had his office in Melbourne, had already given instructions regarding the project. Alan had accompanied many bush-bashing camps of ours on the early extensions of the Woomera Rocket Range and was the originator of many joke sayings we still often use. Once, we were sitting around a camp fire in the sandhills discussing radar, and how flying cave dwellers use the same system in avoiding collision with the dark, dank sides of their caverns. Just at this point something whistled past one of the member's ears causing him to

111

start violently and ask nervously what it was. The Chief Scientist, who was an authority on the subject of radar in its early development, explained carefully in a very precise English voice that all was well as it was 'only one of those bats with his little radar set.' Another time a member of the party who had cooked the sausages for dinner asked him how they were. 'Pretty well bre(a)d,' was the reply.

Apparently now however, the site required was to be in an area roughly 500 kilometres from Woomera in a place where radiation would not interfere with the future missile range work. On paper it fell in an area which I knew from many expeditions to be just a sea of high sandhills covered with dense mulga scrub and nearly 320 kilometres from the last cattle station homestead in that direction. The description of the site went on to say the immediate area would need to be about 8 kilometres in diameter, and clear of sandhills so that work in progress would have the maximum accessibility and so that instrumentation could be located wherever required without topographical obstruction. This was going to be some task in this region, though one possible area sprang to mind immediately. This was a iron-hard claypan about 1.5 kilometres long which we had discovered, smooth as a billiard table and on which aeroplanes could easily be landed. It also had the advantage of being within the desired boundaries of the forthcoming event.

There was as usual a date set when the site should be ready for inspection and this was arranged to coincide with the arrival of a team of scientists from England who would be conducting an atomic bomb test at the Monte Bello islands off the north-west coast of Australia. The team was to be led by a Doctor Penney whose name was already known in connection with the nuclear physics of these tests and with whom I was soon to have many pleasant dealings. It seemed that there was time for the project with which I was then concerned, the bombing range at Woomera, to be completed. This would only take a further fortnight's surveys, and in the meantime I could plan for the new one. Vehicles could be made ready and equipment ordered in by another member whose help would be allowed as long as the main reason for it all was not divulged; he could be given to understand that it was merely an extension of the range.

I had that member already in mind; he was someone who had been with us often on hard trips and was tried and proven. I determined to ring him up before flying back to Woomera next morning to finish the bombing range.

I had a few more queries which were answered in hushed tones. Then I described the area under consideration from memory. The closest track or road of any kind was 250 kilometres away through bush and sandhills, and there was no surface water for the entire distance, almost from where

Top: The Emu claypan and the finished airstrip alongside. Near the site for the first atomic bomb tests in Australia, the claypan could be used for landing purposes while the airstrip was being constructed. Bottom: Sir William, later Lord Penney, waiting for the right winds before the atomic detonation

we were sitting at the present minute. It was not too different from what we'd been up against since the whole missile project had begun, however, and we'd do what was possible despite the odds.

After padding out of the office with the carpet engulfing the soles of my hobnailed boots, I found a telephone to have a yarn to old Bill Lloyd. He was the one I'd planned to take with me, and although he was currently employed by the Air Force I knew a brief talk to his commanding officer would be all that was required to release him. When I got him on the wire and told him who was calling I was assured of his acceptance immediately. His words were breathed with a heavy sigh of relief, 'When do we go?' I replied I'd see him in an hour after the talk with the C.O. The C.O. also heaved a sigh — but this was one of resignation to the inevitable; we'd better take him straight off, he said, as it always finished up that way in the end anyhow. With a 'Good on you Mick,' I was transferred by the operator back to Bill who had already packed his toothbrush and said he'd come over to meet me. He was stationed only 3 kilometres away.

While sitting in my car waiting for him at the guard gate I got to thinking of the immensity of this project and what would be involved with every aspect of it. The major part of the task would be supplying water for several hundred men for a year. We'd have to make an access road out but this wouldn't be so bad, apart from all the sandhills, and food could come out on a series of planes landing on an airstrip we could make once the bulldozers were on the site. The claypan could possibly be used for a while for bringing the supplies to the immediate area, and a shorter road to the site itself could be made if need be, but whatever we did an access would have to come in from the main road. It was plain to see we'd somehow have to get a boring plant to the site for the water problem, drilling down to try our luck with the sub-artesian supplies; though, if the quality of the water was as poor as I thought, it was going to add an enormous burden to the project both in work and expense. Generally, water could be discovered at 30 metres or so, but drilling was slow and only limited supplies could be expected. The neat bore water, barely fit for stock, could take care of the washing arrangements and most of the construction, which was after all the bulk of the consumption needed, but either way that was going to be a big part of the job.

So far we didn't even have a site but that couldn't alter the fact that the whole region was waterless — I knew this from six years of battling with it doing astronomical observations for the ground control of aerial photographs which had resulted in the first detailed maps of the area. Sometimes it would take weeks of working over the desired area almost

The author surveying instrument layout for the atomic test site tree by tree to pinpoint a position on the photograph which coincided with the one on the ground. As hundreds of these pictures were of nothing but a grey mass of mulga scrub it was understandable that we knew what we were up against now, especially as our area lay a further 150 kilometres from the extremities of these maps.

So intent was I on all the problems involved that I failed to notice the arrival of Bill who opened the door with a, 'Good-day, wasn't I glad to hear from you?' from which I gathered he had not had a very interesting position at his base job. A few minutes was all it needed to arrange things; we had his truck at Woomera where most of the stores could be obtained so he would fly up with me the next day and start getting together such early supplies as we would need while we looked for an area for a 'Woomera job.' He didn't know and it didn't occur to him to ask where we would be going or for how long; the only thing that concerned him was how many tubes of toothpaste he should get. We had a joke that we'd measure the length of time we'd be out by the number of tubes of toothpaste.

I spent the rest of the afternoon gathering what extra instruments and calculation books I would be needing for star work as the others were still at Woomera for use on the jet range. As I worked, I couldn't help wondering what an atomic bomb looked like. The rumours that went around the troops in the army at the close of the war would ultimately be confirmed or otherwise, but somehow I thought it would be 'otherwise.' Some maintained it was the size of a tennis ball and others were sure it was no larger than a house brick, but there was no end to the speculation. And we might actually be seeing one! To think that for the first time the mulga country site somewhere yet to be found was to come to life in the blinding flash of an atomic explosion which was capable of razing a city was awesome enough in itself, but the knowledge that the responsibility of finding a place was mine caused me many disturbed and sleepless nights.

I had my built-up Land Rover put in the workshops for a complete overhaul by our faithful mechanics who always realised how much we relied on it in the bush, and, after booking two seats on the Woomera Bristol Freighter for the next day, I started drawing up some lists.

The next two weeks seemed to race by as I finished the surveys for the jet bombing range, and, after the buildings for the instrumentation and tracking apparatus were under way, my work there was over. Bill, with much paper work and signing of forms, got most of the stores organised. These included head gaskets, dish cloths, petrol, frying pans, and rifles, and we put them together in a corner of a shed where we could lay our hands on them in a hurry on our next pass through Woomera with our two vehicles. As far as everyone, including Bill, was concerned, we were just going on another routine reconnaissance into the bush. It was a terrible secret to have the responsibility of keeping but it was very obvious that was the way it had to remain until it was decided at very high levels to release the news. Actually it was almost a year before it was officially made known, although some people guessed pretty accurately what it was all about beforehand.

Then came the time to set off on the first stage of the work, which was to find a site for an atomic town to mushroom in the mulga within the required distance of a suitable topographical standpoint for the actual blast. It also had to be in a direction dictated by the general prevailing ground winds which in turn meant that the trend of the upper stratospheric currents had to be taken into account. It was important that the deadly radioactive fallout be carried away harmlessly into the desert. Once I got used to the initial excitement caused by the magnitude of the task, I was more than ready to get on with it, and, after another trip to Adelaide and brief talks to the powers there, we headed off to the sandhills.

Rain poured down the day we left Adelaide and by the time we arrived at Woomera late that afternoon it was so widespread that the road was made up mainly of a series of small flowing rivers. Large heavy balloon tyres for the sandhill crossings saved us time and again from being hopelessly bogged.

We struggled into Woomera covered with thick red clay, the windscreen wiper quite inadequate to cope with the sheets of liquid mud, and went in for a late tea in the mess. I was discussing with the doctor there various parts of a special first aid kit he had put together for us for the trip when the phone rang for him. He came to me minutes later to say a little child was very sick at the near-by rail siding at Pimba and her father had managed to relay the message to our hospital. It was only 6 kilometres away but the road was under water most of the way and it was still raining down in sheets. I offered to try to get through immediately — no other vehicle would have a chance of making it. The hospital could ring back for her parents to watch out for me and have the child ready.

Within the minute I was on my way on one of the most nightmarish trips I can remember for its relatively short length of 12 kilometres return. Time and time again, while the hospital staff prepared for an emergency, I found myself moving at a snail's pace through mud to the floorboards; water cascaded across the road in the usually dry creek beds. In the pitch black of the night I had to guess where the road was for thirty metres at a time, and often with the momentum of trying to get through an unusually soft spot, the vehicle would slew about in the mud with volumes of water making the engine miss many beats. Somehow luck was with me, and I came out at the siding after what seemed like an age to be greeted by the parents waving a torch in the rain to indicate which cottage to make for. I went in with them and wrapped the pathetic little figure, white-faced in the lamp light, in a camp sheet and carried her out in my arms to install her in the passenger's seat I had cleared for the occasion. There was a radio transmitter there, so asking them to let the hospital know, I lost no time in turning around and starting back, one hand on the wheel and the other over the radio supporting her against the seat. I determined to get, if not right back, then as far as the vehicle would take us; I would have to carry her the rest of the way.

There were still 3 kilometres to go when the engine spluttered to a stop and refused to go at all. This was caused by an unusually large sheet of water swamping up over the bonnet. However, with a canvas camp sheet, the driest rag I could find and some work on the soaked distributor, it coughed back into life and we resumed our evening drive. The little girl, clutching on to my arm with a tiny wet hand, endured it all wide-eyed and pale in the glow from the headlights. At last we reached the tarred section of the streets of the village at Woomera and with a sigh of relief I drove on to the hospital where the doctor and staff were waiting at the entrance with a stretcher. After placing the girl on it and unwrapping the canvas, my part of it was over and, thanks to that cross-country vehicle, the grateful little mite was in safe hands at last.

The next day Bill and I called for his truck we had already prepared, loaded on the stores from the shed, and started off, this time in the sunlight, though the country was a quagmire. We drove in and out of bogs all the way, pulling each other out, until we reached the last of the cattle stations we would be seeing which also meant the last of the made-up 'roads!' It was at this station, Mabel Creek, that the 'creek' actually became a river with water in it instead of the usual dry depression. As we drove towards it, it looked as though it was going to block our way. With the recent downpours of rain it was nearly 30 metres wide, and was flowing rapidly right across our path. It seemed as though the back country was making a final bid to save itself from an atomic attack.

Taking note of where our previous wheeltracks crossed over, what dry mulga tree to make for, and which side of it to detour, we gave it a try, first in my lighter Land Rover with the truck high and dry on the other bank. It could at least pull me back out of the 'creek' should the attempt fail. I remembered the deep billabong alongside the wheeltracks to the north and knew that if I slid into that I'd really be clean out of sight. After trying it first on foot and placing a marker on the opposite bank I removed everything liable to be water damaged from the floor-boards, started the engine, and slowly plunged in. As the level of the water had been above my knees when I waded through, I was not at all confident of success. As I edged forward I couldn't help thinking about the bubbling submerged exhaust outlet which would suck in water if the engine stalled, but eventually I struggled up the far bank, the level of the water coming over my boots in the cabin. The good old vehicle lumbered up the bank pouring out water like a cumbersome black walrus. Then the engine began missing violently and finally coughed its last. Fortunately, the Land Rover by this time was clear and on the dry level beyond the edge. I think disconnecting the fan belt would have helped to reduce the splashing but at least I was through. Now I could dry out the wiring so I could lend Bill a little weight if he should stop mid-stream, although with the higher frame of his truck we had hoped he would have no trouble. These hopes were soon justified.

So it was we were at last on our own to battle with the odds in front of us. We would see what could be salvaged out of this country for a project as yet undreamed of in the minds of all but a handful of men.

An area of about 20 000 square kilometres of country beyond the furtherest expeditions to date seemed, by inspection of a map of Australia, to be a suitable geographical location for an atomic test.

This was found to be some of the most inhospitable country in Australia, with its endless horizons of 30-metre high red sand ridges covered with a thick carpet of mulga scrub. Activity of any nature would require room to move without the obstruction of mountains of sand at almost every turn of a wheel and with the range centre line in mind and countless astrofixes, it had taken half a year of exploration to discover such an area. Extreme difficulties with food, fuel, and water dogged the operation, which was solo owing to the nature of the security surrounding the project, but eventually a claypan was discovered capable of landing any weight aircraft on it without any preparation. It was an iron-hard, 1.5-kilometre long ribbon of clay within 30 kilometres of the only spot located free of sandhills in this limitless wilderness. This perfect combination had taken six months to find, and happened just at the time of the British atomic team's visit to Australia to conduct its first trial on the Monte Bellos.

The chief atomic scientist Dr Penney (later Sir William and then Lord Penney) and a few selected colleagues and politicians flew out to the claypan under a cloud of secrecy to be shown the site which was approved before they flew on to their work off the north-west coast.

Preparation, in boring for water, planning a future tent town, and locating an overland route for a road, occupied the remainder of 1952 and work resumed in earnest the following year . . .

118

11
Paving the Way

The new year of 1953 saw us back on the claypan. By February the bore-sinking programme was well under way, only this time at the new place recently named Emu. We had gone to Dingo on our old sandhill tracks through the scrub and collected as much of our old camp as we could heap on to the blitz truck and my Land Rover, as well as some boring equipment. The drillers, Bill, and I pressed on along the new tracks past the food-can signpost, to Area A via the four-poster bedroom, and across to the claypan. The straight line route I had taken with the four Rovers had settled in my mind which way we would return in the new year. With the drillers installed at the most likely site complete with their plant, Bill and I returned to Dingo after dropping off several old diesel drums of salty water we had collected at the old sites. These would enable them to start operations while we went for another load before withdrawing the pump rods and pump from the old cased holes at Dingo, thus cutting off our last source of supply of water. We also dismantled the engine and pump jack rig which we'd spiked to logs, and made back in haste to Emu.

There are various ways of picking a site for a water bore in this area. First by natural topography: no one would start on top of a hill. I often wonder if the person who wrote the rhyme 'Jack and Jill' ever visited the Australian backcountry. Having proceeded to the lowest part of the surrounding vicinity hoping the bedrock might follow a parallel course to the surface you search for the additional indications of dry gutters and watercourses, always keeping your mind back somewhere B.C. A point can then be tried, and if it successful, an engine pump jack can be installed easily and the material from the bailer can run off with the least effort. This may or may not give results but mostly seems to produce something even if several tries must be made. Our observations were that water near a claypan, including an 800 kilometre scope in that country, always gave us nearly brine. As this was a claypan job and the village was to be at hand we were quite prepared for what we ultimately got, namely water almost as salty as the sea which corroded the pipes and caked salt around taps. The pipes connected to the distilling plant filled with mineral until only a trickle came out; they had to be hammered constantly and cleared with compressed air from a pneumatic drill plant.

I did, however, after a learned talk with Tom Barnes, at that time the field geologist handling the operations, try to get very technical. I employed the method where, by using a fault line near the weapons area, a closer supply for washing future radioactive material such as clothing, boots, and undersides of vehicles would be available. It was an attempt to select the site by discovering the fault line, resulting in the forming of an underground dam. I found the dip of the strata and marked a point 45 centimetres on the upper side of the fault where all this water might be stored, and the plant was accurately centered over my cross in the dirt. The string of tools went down, and down, and down ... The result was a failure that was known from then on as the 'geological waterhole.' The men insisted on sticking in the hole a signpost saying, 'This is Beadell's fault,' adding insult to injury by forcing me, at the point of a rifle, to paint it myself.

The two bore-sinking teams worked in shifts night and day keeping the machinery constantly on the go, while Bill and I got on with the other phases of the work. They got curious from time to time and asked in incredulous tones what anyone wanted all this water for in this country, being used to boring at stations and farms where there was good reason for their efforts. However, the old 'extension of the range' theme satisfied them and they pressed on, not minding as long as their pay kept on as well.

Concerning their pay arrangements, they would put in their overtime sheets for me to sign and pass on to the Mines Department. I was never sure which was their hardest task: filling in those forms or the drilling. Sometimes the day shift pair would argue until midnight about some point, and listening to them became our biggest source of entertainment. Old Jim Bannerman would discuss it with his snapman, the name given to the offsider of the one in charge of the plant, and the conversation would proceed as follows:

'We worked 'till eleven last Tuesday night on our shift.' This came from Jim.

'No, it was 'till half past.'

'No, that was Wednesday night.'

'No . . . Yes.'

'Yes, then Monday it was 'till ten.'

'*No!*'

'No.'

'Yes . . . that makes it eleven hours Monday.'

They would then struggle through the higher mathematics involved in totting up the number of hours worked and at which rate.

'That makes it eighteen and a half hours.'

'No.'

'Yes. I worked 'er out.' Silence would then prevail while he rechecked his work. 'No, nineteen.'

'Yes, that's right . . . no, nineteen and a half.'

'No . . . Yes.'

. . . and so it would go on for anything up to six hours. By this time Bill and I were so weak with laughter it was necessary to call a halt to this meeting of the 'Emu Debating Society.' I took to noting the times myself and acting as a president to give a casting vote, which they both seemed to find acceptable.

One night a terrific storm hit the camp as the night shift was out. Ironically enough, this was several days after striking our first successful hole, with all our labours bringing water from Dingo. Something had happened to make the team appear back in camp, before they were due, in a near panic of white-faced terror. Long before they arrived we could see their headlights through the sheets of rain with occasional silver streaks of forked lightning contrasting sharply with the usual black gloom of a camp in the mulga. When they sloshed their way in with the Rover and stumbled into the dry interior of my tent where I had a hurricane lamp burning, I first saw their pallid cheeks and noticed them both trembling as with fever, the whites of their eyes showing, and water cascading on to the dirt floor from their hats and slickers. For some time they couldn't even speak as they sought out a box and stool on which to sit while their uncontrollable shaking subsided.

I wondered what on earth had happened to put grown men into such a frenzy. Their first words were to ask me if I remembered the huge old tree alongside the plant where they hung their water bags and things while they worked. I knew it only too well as I had the plant manoeuvred in such a way that this could be of help to them as a sort of hall stand 3 metres away. It was almost a metre in diameter at the base and was tall in proportion. The violence of the storm struck with such suddenness that they had run to the tree for their hats and slickers in an attempt to reach their vehicle before the rain hit. After shutting off the engine with one action of the throttle wire they had grabbed their things from the tree. No sooner had they done so than a bolt of lightning had ripped the tree apart behind them, sending it crashing in flames to the ground; fortunately it fell away from them. They had missed certain death by a few metres. The shock had set in properly by the time they got to my tent, and I think I must have become infected by their urgency as I realised that by having singled out this tree, I would have felt a certain responsibility in the event of a disaster. It was true, storms of this nature were very rare but that wouldn't have helped my reactions very much.

Next morning, after a sleepless night, we pushed the vehicle to the site in the sunshine through the sheets of water and rapidly softening surface of bog holes and found the tree was in shreds; only the rain had stopped the fire from burning it completely. As it was, it presented an awe-inspiring sight.

While this work of supplying the project with its very life-blood was going on, I was free to carry out a comprehensive programme of astronomical observations for a huge grand overall map of the whole area extending 50 kilometres in all directions. Barely a night went by that didn't see me dancing around my theodolite to keep pace with the tight star schedule I'd precomputed. I couldn't afford to waste a night, and I could not spare the time to be away from the instrument except to book the observations and receive time signals, mostly for three hours at a stretch. I could calculate them the next day and be out in time the following night for the next one. When the distances became greater between points I received a very welcome radio message from my old friend Ken Garden at H.Q.

Ken and I had been on many hard trips together, during which we yarned around camp fires. I learnt amazingly enough that ten years or so before he had attended the very same school in Sydney as Len Murphy and I had, and had tormented the same masters. It does seem a small world at times. He had left our H.Q. since, and being a squadron leader in the R.A.A.F. engineering group, had moved to further postings; now he had returned temporarily for this latest development. The message was short but very important for me — 'Could you make use of helicopter for a week?'

In the course of several days during which a Bristol had flown in special octane fuel as well as bits and pieces peculiar to helicopters, instead of bringing them overland, the dragonfly itself appeared. The pilot left it with the trained fitters for servicing, and we had a hurried conference concerning the programme I had planned and the number of days I could expect to retain its services. Seven, we worked out, so I resolved to do seven more remote astro fixes, one per night if I could possibly maintain the pace and keep the tremendous volume of computing abreast of the observing. A word to the fitters prepared them for this, and Jack, the pilot had us in the air mid-afternoon of the same day, complete with theodolite and tripod, chronometer, star charts, field books, stop watches, pencils, and the host of other incidentals necessary for the work in hand. I ascertained in advance that their inbuilt radio transceiver was also capable of receiving the special time signals I used.

The daily programme to make the utmost use of such an unexpected windfall followed a pattern; we arrived in daylight at the identified air photo point I'd be using for an astronomical station, and observed stars at night. In the early hours of the morning we'd fly home, the thick bush carpet passing underneath, to a bright kerosene lamp left hanging high on a tree as a final guide. I would provide Jack with a rough homing bearing which I arrived at from a preliminary calculation from my own astrofix. We could see the lamp for a great distance at night, so only a rough bearing would be needed. As we flew in this eerie contraption with no wings and the chomping sound of the rotors overhead, I would start on the reductions of the observations in readiness for the morning's sums. I could be safe in saying that during these trips, I occupied the most unique computing office in Australia. The fitters would always be waiting for us to guide the last taxiing operation by torch light, whether it was two or four in the morning, and good old Bill would always greet us with a black billy of cocoa. We would loll about sleeping for the rest

of the darkness, sometimes four whole hours, then the fitters would begin their refuelling and maintaining again, while Bill prepared some breakfast, Jack filled in his flying log sheets, and I dragged myself into my tent to get on with the sums. We would take off once more in time to be at another site on my old wheeltracks for a midday sun observation, complete this, and go back to camp to collate all the results. Then an early tea and off again to drop in on another site I'd chosen for barometer height comparisons on the way to the next night's astronomical station.

One afternoon as we flew I found out what would happen if Jack let go of the collective pitch lever, which he normally held in his left hand. He was opening a fresh packet of his inevitable chewing gum and with one hand on the stick holding the packet he tore off the paper with his other. The lever stayed in place for several seconds, then vibration took over and it freed itself and dropped about 20 centimetres. The effect on the machine was immediate as it fell almost vertically for 30 metres or so as gracefully as a house brick. Jack's left hand streaked down and pulled it back up. It was as though we had landed on a jelly and we were once again flying level. He merely grinned as he chewed faster than ever explaining that even if the engine cut out it would windmill down safely. I was unable to reply for two minutes. Another afternoon as a fresh packet appeared in his hand he asked me to fly her while he peeled off the wrappings and let go everything at once. I'm sure no one ever became a helicopter pilot in a shorter time. The slightest movement of anything did *something* so I was glad when Jack thanked me and ironed out my somewhat erratic course by taking over.

This tempo of work continued without a stop for the full week, at the end of which I was almost a wreck, both mentally and physically, having averaged only three to four hours sleep a night. Apart from the observing and computing I would often walk with an axe for a kilometre through the bush from the nearest point at which we could land in the mulga to the point I'd preselected. I would then chop out a landing field for the dragonfly. I was almost glad to see the thing fly away; they were probably just as glad to go, and I suspected they wouldn't relish another such week in a hurry. Everyone had been wonderful, though, and their support had allowed me to complete one of the most urgently needed maps anywhere on any drawing board.

In the ensuing week or so everyone who thought he had an excuse would jump on the old Bristol from H.Q. and come 'just to see what's what' in an important sounding tone. Then as they hurried aboard out of the flies, in good time for take-off, they would say equally as importantly, 'Oh yes, now I see.' I noticed that I never saw them again at the claypan. Sometimes we would stand at the door of the aircraft just inside until it was being shut then quickly hop out and slam the door. That was to trap that particular cloud of flies — flies were a constant nuisance — and air freight them back to Adelaide. However, this procedure never seemed to make any difference to the number of flies left behind which seemed, on the contrary, to be increasing almost hourly.

At this stage I wondered if I should ever live to see the end of the year, to say nothing of writing a book about it. However, we were all seeing results for our efforts, and the drilling teams had several successful water bores equipped with engines and pumps, ready for the later arrivals to connect to the camp; all were of the worst brine quality but still it was water capable of being distilled. Sample bottles of water were sent to Tom Barnes at the Mines Department for passing on to their analyst, as also were many boxes resembling a horizontal nest of pigeon holes full of 'custard' samples from labelled depths. These would be studied by the experts in Adelaide under microscopes and chemical tests, thus adding to the ever-growing number of geological maps of the surface crust of the earth in South Australia. With every government bore sunk, the same tests are carried out, and a dual use is therefore gained from each hole; so some good came from even the unsuccessful 'geological waterhole.'

All this was paving the way for the main work to follow, and in a few short weeks follow it did — with a vengeance.

Almost four hundred men, both construction workers and scientists, flooded into the claypan by aeroplane, which for a time was the only link with the outside world and supplies for their needs occupied half the payloads. Everything had already been planned during the preceding year and teams were let loose on the atomic village preparation firstly in order to house everyone. Water tanks and kitchen, mess huts, tents, and blocks of sheet-iron garages for office accommodation were erected and huge half-round sheds for maintenance workshops followed laboratories for photographic and administration purposes.

All this to date was without the aid of earth-moving machinery which was urgently needed. To this end a large contingent of service personnel was assembled with half a dozen bulldozers, a road grader, sheep's foot rollers, concrete mixers, and trucks, at the nearest point on the Alice Springs road to the scene, a distance of well over 200 kilometres. The only way to bring such equipment to the claypan was along a road of its own making in country never penetrated before the reconnaissance survey of location.

Upon arrival, work began immediately on bulldozing a road to the actual bomb site. Bulk fuel could now come overland in convoys, leaving room on the planes for everything needed in an atomic trial including component parts for a 30-metre steel tower to hold the bomb aloft for exploding.

The time came at last for everyone to be officially informed of the reason for all their work, although by then most had guessed, and this opened the way for a weekend of entertainment planned by the claypan camp for the support teams from H.Q. 'down south' . . .

126

12
The Concert

So many men, both at the bomb site itself and at the headquarters at Woomera and at Salisbury, had done so much constant work with such willingness, many far beyond what was required of them officially, that ideas for a short relaxation of the tension began to take shape. A 'concert committee' was formed with the full sanction of everyone involved. It was to plan a never-to-be-forgotten event in the life at the claypan and invitations were to be extended to all who had a hand in the smooth running of the programme from their desks at H.Q.

The idea caught on with immediate success and Luke helped with whatever was needed for the occasion. The actors and performers would come from the camp, volunteering whatever talents hidden or otherwise they possessed. Soon an impressive list of artists was drawn up: Lorry Hogan, an airfield construction foreman could play the bagpipes which Chinny McWilliams promised to obtain, Ken Hurne, the cook mostly to be seen peeling onions in the kitchen, was a hypnotist, the once 'dead' tip-truck driver could sing, and an orderly room sergeant was an expert on the piano. Of course, the fact that there wasn't a piano for many hundreds of kilometres didn't present any problem, as Luke was to confiscate one from a source he knew about and have it flown out to the claypan specially for the event. A heavy equipment fitter, strangely enough, could tune a piano but couldn't play a note. I added what I could to the programme by volunteering to draw with wax lumber crayon on huge sheets of butcher's paper caricatures of various well-known members of the camp. Throughout the project so far, John Stanier had been taking reels of colour movie films of the boys as they worked, so he was to fetch them along with the equipment to give a local film show on the night.

All the preparation for the concert, planned for several weeks hence on a Saturday night, was done by the ones concerned, with ample help from the others by lamplight after their normal day's work. The first essential was a stage. Carpenters set about building this with whatever materials they could find. The platform was comprised of a number of tent floor boards. A white picket fence screened off the future 'orchestra pit' and the whole thing was built at the foot of the hill where the village had sprung up. It was complete with side-walls and a roof with a butcher's paper lining on which I drew the stage props. Maddock and his team supplied a microphone and stand wired to loudspeakers tied to the mulga trees. These were probably the most easily obtained pieces of equipment present.

Looking at the finished product I was reminded of an incident which had occurred before in a bush town where the people suddenly required a similar sort of stage for a visiting entertainment group. A man returning to his house one afternoon was astounded to see only a vacant block of land where the house used to be, so he hurried to the small police station to report that he had a complaint to make. When the constable asked what it was, he replied, 'Some coot went an' pinched me 'ouse.' No one could find the house anywhere, but as the man was sitting watching the performance that evening he recognised parts of the stage as being from his front verandah. On closer inspection he discovered the whole structure had been built with the component parts of his bachelor dwelling.

As soon as the set of bagpipes arrived, Lorry started rehearsals and kept them up for so long at a time that various members seemed to think they would like a spell from listening. Eventually one of the chemists poured a test-tube full of some mysterious liquid down one of the drones. This proceeded to eat great holes in the bag itself until it was nothing more than a network of openings held together with strips of hide. Lorry was very disappointed and brought what had once been his bagpipes to me to see what could be done.

I happened to have a well-tanned kangaroo skin in my box so offered to try to make a new bag for the instrument. Carefully taking what was left of the old one and unpicking the stitches I laid it out on the 'roo skin and cut out the pearshaped piece to fit. The bullet-hole in the skin could be manoeuvred until it coincided with one of the holes cut to take a drone, so it would be completely airtight. With waxed string and huge sail needle from the cable joiners' kit, I sewed it together and tightly tied each drone, the mouthpiece, and the hand reed tube into place. Dressed it

The atomic bomb was on the top of this 30-metre steel tower which disappeared completely in the first atomic blast on the Australian mainland

with its tartan sack covering it looked quite as good as new, although I had never seen a set of pipes before. Only then did I tentatively try to blow it up. Alas, all the air I could muster seeped out of the needle holes as fast as I blew it in, and each time my only reward was a feeble sound like a duck dying. I called Hogan in but he was quite unperturbed. He said that this often happened and was easily taken care of by the insertion of a weak mixture of treacle and hot water to heal over the holes. Sure enough this worked like a charm and, much to the sorrow of the chemist, Hogan was soon practising again. The only thing wrong was that as the sweet goo oozed out on to the tartan jacket, the whole thing was constantly set upon by ants and flies, forcing him to carry a tin of repellent in his camp-made sporran. He nevertheless refused to let it out of his sight from then on, sleeping and working with it literally under his arm all the time.

Next came the Scottish dress and kilt to go with it for his big stage act. The tartan for the kilt, cap, and plaid was made by spraying a red-lead soaked scrubbing brush over a piece of yellow survey bunting cloth which was placed under a piece of steel concrete reinforcing arc mesh. This gave a square red pattern and the lines in between the squares were hand-painted with a toothbrush dipped in a huge mulga green paint pot. The black belt across the chest and around his waist was made from the tarred malthoid that is sometimes used for fowl house roofs, cut into wide strips and dipped in petrol to make them a shiny black. His sporran was composed of a row of frayed-out manilla rope trimmed to length with an axe, emerging from beneath a half section of an aluminium saucepan lid, engraved with the end of a wood rasp. Tucked in his spats made of army gaiters dipped in whitewash, was the traditional dirk which was really a cook's carving knife. He was to wear some pink lace underpants rescued from the sack of bulldozer engineers' cleaning rags. From a relatively short distance the whole effect was as perfect as we non-Scotsmen could wish to see.

One day the piano appeared among the loading on a York. Many helping hands got it aboard a waiting lorry, rolling it along on lengths of bore casing and unloading it in the 'orchestra pit' by the stage. The sergeant musician soon found it to be well out of tune so the bulldozer mechanic spent a good proportion of time fixing it up. Finally, he declared it to be in tune and the sergeant was overjoyed to find that it really was. A large canvas camp sheet tied down over it kept off the sun until the night. A long length of fencing wire was stretched diagonally over where the audience was to sit in a natural amphitheatre on the slope of the hill, and a large steel outline of the project's code number 'X200' was made by the welders, and was joined and attached to the wire by rollers. This was bound in yards of potato bagging wired into place, the idea being that at the

Six kilometres distant and one minute after the explosion at the Emu claypan (*Courtesy Atomic Weapons Research Establishment, Aldermaston*)

opening this would be soaked in petrol, ignited, and released to roll slowly in flames on the wire over the patrons. Most of this was for the benefit of the unsuspecting visitors from H.Q. of course, as we wanted them to have some stories of the claypan hospitality to take back with them.

Tents and stretchers were prepared to accommodate them overnight. Chinny and I tied two bundles of gelignite to two myall trees just safely over the rim of a small vertical cliff at the end of the tent lines. These were to have detonators and different lengths of safety fuses attached which would be lit by us simultaneously at five o'clock on the morning following the concert. The theory here was that when one fuse gave out and set off its bundle of explosive, the visitors, still half asleep, would probably land on the floor of their tents from the shock; then, as they struggled back into their blankets in a daze, they would be allowed a minute to settle in before the next fuse came to its end, thus initiating the next and more violent explosion. We visualised the unfortunate H.Q. men sitting trembling on the edge of their beds nervously awaiting the next one but there were to be no more. All the claypan members had been forewarned, as we had to live together for a long time to come. Sir William Penney was tickled pink at the ingenuity of the diabolical scheme.

Three whole cases of gelignite placed in an oil drum were set at a distance worked out by Chinny who was in charge of the explosion. To start the show off with a bang they were all to be ignited at the same time at a signal given by the petrol-soaked blazing inferno of the 'X200' sign glowing up into the sky. The lighting and rolling of the sign were to be initiated after twenty coloured phosphorous Verey pistol flares were fired in a criss-cross pattern over the 'theatre-goers' heads, and to make sure the men ready to release the sign did not lose count, the last two shots were to be of a different colour. Only accurate timing would produce the best effect, and the differently coloured flares would also be the signal for the exact length of safety fuse at the oil drum to be lit to give McWilliams time to drive away in a hurry before it exploded.

I was beginning to think the preparation for the concert was giving us more work if possible than the preparation for the atomic bomb itself, but it kept the morale at its usual high level.

Once a date was set for the night everyone started secretly rehearsing plays and acts in earnest. Ken Hurne tried out the best subjects for his hypnotic act and demonstrated his powers to us from time to time, soon proving he was quite expert in the art. Apparently he had worked with a well-known performer before he joined the army as a cook.

The amount of talent to be found in a camp of this nature was amazing — it looked as if we would be able to put on a good bush show. I selected a dozen of the boys from all spheres to cartoon on the stage from 'memory' but really I had already made a number of sketches beforehand for the best effect. Among the subjects I chose were the Whip, Luke, McWilliams, Flip, and one of the tall thin plumbers with the baggiest overalls I had ever seen.

The three Yorks made available to fly the visitors in began arriving on the morning of the concert. Everything had been planned — as well as the short nerve-racking journey from the aeroplanes to the village. Being organised by McWilliams it consisted mostly of gelignite and revolver shots. The security section, looking as stern and official as they could, met each visitor as he emerged from the plane and inspected his pass. This was routine but they really did not have to wear shiny leather shoulder holsters holding huge .45 automatics. The office workers stared wide-eyed at them and moved obediently into their allotted trucks to proceed in convoy to the village.

Mountain Lowrey led the convoy in a utility buckboard at a pre-calculated speed of 10 kilometres per hour, arriving opposite a thick clump of myalls at the exact time a bundle of buried explosive was set to go off. The signal to light the fuse was given by a security officer who fired three quick shots from his automatic as Mountain left for the village. Just the right-sized shock wave blasted the sides of the trucks and anyone wearing a hat suddenly found himself bareheaded. This was to condition them for the evening's events.

They were shown their tents and as they beat at the clouds of flies and gratefully sat down for a rest after the long flight, they were completely unaware of what was to come. When it came to retaining secret information, the Emu boys were tops. After a wonderful meal put on specially by Ozzie and his boys, it was time for them to take their places at the amphitheatre, and by five minutes to eight everything was ready for the performance.

At three minutes to eight the bucket of petrol was sprayed over the sign and the hessian was well soaked, as, to the obvious surprise of the audience, the phosphorous flare signals began coming from all directions. With the second one of a different colour a lighted match was thrown at the sacking around the sign which burst into flames shooting up into the night and the thin retaining wire was cut by a mechanic with a pair of pliers. The roaring 'X200' slowly passed over the heads of the terrified visitors and at the precise moment it plunged into the lower myall tree, the oil drum containing the three cases of gelignite on a rise a kilometre away exploded in a sheet of white hot flame. Seconds later the roar of the shock wave carrying the violence of the blast, hit the group sitting in surely one of the most unusual theatres ever. By this time most of them were as white as the scene on the ridge, but then the floodlights were switched on bathing the stage in a glare of the same old shade of white and the sergeant opened the proceedings with a burst on the piano which had been uncovered in the darkness. The 'live' corpse came on stage to the microphone with a very professionally rendered song to the accompaniment of the piano, and the show was under way.

One of the members of the stone-picking group of engineers, a short round and jolly corporal, was M.C. He had compered many army gatherings in the past and did an excellent job keeping the periods in between acts bubbling with jokes. I felt sure the colour was returning to the faces of the visitors at last.

The Cinderella opera was next on the programme. Although this particular version would hardly be suitable for the drawing-room, it was cleverly done; a lot of work had been put into it. The hobnailed boot 'glass slipper' which was attached to a myall branch overhanging the stage, almost hit Cinderella on the head, but glanced off her shoulder as it fell.

After another piano item Ken Hurne called for complete silence which the visitors were more than willing to give. He mass hypnotised his six subjects and put them through a variety of harmless acts. One was so successfully hypnotised that he was laid with his shoulders on one chair and his feet on another, and a man standing on his belt line didn't even bend him. The whole act was a most interesting addition to the show and all onlookers were suitably amazed at seeing such sights in so remote a setting.

My caricatures came next amid much yelling and comments as the various ones were recognised. I think the Whip drew the most vigorous reception and after I had finished up with Brigadier Luke everyone called out that I would be out of a job the next day. Actually he asked for a smaller one to keep for himself later. I was forced to hurry with each one because the soft wax lumber crayon tended to melt in my hand with the heat of the lights.

Lorry Hogan carried on the show with a very well put over bagpipe solo. He looked no different from the lone piper who appears at the Edinburgh Festival — that is to anyone who hadn't been there. Old Jock, who had won the old codgers' race, might have thought otherwise but it was still an excellent performance. He finished his act in the middle of his rendition of 'Nut Brown Maiden' by suddenly stopping and gasping loudly as he trudged off the stage for all to hear, 'That's all fellers, I've had it.'

While the movie projector was being prepared, the pianist and the M.C. kept things going. Then, with the white tent fly unrolled for a screen, the colour movie started rolling, with all the 'film stars' sitting right in the audience watching themselves and each other. A roar went up as, one by one, the boys appeared on the screen, and friends yelled appropriate

remarks about each character. There were some action shots of the army engineers at the bottoms of excavations shovelling out rubble and if the one on the shovel happened to stop to lean on the handle for a spell, the audience would bawl a phrase they had heard the Whip use, such as 'Get working down there, this isn't a convalescent camp; move about now.' Although Ken Garden had his sense of humour, he was seldom to be seen other than serious-faced with the numerous things on his mind, and when he appeared on the canvas smiling, a particularly rugged air force member of the airfield construction team yelled out at the top of his voice, 'There y' are, what did I tell you blokes, it *can* laugh if it wants to.' It was all taken in good part by everyone and this was a highly successful finish to the most lively and appreciated concert that could be found anywhere in Australia.

The visitors were delighted to have been invited to it and would return to their desks at H.Q. with a renewed interest and understanding of what was involved. Until now they had thought of the project only in terms of impersonal code numbers and reams of paper work.

Finally they trudged wearily to their tents. They were unused to this sort of activity and they had already made a long flight that day and would be leaving the next morning at first light. Soon they were lying on their beds, exhausted and rapidly drifting into welcome oblivion. But Lorry Hogan was not going to let them off so lightly — he walked slowly up and down their tent lines vigorously playing 'Nut Brown Maiden' on his kangaroo skin bagpipes. The ants would have to wait for their treacle and water supply; even we thought it might be nice when it stopped. Eventually it did — at three in the morning.

At half-past four McWilliams crept into my tent and we prepared to go down to light the fuses on the bundles of gelignite hidden by the small cliff at the end of the camp lines. They were to go off a five a.m., so, at that time, with match heads placed firmly on the ends of the angle-cut fuses, Chinny and I drew the edge of the matchbox across them simultaneously and raced for our respective tents. A minute later a violent explosion rang out. This was followed by a shock wave making the tents shudder in spite of the slight subduing caused by the cliff. Things were quiet for the succeeding minute during which time we could only speculate on the reactions of our friends. With watch held tightly in hand, I counted down to the second and bigger explosion. Within seconds of the allotted minute which seemed an hour even to us, the next bundle went off and this all but blew the nearer tents down. Now those who had been warned could resume their interrupted sleep. Not so the visitors who could be heard gasping and asking each other what on earth had happened. As we had expected, they waited in vain for the third.

Soon, however, the whole camp was astir and willing hands began moving the heavy piano from the orchestra pit to the aeroplane. It was loaded and securely tied down to the holding bolts in the York. By this time Ozzie, Ken, and the kitchen staff had a great breakfast prepared.

The visitors were then shown some of the 'sights' of the claypan. They saw the fly-covered rubbish dump, and the 'Tiefa' machine that was used daily to force clouds of white fumes into the middle of swarms of insects in the quarry and at the water bore sites. A visit to the forward area was not included in the itinerary but an inspection of our prized new concrete mixer filled in the time until the accompanying aircraft fitters had their planes serviced, refuelled, and ready for the return journey to Woomera and Adelaide. We couldn't quite fathom the reason for the gleam in the eyes of the pilots as we drove the thoroughly weary but still smiling passengers down to the claypan. They gratefully handed in their temporary passes, had their names checked off the lists by the security section who kept up the atmosphere to the last with their grim faces and their .45s in shoulder holsters, and disappeared with a wary backward glance over their shoulders to sink into their seats.

The whole thing had certainly gone off with a bang, and stories of the rugged claypan camp were to be heard at H.Q. for weeks to come. But the most important thing was that they all had actually survived and were really glad they had come. The engines of the three planes started as soon as the doors had been slammed shut, a little too soon, we thought, but the haste went almost unnoticed. They taxied to the extremity of the claypan, turned, warmed up their motors, and commenced their take-off runs one after the other. We could almost hear the sighs of our friends as they waved from the windows.

However, the master touch was yet to come. The three huge aircraft circled and seemingly got themselves manoeuvred into one straight line, nose to tail as would a ground convoy, and made what we thought was a final pass over the claypan, as we watched from the ground. Then, without warning, they made a graceful sweep a kilometre or so on the Woomera side of the camp, and flying lower and lower as they approached the lines of tents, screamed a tree-top level over our canvas bedrooms. The first one loosened most of them in the slipstream, the second demolished those and handled others, and the third, exactly in the same line as the others with propellers almost touching the tail rudder of the one in front completely flattened most of the remaining tents, keeping up and increasing the violent suction of the others' slipstream. As the three monsters rose from the trees with a well-timed banking operation they put their noses down once more and really excelled themselves at low formation flying as they all made another obviously pre-planned pass over our humble, flattened abodes, dealing with several on the outskirts which had so far survived.

When we reached the scene of utter destruction we could almost hear those pilots and passengers saying, 'That'll teach you,' as they rapidly became three black specks in the sky on their way south. It had been our turn to be on the receiving end and, as we sat among the wreckage, we laughed until tears came to our eyes. It had surely solved the riddle of the gleam in the pilots' eyes and the eagerness with which they had started their engines as the doors slammed.

So ended what was undoubtedly the most raucous weekend that could have been endured anywhere on our planet, and one that could not have happened anywhere else but in the remote outback setting of the Central Australian bush. Everyone on both sides had been 'entertained' to the limit and a more fitting and well-earned lull in the pressure on all those present, could not have been possible.

As we began the job of rebuilding our village, I overheard one of the weary boys remark, 'When Hogan's bagpipes break down again, we'll sure make him a new bag, but this time it will be out of Beadell's skin.'

The explosion of an atom bomb in a trial requires much more of an operation than just pushing a button. Thousands of kilometres of planned grid lines must be laid out for specially equipped teams to take radiation contour readings to determine the rate of deterioration. Hundreds of cameras have to be positioned to photograph at all speeds, the blast for intense study afterwards, and thousands of specially designed instruments have to be arrayed in the immediate vicinity with an exact knowledge of their distance from the bomb itself to produce specified results of heat, velocity of shock waves, and pressure effects.

Then as the year progressed the astronomical cost of supplying the claypan became apparent and as further bombs were to be tested, a new site was being considered for the subsequent experiments. While the British atomic scientists were on the doorstep, an expedition was to be arranged just prior to the first atomic blast on the mainland of Australia at the claypan site to endeavour to find another site.

As a railway traverses the remote Nullarbor Plain, in the main quite free from habitation, the idea that freight could be brought by train much cheaper than aeroplane, soon appeared to be reasonable if a site could be located closer to it. The expedition covered almost 800 kilometres altogether and the atomic site of Maralinga resulted.

The British team were delighted and everybody reassembled at the claypan, where there was nothing more to do than wait for the right winds before pressing the button . . .

136

13
The Atomic Climax

There was an air of expectancy and excitement in the whole camp. Everything was in place and ready at every installation. The underground structure at the end of the co-axial cable was crammed with instruments and a movie camera. All the toothpaste tubes had been inserted in the baffle plates and the camera towers were equipped with their dozens of cameras, some colour movie, some fast, others slow — every combination possible. Each would be automatically set going at the time allotted to them before and during the final count-down.

Maddock's 'stuff' was in place and had proved its efficiency in many exhaustive tests. Loudspeakers had been placed in mulga trees wherever they would be needed and wired to Maddock's microphone at the firing panel, while both ends of every forward building had been removed. Each vehicle scheduled to be up front on the day had been identified and labelled with a large white number or letter fashioned on the passenger's windscreen with sticking plaster and the respective owners and passengers listed. Every man in the camp was listed and was ordered to be in a special position at the count-down, to be checked off on duplicate lists by section heads and the security boys.

Already full-scale rehearsals had been carried out to the letter. Even to the time when everyone would be up by midnight and off in their fuelled vehicles to carry on with their respective tasks, loading each camera with live film, joining wires at the tower base, locking the massive steel doors of all the underground concrete block houses. Maddock and Frank Hill were in place at the firing desk and vehicles and personnel double-checked. In fact everything had been done except arming the bomb which was hoisted, harmless, to the top of the tower. This proved the winch arrangements. The engines in the Centurion tank were started up for tests to observe whether they would continue moving or be snuffed out, and it was even equipped with 'Cecil,' the straw dummy propped up at the controls. It has been stressed before that this tank could have been placed in a position where it would have melted, but more knowledge could be gained if there was something left of it to study. Each group listed to be in possession of the personnel keys was handed them; after the rehearsal they were checked off by Maddock who was powerless to do anything unless he had regained charge of each one. This also went for the master key held by the men on top of the tower.

Nothing must go wrong when the moment arrived. An enormous responsibility rested on every man because even a day's hold-up at this stage meant thousands of pounds. The main problem was the weather, for if the wind was not exactly from the right quarter nothing would induce anyone to consider the explosion. Actually the final decision rested with Sir William alone. After all, the eyes of the world were upon Emu Claypan at this stage. Newspapers from every country which continued to pour into the ante-room, had headlines such as, 'Penney's packet ready to go.' One with 8-centimetre high black lettering read, 'Tomblin — Wind still wrong,' and so it went on with cartoons and facts which only helped to heighten the excitement at our 'haunted goanna hole' village.

Slowly and dramatically the hours ticked away into days until one evening a weather prediction was handed in saying that the wind was going to come from the south-east the following morning. That was the news around tea time. The weather boys both at the site and everywhere in the Commonwealth were the ones governing this phase of the procedure — a job few would envy.

On this night, however, tomorrow seemed to be *the* day, and everyone in the camp was so tensed up that I doubt if one member had even the suggestion of sleep before midnight when the activity was due to begin. The decision was being backed by each weather report that came in. Seven o'clock was the time scheduled for the firing in the morning, but even that time would not stand if any doubts whatever arose. When these electronic timing wizards said seven o'clock they really meant it, with some fantastically small proportion of a fraction of a second for tolerance, and the equipment was checked and rechecked by an automatic system coupled up to a precision time signal. Nothing that could possibly be done electronically was done by hand — tense nerves could mean errors.

On the stroke of midnight as if everyone had not been studying a watch dial for hours, an ear-splitting siren sounded out over the camp and loudspeakers boomed; the final preparation had officially begun. Fully clothed men were in their vehicles which were abrim with petrol in minutes, and off they went to their well-rehearsed jobs. I took my old Rover and reported to the small group who had drawn our personnel key while the other keys were being given out to the correct people. The battery of rockets was connected to the system, cameras were being carefully loaded by trained fingers, the cipher room which somehow had an open line of communication to Britain was buzzing with excitement; this was near the hydrogen loading meteorological balloon building, from which balloons were being sent up at a great rate to be tracked by met. theodolites and radar to their limit of height.

Cooks, mechanics, and men who could stay at the village to lessen the quantity of checking work at Area A were out but still had to be marked off the lists. In fact they were to obtain a more spectacular view of the fireball and mushroom than anybody.

There was no rush or panic as each man methodically went about his role in this drama of dramas. I had said, when I was asked, that I should like to stand on the bluff if it were feasible — I knew it would give a good commanding view of the scene. It appeared that that was where Sir William, Luke, and a selected group would be standing as well, so my ideas conceived when this was all virgin country were being maintained to the very end. In fact everything that had been done through the year had confirmed my mind's eye picture.

The darkness wore on with lights from vehicles and torches flashing about in the mulga. At dawn, when grey streaks of light heralded the commencement of this most historic day in Australia's history, my allotted group gathered to proceed to the very base of the bomb tower. The ominous black shape had been winched up to the top and was now a fixture. Three intrepid scientists were readying it for the last time. As I saw the tremendous steel structure of the tower I recalled my guess as to the ultimate damage it would suffer. Top blown off, middle third strained, and lower third barely marked. I also remembered the grinning faces which informed me 'You'll see.' I hadn't long to wait.

We got out, leaving the engines running, and secured two wires at the foot of one of the legs and joined them up securely. In the micro-second of detonation this device would send a container, which would snap shut in a calculated fraction of a second, through the atomic cloud and high into the air, clear of the heat, with the object of collecting radioactive dust and sealing in a small portion for later studies. We jumped into the Rovers waiting three paces away and as we sped off I took a last glance back at the dreadful black mass at the top of the tower. What was it capable of?

Back at the hut housing Maddock's stuff, a growing collection of personnel keys appeared near the row of key holes, but still the gaping hole where the master key fitted was empty. With half an hour to go, I drove up to the bluff to get into position. I aimed the rear of the vehicle to the tower as I wasn't sure what would happen to the glass windscreen. Various clipped sentences came from the loudspeakers explaining each particular phase. At this stage I was issued with a pair of arc welding goggles. Sir William greeted me and we recalled how we had stood on this very spot discussing aspects of the project exactly a year before. How much had happened since!

Phase Wallaby or some such Australian animal name had now begun and the time seemed to be racing. Through binoculars I looked at the tower 7 kilometres away, and could easily make out the bomb mass that gave it a top heavy appearance. Sir William told us to be careful in the use of the goggles. He did not think it was entirely a good idea to look at the fireball at the instant it formed, so everyone was to be facing exactly in the opposite direction to it. Only after the flash could they turn around with safety to observe the formation of the mushroom. I was told that to look at the flash would be like looking at the sun itself from a few kilometres away, and I began to wonder at the wisdom of being there at all. There were five minutes to go which meant the final count-down would begin in a minute.

At last the clipped 'four minutes to go' came over the air for all to hear, including the Canberra jet bomber streaking across the sky, scheduled to rip through the atomic cloud, when it rose high enough. The pilot was to fly away from the bomb in the last few seconds before the explosion, then bank when he saw the flash, and guide the Canberra at full throttle through the centre of the mushroom, snap shut some wing-tip canisters, and report to a coupled tape recorder any sensations he felt as he flew through the mass. He was then to scream at wide open throttle to Woomera where a cordoned-off area at the end of the cleared strip would be his parking place, and tumble out to a waiting ambulance for immediate medical checking. The plane would be attacked by a scientific team equipped with goon suits and geiger counters and studied minutely from nose to rudder while the wing-tip containers were handled by other experts loaded with instruments. The value of the results of such a test were obvious. Flying into such a cloud of unknown composition called for sheer courage but many volunteers had come forward.

'Three minutes to go!'

There was no doubt about it — the atmosphere at this time was hushed; everyone had his own imagined idea of the outcome. There had been an intense build-up to it all, starting from the day of the Eyebrows con-

140

ference with Bill Worth as far as I was concerned, and with the first invasions for everyone else. The seconds ticked away on the belt watch I was clutching; the welding goggles lay loosely around my neck. I wasn't going to risk the use of them at all after Sir William's remark.

'Two minutes to go!'

This was fast becoming unbearable. Maddock's stuff began actuating on its own the things designed for it. I could picture his control panel, keys turned on over the master key in place, rows of lights flashing from phase to phase, and Frank Hill anything but 'gloomy' flicking his eyes over the dials and cathode ray patterns.

'One minute to go!'

I nearly jumped a foot as it penetrated that the end of eternity was so close; I had been too busy thinking to look at my watch. Suddenly an Admiral covered in braid standing alongside me turned to Sir William. 'I say,' he said 'what if it doesn't go off?' Sir William gazed sleepily at him over the top of his black-rimmed glasses and broke the silence of the group with his confident and almost yawned reply, 'It'll go off all right.' That was that — emphatically. I couldn't have come out with a question like that, at a time like that to the man on whose shoulders the complete burden rested, for all the shady tea in China. Kevin Connolly had arrived, and as Sir William added, 'This isn't my show, I'm just here for a look.' Kevin whispered to me, 'It takes a big man to say that.'

'Thirty seconds to go!'

Someone pulled his collar up around his ears as you would to keep out a cold evening and it struck me it wouldn't help much unless it was made of reinforced concrete. Hardly anyone wears a reinforced concrete collar these days anyway.

'Twenty seconds to go!' Silence!

'Ten seconds to go — nine, eight, seven, six, five, four, three' — a loud generator started up alongside me and I nearly died on the spot, as I flicked an eye on the tower and back again before he continued, 'two, one, NOW!!'

Great Scott, what a sight! The entire sky as it domed out and down past the distant horizon lit up in a blinding flash of fire and we felt the heat on our backs for a fleeting fraction of a second. No noise yet, apart from the screaming jets of the Canberra bomber, as it made its run in. In just over a second we all whirled around to witness the end of the fireball and the boiling cauldron of deadly radioactive dust fighting for room to expand all at once. It surged, enlarged, and began its skyward path to write its mushroom signature in the heavens.

The bright sun was about twenty degrees high by now in an otherwise cloudless burnished sky and the mushroom began to obliterate it as the screaming silver streak of the Canberra closed the distance to the thickest part of the mushroom. We saw it again as it raced out of the other side and rose above the line of the mulga trees. As it banked the pilot indicated that he was going to have another go at it. Then, without as much as a goodbye, his silver bullet lit out for Woomera.

Gosh! what a morning. During all this we had temporarily forgotten that there was supposed to be a noise and shock wave accompanying it, but we were soon reminded. At least there was a little warning — we saw a difference in colour of the mulgas as they bent reflecting the sun at a different angle. This change in colour from normal dull green to almost light grey neared slowly at first as we were looking at it obliquely. Then when it got to within a kilometre it seemed to race at us and we were nearly pushed over by its force. The blast was the loudest I had ever heard; it sounded like a case of gelignite let off by Chinny in a room.

It was over. The results of a year's all-out effort manually and mentally gone in the fraction of a second. But what a climax! It surely lived up to and surpassed our wildest guesses, and one and all agreed that they were proud to have been associated with it.

Old Luke had a little joke waiting at this stage for the reporters. 'Look,' he shouted pointing at the atomic cloud, 'do you see it?' Everyone whipped around to direct their attention to the cloud. 'A perfect portrait of a myall blackfeller written with atomic dust; the new and the old have come

142

together today.' He was so enthusiastically serious that one by one they agreed that there was no doubt about it. Sure enough the newspapers printed the huge headlines: 'Myall black man written by atomic dust in sky over Emu.' Good old Luke.

Suddenly — for all this interchange had only taken several minutes — Sir William leapt into a waiting vehicle and raced for the cipher room. Churchill in Britain probably had the news minutes later on the wide open line from the haunted goanna hole to him. I drove back to the claypan where there was a York plane waiting with engines going, and George Pither and several others, including me, crawled aboard, and we waited for Sir William before taking off for a quick flight over the scene. It was still a very hot radioactive area and we lacked the speed of the Canberra, but all the danger of the cloud had dispersed by now.

The York was lined up at the right end of the strip for the light breeze. Then we roared off down the runway for an immediate take-off. Flying to the forward area took a couple of minutes, but soon we were looking down at the devastation. Small fires were burning, and long radial streaks of bare destruction emerged from a centre. It looked as though a giant paper bag of grey flour had been dropped and had burst.

Where was the tower? There was absolutely nothing whatever left at the centre of this schemozzle. Just smooth saucer-shaped ground. I couldn't believe my eyes ... that huge steel structure which I thought might become a little 'strained' ... I laughed aloud at my naïvety. The whole thing had melted and vaporised in a decimal of a second; later, when I visited the scene in a goon suit, it still seemed impossible.

I was sitting next to Sir William as he looked down over his glasses. I saw him rubbing his hands and heard him murmur one word, 'Whacko!' He should have been an Australian.

We felt the plane bank as we came over for a last glimpse of our year's work. Then back to the claypan where we and aircraft were run over with geiger counters. They did not respond.

Frank Hill came to me with head bowed, eyes lowered, and uttered a long, a soft, drawn out 'Gloom!' He had lost a prized lizard in the fuss. In a day or so Sir William boarded a special aeroplane and began his return journey to England to wind up the details on paper. He farewelled me in his tent saying that we would meet again in due course at Maralinga.

Later that morning I was talking to Maddock in his tent, and the sight of his diary gave me an idea. It lay open at the present day's date, 15 October 1953, and, while his back was turned, I helpfully entered up for him his movements of the day:

Up early to darn my socks, brush teeth, and fold my washing; let off atom bomb and iron my hankies.

A year and a half of intensive survey work and mapping to provide a framework upon which Maralinga could be based followed closely on the heels of the first atomic trials at the claypan, which had been named Emu. Not only the main bombs were to be tested but their trigger devices proved and various other developments akin to the nuclear experiments had to be planned and laid out in the field. Then the practical problem of what to do with the equipment left at Emu arose.

Much of this could be put to similar use at Maralinga including the prefabricated buildings, and since it would be a gigantic moving job involving a distance of 2000 kilometres return, a shorter road was clearly needed linking the two sites, as just over 200 kilometres separated them. When the connecting link had been completed, convoys of trucks transported the expensive items to the new site.

Radiation readings were still needed on an even larger scale and this new road also provided instant access to the north. Additional similar access was still required and further roads were requested westerly to continue on with the original road to Emu. The overall geodetic survey of Australia for the two projects was also urgently required and Woomera and Maralinga combined finances to carry out the access to make this possible.

The country became even worse as the team pushed out west and some of the original members of that first little team remained on that work for the next eight years . . .

14
Vokes Hill

As I scanned the unbroken horizon of red sandhills and mulga from the top of Vokes Hill after finally rediscovering it, my first impression was that here at last was a place free from tax collectors and hydrogen bombs.

Binoculars were useless, as they only magnified the heat shimmer which converted the skyline into jelly as the sun blazed down on the already baked country extending for hundreds of kilometres in every direction. I was at the time in the middle of a hundred thousand square kilometre belt of dense mulga-covered sand ridges, completely bare of life apart from the few lizards moving from one saltbush to the shade of the next, with the nearest track of any sort some hundreds of kilometres to the south on the Nullarbor Plain. There was nothing at all to the west for almost 800 kilometres and 500 kilometres to the east lay the opal fields of Coober Pedy, on the road from Adelaide to Alice Springs. Several hundred kilometres north was the road my little camp of six bush bashers had made, extending for nearly 1500 kilometres east to west. This was the first road bulldozed across Central Australia and was named the Gunbarrel Highway. I had originally called our band of men the Gunbarrel Road Construction Party as a joke because, wherever possible, we liked to make our roads straight, and we felt quite honoured later to see the name Gunbarrel on the official maps.

It was at my present position in that stretch of desolation, where I did not exactly have the feeling of being hemmed in, that I had at last found the only labelled pinpoint on an otherwise bare map. By a series of astronomic and sun observations, I had been able to draw closer to the plotted position of Vokes Hill, observing stars with my theodolite at night, calculating the results by the lights of the Land Rover, and bush bashing it on the new bearing during the day. The sand ridges made it almost impossible to keep to any computed direction other than east or west, as that was the way the ridges lay, but by deflating the tyres to a point where any less would withdraw the tube valve, I was able to veer a little north and south.

Finally, I could sense the country rising, as from the top of some sandhills the visible horizon extending farther, with the sandhills and ridges becoming gradually more confused, lying one on top of the other, each starting before the other cut out.

The pattern was changing. That indicated that something had happened in the past geological ages to cause it all, in this case a build-up in altitude starting from many kilometres around and culminating in a crescendo of sand. A long time before, an expedition had been drawn towards this spot on its way — probably on camels — to a place where some mineral deposits had been mentioned by an explorer of the previous century. The word 'gold' had been the incentive. This highest point in the turmoil of sandhills had been named Vokes Hill, after the man who had organised the trip. The expedition had struggled northwards from the bare Nullarbor Plain. At this moment I would gladly have exchanged my motor vehicle for a camel.

The night before, I had calculated my lat. and long., and after plotting them had found that the hill lay only a few kilometres by scale to the north-west from my lone camp. After mending the staked tyres and eating some bully beef from a tin, I lay on my swag in the saltbush, impatient for morning to come so that I could get going once more. I planned to move west in a sand valley, following the ridge for a kilometre or so, then abandon the Rover in favour of hiking north for about a kilometre to find this elusive summit.

By first light next morning I was again bush bashing through the heavy scrub in my unfortunate vehicle which I'd had modified with special reinforcements. Stopping a kilometre to the west, I took binoculars and compass and climbed up on to the first high sand ridge, from where I could see at least 80 kilometres south, but to the north all I could see was the next sand ridge a hundred metres away. Clambering up that, I could in turn see over the previous one, and after six more I began to see parts of a similar horizon away to the north. Plodding up on to each next obviously higher point, the time came when only one small section of the skyline out of the full circle was obscured. When I arrived at the base, where this final mound of sand met the confusion around it, I

knew I had at last rediscovered Vokes Hill. It was impossible to walk up this last knob of forty-five degrees, so I crawled up on hands and knees with the sand not held by mulga roots cascading down around me. When I was next able to stand I was on the summit. The endless desolation, unobstructed in every direction, stretched away into the heat haze. I had no one with whom to share this final victory. In fact I hadn't seen anyone at all for a week, and then it was only the few men of my camp working at the head of our new road, servicing the bulldozer and trucks in readiness for the next onslaught which we had to make on the bush.

This was why I was here in the first place, to build a second road across Australia, also 1500 kilometres long, which would divide the continent halfway from the Nullarbor Plain to our original Gunbarrel Highway. The road was to provide access for a further series of surveys adding to the overall geodetic survey of the unexplored parts of Central Australia. The information was required for our rocket range projects at Woomera. Owing to the vastness of the wastelands in the semideserts of Australia, such large-scale surveys had been next to impossible before the advent of bulldozers and four-wheel-drive vehicles. As these tellurometer traverses (so named after the new radar-style measuring instruments) require hills or high country from which to cover the distances, I had decided long before to make the road pass as closely as possible to the only point shown as a hill. This would help the parties from the National Mapping

Council of Australia who would eventually follow in our wake to drive their heavy equipment near to any high areas.

So far the new road had progressed west from Emu, a site I had discovered for the first atomic bomb trials held on the mainland of Australia, to a distance of about 100 kilometres, and it was there that the bulldozer and camp now lay. Emu was joined to the Alice Springs Highway near the Coober Pedy opal fields by a bulldozed and graded road I'd surveyed and made several years before, so we now had over 300 of the present 1500-kilometre project finished, leaving only a mere 1200 kilometres of road to make.

This we had planned to join over to Laverton in Western Australia which was almost a ghost gold-mining town due west of Coober Pedy. Vokes Hill just happened to be right on line. That explains the trouble I'd taken to find it in that inhospitable wilderness. Astrofixes were positively the only way to do it.

Once the road was through and our survey needs satisfied, other incidental users of the road such as geologists, oil exploration parties, further state mapping groups, and Aboriginal patrol officers would be sure to follow. The overall help to Australia's future would be considerable, so I put as much care into the construction and survey location of these roads as if they had been much closer to civilisation. I looked upon the

whole undertaking as being much more of a privilege than a job, and would not willingly have changed places with anyone during the eight years I was engaged on it, although the work became very strenuous the farther we penetrated into the unknown.

Much support from our H.Q., the Weapons Research Establishment at Salisbury, near Adelaide, was needed and given to carry out such an unusual and immense programme of work. One clerk turned pale as he ordered in for me a set of dental equipment with forceps and hypodermic needles used in teeth extractions. As I stood by his desk telling him what we'd need, he said he hoped he'd never have to join my camp himself.

The sun was on its way down at last and I thought it was time I should slide down the hill and start the trip on foot back to the Rover. I eased down the sand heap, starting a miniature avalanche which filled my open-topped hobnailed boots with the hot-baked grains. I emptied them for the hundredth time and retracked myself over the ridges back to the vehicle. It was still there, glowing with the heat not only of the sun, but of the reflected rays off the ground as well as the switched-off engine. It had taken several minutes to stop coughing after turning the key, so it all added up to an oven-like cabin. Again I had to shut the perspex windows against the mulga branches and sticks which constantly raked at the sides as I pushed through the scrub on the return to camp. The compass I had carried was only for reading magnetic bearings to distant rises or any features which served to draw up my own rough map as I went, and not really for use in finding my way through the bush.

A tyre had gone down while I had been away, and as I unloaded the ever-ready tools I realised just how thirsty I had become. I could now have a long drink from the tepid water in the tank, something I had made sure of not doing before the hike. It took a little manoeuvring to turn round in the scrub but eventually I was following my own tracks back in the direction of our camp of bush bashers. It was a great feeling to have located the hill at last and my thoughts now turned to that huge bulldozer blade which would soon be attacking the scrub, carving out the final road along which trucks could travel.

Apart from the complete lack of water, the hordes of flies, and the utter remoteness of this wilderness, it was relatively easy camping country. There were not many problems such as hairy poisonous spiders, snakes, or other dangers to combat. All you had to do for a fire was to rake your fingers along the ground and light the resulting heap of hot dry tinder. In other areas it takes quite a project to get a fire going with soggy wet wood, each piece harbouring some specimen of insect ready to bite or strike their venom into unsuspecting fingers. Clouds of the more disconcerting mosquitoes also take the place of our flies which at least go to bed at the same time as we desert dwellers do. It is only one night or two a year that rain disturbs us, although at times I did think a little more would be welcome.

During the quarter of a century of almost continuous camping in the open, I often wondered what another might do while searching the stars every night before sleep took over. I happened to occupy myself with the forming of countless patterns of right-angled triangles with the brilliant pinpoints of light filling the black sky on moonless nights, and it was only on the full moon evenings that I would forcibly have a rest from my geometry.

After more silent, lone camps and a dozen flat tyres, I eventually emerged from the scrub to rejoin the camp at the head of the road to date, and found everything ready to be on the move again. Doug, the bulldozer driver, ambled over to see how I'd got on, while old Paul, the cook, put on a billy. Scotty made an exaggerated burst of running to his grader, as if not to be left behind, and Frank Quinn, the supplies driver, yelled out from underneath his truck that it was about time I got back from stargazin'. Rex, the heavy equipment fitter, knowing everything was in first-class mechanical order, didn't need to stir from his conference with Eric about some worldly topic. Eric's job of cherry-picking, or cleaning the finished road free of hidden roots, stumps, and loose sticks was now about to resume, but he'd been just as hard-pressed helping Rex with the machinery.

They were an extra good group of men whom I had picked from places as scattered as the Maralinga bomb site, the Northern Territory, and farms over a hundred kilometres east of Adelaide; they included a former bush shearer's cook who had been working in Mines Department water drilling camps. As Scotty had once said during one particularly rough period we went through soon after our little band got together: you need bush blokes for the bush jobs! Some of them stayed with me for eight years, under the worst conditions possible, during our work in Central Australia, and then the couple who did leave did so reluctantly for family reasons. Most of us were single, without a tie in the world, but Doug had to go and get married and spoil it all, eventually followed by Eric, and then even myself. Rex just sat back contentedly, telling us how sorry we'd be, but I noticed he was as happy as any of us although he had been married for many years.

We were eventually to make 6500 kilometres of roads through the unexplored Centre, but here now was our latest project, that of joining east to west across Australia for the second time.

A survey link from the Gunbarrel Highway to Emu had been required before beginning this one, which entailed a road of 500 kilometres starting at Mount Davies, a point near the north-western corner of the State. We had finished that. Being in a south-easterly direction it crossed over hundreds of sand ridges with which we were now battling.

Anxious as we all were to get on with our new project, yet another road had to be made from the Vokes Hill area south to the Nullarbor Plain, and we arranged to do that first. It was a direction which meant these sand ridges had to be crossed every hundred metres and the scene as viewed from the Hill didn't hold out any hope for an easy going. The first thing now was to close the remaining gap from the present camp to Vokes Hill and tap the resulting road at the best looking spot for the bushbashing south.

We made a start the same afternoon that I lumbered back to camp, and it was with great pleasure that I watched the huge cat 'dozer fighting with the scrub in place of my relatively delicate vehicle. The first section was travelling with the sandhills, and irrespective of the thickness of the scrub we usually managed to carve out about 6 kilometres each day, double the width of the blade to protect the truck canopies from over-hanging mulga branches.

Ahead of the bulldozer, I had the chance of deciding on a place I'd planned to call Vokes Hill Corner, and settled on a spot a few kilometres short of the place where I'd left the Rover to complete the reconnaissance on foot. It was still in the heavy scrub, but the sand ridge on the south had cut out, giving us a few hundred metres start before attacking the next one, so after the bulldozer had crashed through the trees to that area, we guided it a hundred metres farther on the route to Vokes Hill.

That was to be as far as the road would go west, until the new one was opened up south to Cook, a siding on the Nullarbor Plain on the Trans-Australia Railway Line. Back-tracking then to the exact spot planned for the corner, we cleared the area of scrub ready for a camp and started the bulldozing towards Cook. This was only to put our little base camp clear of the future roads. When the first sand ridge loomed up, the heavy machine again back-tracked and continued east to the head of the road where the trucks were waiting for something to drive on. Vokes Hill itself would still have to wait for its road as it had already done for so many thousands of years.

The next stage was to chop a heavy log of black oak for a sign-post, carry out an accurate astrofix for its lat. and long., and attach the aluminium sign plate I would make for it. When the camp moved up and settled in, it was time to start yet another expedition to see what we'd be in for on this job. While unwanted equipment was being sorted and unloaded, I prepared for the trip. In this country I wasn't altogether looking forward to it, with the dozens of staked tyres I was bound to get.

We planned to have the party move back up to the Gunbarrel Highway to carry out a regrading programme of parts of it that were reported to have suffered in a recent downpour of rain while I was away from them for several weeks after this new expedition.

The reason was that it had become my turn to copy Doug, despite his advice about how to avoid weddings, and I had somehow been included in the arrangements to take place in several weeks' time. All I had done was to allow myself to be persuaded into purchasing a house in which I had no intention of living and had returned to the bush leaving behind a family kind enough to occupy it for me. The fact that they had a daughter led eventually to this present planning at Vokes Hill Corner.

After the expedition then, provided I got through alive, I would be going to Adelaide, and as I ploughed off into the scrub I was not sure just what the sad expressions on the boys' faces meant, but I made a shrewd guess it didn't have anything to do with the rough trip I had just begun.

The going was quite as hard as I had known it would be, and each high sandhill required a dozen attempts to finally cross over, while the thickly covered carpet of mulga trees raked along the sides of the Rover. One branch pushed right through one of the perspex side windows and from then on I was sitting up to my waist in a nest of dry sticks as they poured in through the jagged gap. The non-magnetic rods I'd designed running from the front reinforced grille to the top corners of the windscreen protected the glass as the bulk of the branches slid up and over the vehicle, but I still resembled a nesting wedge-tailed eagle.

On one crossing, while backing down in preparation for the next attempt, the Rover slewed out of its wheel tracks and I found myself side on to the rise, with the vehicle on the point of overbalancing, held up only by a small mulga tree growing in the sand. I was on the lower side, and the angle the door made with the ground made it impossible to open it enough to get clear. This meant gently crawling over the transmitter and other boxes on the passenger seat to climb out through the other door, and with a shovel and axe it took an hour to relieve the excitement of possibly watching the Rover rolling over and over down the hill.

There were some native wells indicated on the way, which I had no hope of finding on this trip without much observing of stars but which I endeavoured to come close to on my reconnaissance. I would find them later, if possible, and make the road pass by them as a means of location for future parties following along, labelling them with the usual aluminium plates. I carried quite a number of these together with a set of alphabet stamps for this purpose, and when the lack of trees for posts made it necessary to bolt them to lids of empty diesel drums, I'd shoot the holes through with my revolver.

The rippled mulga green carpet effect as seen from the higher ridges stayed with me for 150 kilometres until I detected traces of marine limestone on knobs in the valleys which had been exposed as the wind had blown away the loose sand. This meant the vague first beginnings of the Nullarbor Plain, made up of marine limestone from the middle Miocene period with an age of about 40 million years.

The scrub was still thick, but the worst of the ridges were behind me now, as were the maze of dry salt lakes I'd been forced to weave through, and it was only a matter of time before I could expect to emerge out of this mixed up jumble, known as the Victoria Desert, on to the bare plains.

It had been a week since I'd left the boys and I could see a lot of hard work ahead to make this access a reality, but it was a challenge as well. The mulga was as thick as I'd seen it growing anywhere, and camping in it this last week made me eager to see proper daylight around me each morning, instead of the gloom of the mulga jungle, as I emerged from my swag roll. Gradually the scrub opened up as the outcrops of limestone took over, until suddenly it stopped, as if a giant mower had been used, and I could see a 80-kilometre clear horizon for the southern half of the circle. The last bush-bashing and sandhill expedition I was to make as a free person was over.

After driving across the plain to Cook and continuing on in the direction of Adelaide, 1300 kilometres away, I began to wonder nervously if it were not, after all, easier to cope with the country around Vokes Hill.

The little Gunbarrel Road Construction Party was, by choice, comprised of young, single men without ties and as free from commitments as anyone in the world. The combination of this requisite and the fact that they could very efficiently carry out their allotted tasks in the bush with the added willingness to live as Aborigines in the most primitive and harsh conditions to be found anywhere, made it an ideal and happy band. The unprecedented nature of the job went a long way towards keeping the atmosphere in their camps on a level bordering excitement.

Inevitably as time went on and in the very brief spells 'down south,' sometimes for only a few weeks once a year, the members married but they still answered the call of the bush and carried on with their work with almost increased vigour.

The author couldn't believe what was happening to his camp up until the time he followed suit and in a move totally unparalleled in the history of the project, brought his wife and five-month-old daughter out with him. They camped in the most remote parts of the Great Victoria Desert for nearly half a year while the road making proceeded and even helped in booking readings for the astrofixes.

Part of the current programme involved making a road link over 600 kilometres long from the little siding of Rawlinna on the Trans-Australian Railway on the Nullarbor Plain, north to the most isolated Aboriginal mission in Australia, Warburton.

Being the first white baby in that most desolate region, the resulting road was named in her honour . . .

154

15
The Connie Sue Highway

With the new access opened up, another source was now available for supplies which could come from Giles as well as Maralinga, so without further delay, Quinny was on his way. I had radioed Giles news of the completion of the road and asked them to expect our truck for a much-needed load of diesel and petrol. I informed the Woomera base to send the usual set of teletypes to H.Q. about the finish of the new road, and after replenishing all our water tanks, we turned around to begin the long trek south. It was 650 kilometres to Rawlinna, half of which was over our freshly-made road, leaving 325 kilometres to be surveyed and laid.

At one spot on the way down we drove west off the road at an interesting looking formation of escarpment country, judging by the air photographs, and discovered a small but rugged ravine in the cliff edge. With Connie riding on my shoulders, Anne and I climbed down to see if there were water present, but although there was none, we were delighted to find some Aboriginal ochre finger-paintings on the walls of several small caves. We would have been the first whites ever to have set eyes on them, and the thought that Aborigines had been here in ages past made the area something to be remembered. Also possibly no one would have seen them since, in such a remote miniature canyon, and this would have preserved them from destruction.

One day, as we were waiting by the fire we had made for a dinner camp in advance of Paul's truck, we saw an extra large cloud of dust approaching from the direction in which he was coming. With the knowledge that it couldn't be the bulldozer, as that was crawling along behind at 5 kilometres per hour, we began wondering what could be stirring up so much dust, when Paul's truck came into view. The dust cloud was coming from behind it but nothing could be seen through the volumes of fine dust billowing up in a much more spectacular way than usual. As he drew nearer we heard loud banging and clattering noises above those made by his truck, and soon, as he slowed to a stop by our fire, we saw the cause of it all. He had been towing the trailer since our last sighting 6 kilometres back, upside down. With its wheels in the air, the loading was almost a wreck, although only some of the ropes holding it in place were worn through. We saw there were no folding legs left on the table on the top of the load as we pulled it over, back on its wheels with the Rover. The stove, which couldn't fall out of the back, had been taking a good share of the battering.

I went back along the road to the point where we'd last seen it on its wheels, before an ant bed had flipped it over as he drove, past all the debris scattered about. By the time I rejoined the trailer I had the Rover covered with old table legs, bits of stove hot plates, and a bent and battered flue pipe. Rex had already begun the repair operation with his oxy-welding torch alight, and soon one set of legs were in shape to replace on the table. The other end could be propped up on the second table for the rest of the year as the woodwork was quite beyond salvaging. A crowbar straightened the flue, and with a bronze welding rod the hot plates were brazed together. At first it had looked hopeless but already we were seeing our way clear. No damage had been done to the trailer. In fact, Paul remarked that he had saved wear on the tyres for a full 6 kilometres.

Soon the bulldozer lumbered in and Scotty, covered in dust, could have dinner while Rex serviced the 'dozer.

A week after leaving Warburton country, we had all struggled into Neale Junction, which now consisted of a road to the east joining on to the main Alice Springs Highway, a road north right into Warburton and on to Giles, a few yards of road south and the same west. Before starting the road south, we decided to make a little further use of the 'dozer while we had it to lead out west past some heavier scrub. After a day at the cross roads servicing the equipment, we left the camp where it was and bulldozed west towards Laverton until the machine emerged through the thickest of the bush to a relatively more open area, 22 kilometres away. Then reluctantly we turned the bulldozer around after clearing the lead out in preparation for the grader to carry on when we returned with it from Rawlinna. That Laverton road would still have to wait for its completion, but having carried out the survey reconnaissance for it I knew I could carry it right through with the grader only.

157

The year was slipping away almost unnoticed. The harder we worked the quicker the time seemed to go, and we still had 500 kilometres of road to make. Within a day or so of the beginning of October we were back at Neale Junction with the bulldozer blade heading at last for Rawlinna siding. The heat was well upon us now, and each day Connie was having a hard time remaining white, as each day the dry dust turned her little body to a coffee colour and her face, beaded with moisture, was crimson. She was certainly having a rugged introduction to life, but was otherwise healthy and as happy as any eight-month-old baby could be. She was now living in the 'Mickey Mouse' shorts Anne had made out of my old shirt.

We had no sooner started on the Rawlinna section of the Connie Sue Highway when the time had arrived once again for shearing, and as I cut everyone's hair I thought how short a time it seemed since the last session. It seemed more like a few days than a month.

Then, not 30 kilometres on our way, the steel cable on the bulldozer blade lift snapped and the winch brake fell to pieces. Rex was along in no time after I'd returned for him in the camp, and with everyone levering and hammering we helped him restore it. The following day was accompanied by a raging dust storm and we were glad the work on the winch had come when it did, as a day later we couldn't have seen it for the swirling dirt, let alone work on it.

Quinny was on another supplies trip to Maralinga as we approached 150 kilometres south of Neale Junction, and I learnt from a radio contact that he had arrived safely, loaded up, and was on his way back to us. Although it was a 1100-kilometre trip via the Serpentines, Vokes Hill, and Emu as against 800 kilometres to Giles, I used Maralinga, as their own stores came to within 30 kilometres by rail. On the other hand, fuel which reached Giles had to be carted from their nearest rail siding which was 800 kilometres away.

Several days after his leaving Maralinga we heard Quinny's engine groaning along under the full load of drums of diesel and petrol 1400 litres of water, and boxes of rations, and as always, I was thankful that he had made it once again. As the noise grew louder we walked out on to the road to see him coming, outlined against a background of volumes of dust, but something looked different about the front of the truck. For a long time we couldn't quite see what it was. Half the front seemed to be missing, and as he drove closer we were astounded to discover the truck had no radiator at all. Where it had been was now only a gaping hole with the engine itself in full view. We were still wondering how it could go at all as it shuddered to a stop at the camp. Quinny climbed out of the cabin covered in sweat and grease and gave us a cheerful greeting of, 'Good day! What are you all gawkin' at?'

He explained that after leaving Maralinga he had done 150 kilometres when two of the fan blades had snapped off and chopped his radiator to pieces. Most drivers to whom this happened would have sat down to wait for help, but not Quinny. He crawled the truck into Emu by constantly pouring buckets of water into the gashed radiator, while stemming the main flow out of the holes with a thick mixture of flour and water. It was only about 40 kilometres, so he persevered until he arrived at the old atomic ghost camp. There he had visited the rubbish dump and discovered several lengths of flexible tubing we once used on the bore water distilling plant. These gave him his solution to the problem. Taking the radiator off altogether and throwing it up on the back, he jammed one hose down over the outlet on top of the engine block and trailed it around the mudguard to dangle it into the 1400-litre camp water supply tank. Then forcing another over the water tank tap, he trailed it also around the mudguard to push it over the lower inlet casting of the engine. The leaks were all taken care of with rags and leather held tight with many wire twitches and after turning on the tap, he drove the remaining 800 kilometres to us with the camp water supply flowing through the cooling jacket around the engine.

It was one of the most ingenious bush improvised jobs imaginable which had got him right back to camp with the much needed diesel to carry on with the road making. With my little camp of 'gunbarrel bush bashers' made up of men like these, I always felt proud and pleased to be associated with them. I'm sure none of us would have changed places with anyone throughout, and each one of us had a high regard for the other's ability, even though it was outwardly taken for granted. They must have even had confidence in my 'star gazin'' as no one ever questioned where we were or where we were going, knowing that all in good time, even though it might take a year or so, we would eventually break out of the scrub through to our destination. It took this kind of teamwork to make it possible, and the completion of each project brought us each so much satisfaction that it was enough to compensate for the rough lives we led and urged us on to even greater efforts.

That was to be the last supply trip back along the road because those two dozen drums would carry us as far as the Nullarbor Plain, where we could drive forward on a compass bearing to the Rawlinna rail siding for more. That would be our base for the rest of the year's work until we turned for home after joining Neale Junction to Laverton.

After the beating the supply truck had suffered with those long hauls, capped by the radiator episode, I arranged by radio for a replacement truck to be made available at Maralinga when we had a chance to go there and collect it. In the meantime Rex could keep the old girl going until we reached the railway by blocking off all the leaks with kilograms of solder. The weather was going through one of the worst phases of the year now, with constant violent dust storms lasting for days between periods of intense heat, and even one hail storm with a deluge of rain hit the camp, turning the country into one big bog. One night the wind came during the early hours when we were all asleep. It turned our old canvas tent fly into a collection of frayed strips adorning the mulga trees after wiping everything off the table and sending the loose dishes and pans away into the bush. The only way to find them again was to drive up to a kilometre in the direction the gale was headed, and collect them from where they had been deposited.

It was time once again for a last long reconnaissance survey trip out on to the Nullarbor to see if there were any obstructions for a straight line run in, so Anne, Connie, and I set off from the camp 140 kilometres north of our goal. Connie was still eating her tinned food but drinking a great deal more water than in the winter. She had survived all the seasons from ice to heat so she would be all right now until we finished off this section of the job. The boggy country hadn't hardened properly as yet but the heat and wind were quickly restoring it to its usual dust, and the flies were now constantly with us in their millions.

Not long after we had started on this expedition we broke out of the heavier scrub on to the patches of marine limestone which was the usual forerunner of the Plain, and we could observe horizons in some directions as far as the eye could see. Then, only half a day out, we saw a wall of dust approaching, whipped up by what looked as if it was going to be the most violent of the gales we had encountered so far. Everything was still and calm at the Rover, with the sun shining, but the amount of blue sky was diminishing every second, until the dirt wall hit us. We had covered Connie over with a towel and shut all the windows and vents on the vehicle tightly in anticipation of the advancing turmoil before it struck, and from that moment onwards for three hours we just huddled down and waited. The Rover was rocked from side to side on its springs as the gravel-impregnated dust lashed it with all its fury until I thought it might overturn. Nothing could be seen out of any window, and we were forced to block off the top of Connie's tea chest completely with a camp sheet so that she would not be suffocated in the powdery dust still entering the cabin. The dog pushed its head under Anne's feet on the floor and I was wondering how the camp was weathering the storm. No doubt the boys would have tied down everything movable but we'd all been through these, year after year, so it was nothing really new.

Eventually it blew itself out and we let Connie see the light of day again. She didn't think anything unusual had happened as she was

Top: Anne, the author's wife, and daughter Connie Sue meet their darker counterparts. *Bottom:* Cleanliness might be next to godliness, but in a remote part of the Great Victoria Desert Connie Sue was not so sure

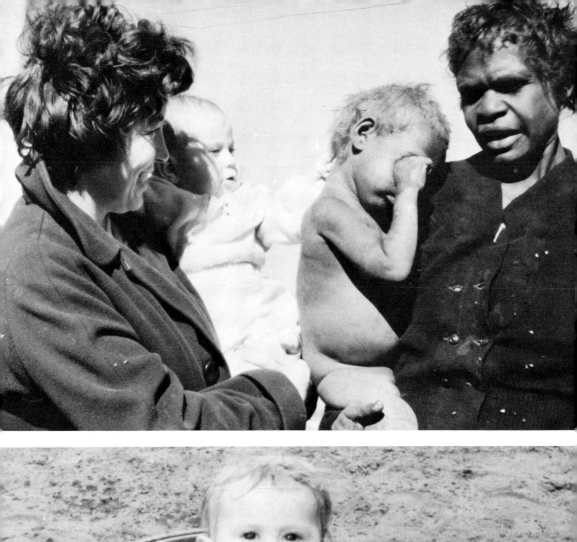

fast asleep in her box thinking night had arrived, but Bonnie wouldn't
stir from the floor. Anne had seen another side of what the outback
had to offer but only remarked that by the time she had finished what
she was knitting it wouldn't be fit to wear. Later in the day we were right
out on the open Nullarbor Plain, struggling along over the stony ground,
when down we sank into a bog hole caused by the recent deluge of rain.
A pool of water gathered around the vehicle in the wheeltracks as I jacked
it up and wedged in rocks from the plain, shovelling, and generally
covering myself with mud. Even Anne got out to act as stone collector
and tool washer as the shovel and jack became shapeless lumps of mud.
In the middle of this Connie woke up due to the unusual stillness of
her bedroom, and we decided, from her tone, that she'd like something to
eat, bog or no bog.

It wasn't till the following day that we dragged ourselves into the
Rawlinna siding, still caked in drying mud, and arranged for diesel
and petrol to be collected whenever anyone came in for it, leaving the paper
work till later. They'd all heard of this road coming down from Warburton
so we received the fullest co-operation of everyone. Anne thought she'd
take Connie over for the nursing sister to see and was told that if she'd
survived all that for almost five months, then she must be healthy. We
told the Sister we gave Connie a rinse in a bucket of water every month,
after which the water was poured into the radiator on the bulldozer.

We had a long way to travel back to camp, so leaving other details
till later, we turned and headed north as soon as possible. Our old grader,

Top: Keith, an Amata piccaninny, inspects a copy of one of the author's books. *Bottom:* During
the construction of the Sandy Blight Junction Road, the author instructed Doug on the bulldozer
to head straight for the point of the bluff on Mount Leisler

which we had railed to Rawlinna, was there waiting for us, tied to the flat top carriage on the siding, and we planned to drive it off, replacing it immediately with the bulldozer, if we ever made it.

Two days of bush-bashing passed after we again entered the scrub belt before we pulled into our camp as tired and hungry as it must have been possible to become, but at least the way was now clear to carry on. There had been nothing to prevent us from calculating a bearing straight for Rawlinna, and remaining with it for at least 130 kilometres, so after another of Paul's welcome teas, and bone weary as we were, Anne volunteered to book a complete astrofix that same night as I observed the stars for a latitude and longitude. From this I could compute a bearing from where we were at the head of the road which was now 210 kilometres south of Neale Junction, and lay out a line of markers which would set us off on our last direction. Once started we could carry this on indefinitely, if need be in the same straight line.

As it happened we ran that bulldozed road dead straight for 130 kilometres, after which I came in for a certain amount of criticism from later users. They told me that all they saw out of their windscreens for days was the road in front disappearing into a hazy skyline and asked why I didn't put even one bend in it as something to look forward to. I explained it simply by pointing out that I didn't want to make Australia look untidy.

Several days later another violent storm hit our little group with not so much rain but lightning and crashing thunder. Bonnie was considerably upset, thinking it was more of those signal flare shots. This country was not going to let us off till the bitter end, and the farther south we progressed with the road, the more we were open to such weather which constantly batters the Nullarbor at that time of the year.

Connie had taken to crawling right out of her box by now, and some mornings she was to be found forging her way through the array of clutch and brake pedals, accelerator and gear lever, having dropped over the edge of the box to the seat and on to the floor. One dinner camp brought Scotty over to us in a great state to inform us Connie was right out of the Rover on her own, fighting her way along through the spinifex. She had climbed out of the box, edged along the mattress to drop on to the open tail board. It had then been a simple matter for her to fall the rest of the way on to the sand and head off into the prairie. It was lucky the tail board didn't happen to be over a clump of thorny spinifex as we would have been picking spikes out of her for months.

Then one day the 'dozer became bogged deeper than the caterpillar tracks in a ditch on the Nullarbor which had become bottomless mud again from the recent rains. We camped by it for nearly a week, feeding rocks collected from the plain in under the plates as they slowly turned, sucking them under. It had taken half-a-day to shovel the gluey mud away enough to first remove the blade holding-bolts, thus allowing the tractor to move more freely without the extra burden on the front. Connie added her share of stones when she saw what was needed, throwing her pebbles in with the others. Eventually, after six days of solid work, the heavy machine began to move and soon was up on the harder surface, dragging the five-tonne-blade towards it by its own winch cable.

The radio aerial masts of Rawlinna were now visible across the open plain and as the blade of the bulldozer was no longer making any impression on the iron-hard sheets of marine limestone, it was raised for the last time and driven straight for the loading ramp at the siding. Rex had already fuelled and serviced the grader still waiting on the flat top and we started it, drove it off and down the ramp. Then our faithful old 'dozer trundled up to take its place on the rail carriage.

For the first time in history, a vehicle could now travel by road from Rawlinna via Warburton and Giles to Alice Springs, using a 1600-kilometre road made by the Gunbarrel Bush Bashers.

As the fiery summer months approached, the camp had to return to its normal quota of members and after the visitors were reinstalled in their house 3000 kilometres away, the work continued as usual.

From a point midway along the Connie Sue Highway, which had already been linked to the Emu atomic site with an 800-kilometre road from the east, a through access to the west was the next stage. The survey had been done in much detail during the winter months with the help of the visitors, and with little time to spare before the mid-summer cessation of operations the way was opened up to the Western Australian road system.

This provided a road clear through the centre of the Great Victoria Desert from the Alice Springs Highway to Laverton, which in turn had been long since joined to Perth. It also provided the second road across Australia made by the party after the completion of the Gunbarrel Highway, and again the first ever to be attempted in those latitudes.

16
Out There Now Leads to Here

It was during one of the delays caused by the numerous staked tyres suffered by the grader that I had the first indication of an alarming story which had begun at Woomera about myself. Apparently it had gained much momentum by the time it came out there to me over the transceiver when I thought it was about time to give them a call. After the aerial was in place, I plotted our present position on the ragged old map in order to ask them to reposition the coloured map tack indicating our whereabouts and progress. Then depressing the switch on the hand microphone I called the operator at Woomera and listened for his reply. None came, so I called again and released the switch to receive, only to hear the most eerie tone I'd ever heard him use, asking in a shaky whisper if that was really my call sign on the air. I was able to convince him that it was, and the quivering voice of the operator came back through the loud speaker in a most distressed manner stumbling for the right words. 'We, er, that is I, ah, well the story around Woomera and Salisbury is that everyone seems to think that you had, er, er, oh dear, well they thought you had expired!'

I came back on the air to him with a burst of laughing, and when I was able, mentioned to him in passing that I was quite alive and asked him what had happened. He was regaining his composure a little I could hear from his next transmission and told me everyone was quite sure I had died suddenly with a heart attack. Inquiries were coming in from interstate requesting details. When he heard my radio call coming over the air he was in such a state of mind that did not expect ever to hear it

165

again, and after turning white, thought it had come back to haunt him. I could hardly answer for laughing, which eased his tension, and I wondered aloud how such a story could have started. He didn't have an idea, but he had been flooded with teletypes as to when he had last heard from me and where I was at present lying, bleaching in the sun. Of course all he could tell them was the fact that he hadn't had any radio transmission for several weeks, which, he added, wasn't really unusual for me. But as the requests for information kept coming and his phone kept ringing with the news, he became uncertain himself, until suddenly out of the ether my call had roused him.

I was really feeling quite touched at everyone's concern, and as I wondered how the rumour could have started, I suddenly thought of Anne and how she would have been informed about it also. Such news travels fast and with the many Salisbury contacts we had she couldn't possibly have not heard, so I asked the operator if he would send her a telegram. The wording was going to be a bit awkward as I had no way of knowing how much she'd heard, so finally sent a message which read: 'Roses are red, violets are blue; don't believe all that is told to you.' If, by some chance, she hadn't received any indication of the expiry date, she could only think that I'd been too long in the bush.

Actually I learned later that someone who fitted my description and was living where I had stayed in Woomera, had died suddenly from a heart attack, and our identities had become confused in the retelling. Anne had been told of it all but having just spent five months out in the scrub with me didn't believe a word of it and waited for just such a message from me. The story had far-reaching results, as I was to discover with disturbing frequency when I did finally return to Woomera. Once, when I was walking along outside the store in the village there, a lady came out of the door carrying a bundle of groceries, took one look at me and dropped them all, turning light grey as she did so. She was so visibly shaken that I fought back the urge to explain to her in fun that I was really quite a friendly ghost. This was to go on in varying degrees with everyone I met who hadn't been told anything except the first part of the drama, and I reached the stage where I never knew what electrifying effect I could expect wherever I went. The most moving reaction of all came from a small girl who ran over to me near the school one morning, clutched my hand and said, 'I heard you were dead and I was sorry.'

By the time I'd finished this radio sked, the grader tyre that had been staked, causing the current delay, had been mended. I told the boys the news, adding how unsportsman-like I felt to disappoint them by turning up again.

Slowly we graded west, and the vast difference between the two machines was shown to us at every turn. Bushes the 'dozer wouldn't even notice, as it waded through, became obstacles enough to stop the grader, and the resulting road no longer fitted the name that our Gunbarrel Bush Bashers had acquired. It was a graded access nevertheless and a big improvement on vehicles struggling over the spinifex and sand hummocks.

Eventually the road had progressed to the vicinity of the Moreton Craig Range, last seen on the reconnaissance back from Laverton with Anne and Connie. It was now time to alter the general course from west to northerly in an attempt to cut the sandalwood road at Lake Yeo. The staked tyres on the grader were a daily event, and as each one occurred, the mending of it left us at almost the end of our endurance, due to the intense heat. Hammering, levering, and straining with the 120-centimetre diameter tyres in temperatures of 46°C, with the tools too hot to handle, and the subsequent inflating of them, was not altogether something to look forward to so frequently. When the compressor on the grader failed it would take half an hour with the little plug-pump on my Rover to make the tyre even stand up, and while waiting for this the black mist of flies made the most of us.

Daily my detailed reconnaissances ahead of the machine took place from the time it was switched off until dark, and at last I came within sight of the box-like hill alongside which we had camped three and a half months before. We had made nearly 1000 kilometres of new road in the meantime since that last sighting when the weather was at the other extreme in temperature. It was hard to imagine in this present inferno of sweat, thirst, dust, and flies that earlier the water in the billy had been converted into solid ice on the Rover roof overnight.

The dense scrub around the hill made it impossible for the grader alone to penetrate, and much as I wanted to add this point of interest right alongside our road, I was forced to skirt it outside the ring of mulga jungle. One evening just before dark I emerged from the bush, spinifex, and sandhills we had been forced to re-enter, on to the tail-end of the sandalwood road at Lake Yeo, and the reconnaissance surveys for that year had come to an end.

Without waste of time in feeling elated that the finish of our road was in sight I turned and retraced my wheeltracks back to the head of the road in the dark and was able to announce to the camp that the road would be finished on the following day. As usual, they didn't believe me, and I concluded that it must have been the way I delivered the news, grinning as I told it. Nothing could convince them once they saw that look, especially after we had all been battling towards this goal for almost 1500 kilometres over a period of years, off and on between the various delays. It was still too hot to sleep until late into the night but eventually the camp became quiet. The constant mending of those grader tyres in the heat had taken its toll of everyone's energy. Paul was having as hard a time with the meals, trying to keep the flies at bay as he worked, and the added heat of his cooking fire didn't help, but he kept going as cheerfully as he had from the very beginning.

As I lay on the top of my swag before falling asleep, and as the beads of sweat trickled off on to the canvas, I thought how everyone would be rewarded the next day as we finally broke through.

We were all up well before the flies next morning, and after telling Paul and Rex that the camp could stay right where it was instead of moving it to the end of the road as usual, Scotty and I drove off to the grader waiting behind its bladefull of spinifex. As soon as the big diesel was going I drove around it on to my tracks made the previous evening and continued along them slowly as the grader followed. Those last few kilometres passed almost unnoticed with the anticipation of the completion so close at hand, and in no time I had bumped over the last hummock of spinifex and waited on the made road. Looking back to the grader creeping along in front of its accompanying dust cloud I noticed one of the trucks behind again, keeping pace with it. The boys were going to be present at the finish, and that alone was enough to show me how much of a personal interest they all had in the work, not counting the way in which the whole team had put up with all the hardships this country had to offer for so long.

With less than 20 metres to go, I inched the Rover along the existing road as the grader followed it in an easy curve and stopped the length of the machine short of the join up. Lifting the blade clear of the spinifex it moved back away and described a large circle to line up on the road facing the opposite direction. Then the blade lowered as the heavy grader moved slowly forward and completed the curve from the edge of the sandalwood road to the spinifex barrier. The second road made by the Gunbarrel Bush Bashers across Australia was finished on 17 November 1962.

It was almost 1500 kilometres long, starting at Mabel Creek on the Alice Springs Highway, passing through the atomic ghost camp at Emu, threading its way past Vokes Hill, over the Serpentine Lakes on the border, becoming part of Neale Junction, and on to Laverton. We were still almost due west of our starting point. In one way I was sorry Anne and Connie Sue weren't with me on this day, but perhaps the achievement may have lost some of its excitement for them with this forge-like heat bearing down with all its fury on our little group of four men. At least they had been right there at the finish of the Warburton to Rawlinna road, having seen its survey and construction from the beginning, and now I could tell them about this latest in a way they would understand, having been here already on the initial survey.

To round off the job and make the most of the grader's trip back to Giles we decided to drop the blade and grade all the way back to Warburton, a distance of 560 kilometres. The section between Neale Junction and Warburton would then be graded for the first time over the bulldozed cut, and back to the Junction would only be a regrade. It was a long way but if we didn't do it then it might never be done and from previous experience with this sort of operation we could have it through in a fortnight.

Leaving Scotty and the camp to start the return, Quinny and I continued on to Laverton for supplies of water and rations which were needed to carry us all back as far as Giles.

At Laverton we knew that not even the bush telegraph could have spread the news of the final break-through of the new road from the east as it had only taken place the day before, so the old map was taken down from the wall at Don Leahy's place and the details filled in. The overnight stay at Laverton was taken care of by Norman Hopkins, the policeman. He had some spare rooms in his local jail house and he invited Quinny and me to stay with him, to which we agreed, as long as he left the barred doors open and gave us the keys. Knowing him, we could rely on his sense of humour to make it look more realistic, spreading the story he had captured single-handed two infamous bushrangers who were staying with him as the guests of Her Majesty.

Bypassing the fuel pumps at the store operated by the boy who made so much use of 'force,' we went on to Leonora, after a night's sleep on the 'inside,' for the bulk rations and supplies we needed, and once more Eric 'Mr Fixit' James and his wife helped us. Mrs James was relieved to learn that Anne and Connie were back in Adelaide and out of this country, with the summer temperatures as they were, but mentioned that news had come over the air of a violent wind storm which had just hit there and hoped they were all right. I hadn't heard of this, of course, so thought no more about it.

The whole town had heard by now of the completion of the road in advance of our arrival, as the wires leading out of Laverton had been running hot since we drove in, and there followed a session of adding the new road location to many local maps. After loading up with these supplies which had been available to us ever since our leaving Maralinga three weeks before and 1500 kilometres away, Quinny and I drove off to Laverton on the way back to our camp.

The first thing which was handed to me at the Post Office there was a telegram from Anne informing me that in a 140-kilometre-an-hour wind storm which had ripped through Salisbury we had lost the complete roof from our garage. Another night spent in the cells at Norman's 'guest' house and we were again resuming our return to the camp. Driving off Martin's sandalwood road on to the curve which made up the start of ours was done with much satisfaction, knowing that if followed throughout its length, that thread of cleared ground would lead us to the established road system in the east, without the need for astrofixes or compass.

We drove along it for 270 kilometres before catching up with the party already 65 kilometres north of Neale Junction, and the new supply of fresh rations was very acceptable. It was 43°C each day now, and had we not been out for the year in the bush, becoming as hard as hobnails in the process, we couldn't have carried on. As it was, we spared nothing in finishing the work, and eventually within a day of the end of November the grader blade was raised for the last time that year as it tapered off into the Warburton road at the northern end of the Connie Sue Highway.

Before starting on the long trip to Adelaide, which was almost 3200 kilometres via Giles, I decided to install a new spring assembly on the Rover in place of the one which was broken in so many places that it allowed the wheel to rub on the mudguard. It was almost 49°C as I lay under the vehicle to do the job, and when it was finished, I thought again that there must be an easier way to earn a living, not that any of us would have changed places with anyone else.

As we struggled into Warburton we received the usual riotous welcome, added to by the flood of inquiries as to the whereabouts of Anne and Connie Sue. Our stay on this occasion didn't amount to more time than it takes to have a few mugs of tea, and we pressed on towards Giles, driving until midnight to cover some of the distance after the blazing sun had set. My diary entry for that day included how the engine on everyone's vehicle boiled the whole time, that the temperature was 49°C, how the differential on one of the trucks had smashed to pieces, making it necessary to tow it from there on, that a tow-bar had broken off one truck, requiring a long job of arc-welding on the road to restore it, and that Quinny in trying to drag a large water-tank trailer over a sandhill had turned it upside down. As we finally camped 110 kilometres short of Giles from sheer tiredness, I fell asleep thinking that things could only improve, but the feeling brought about by the successful completion of our work overshadowed any of these minor happenings.

Hoping I could keep going myself, I took to driving along behind the string of odd-looking vehicles comprising our party to help see that none fell by the wayside. It was rather like coming back from a war, Several washaways had occurred on sections of the Gunbarrel Highway since we had made it, and once as I drove behind Paul's ration truck I was surprised to see how it stayed on its wheels when one side broke away some loose dirt and dropped into a water-eroded gutter a yard deep. The whole vehicle was leaning at an angle which threatened to lay it on its side at a touch, and in great haste the driver's door opened and Paul was out in a flash. The trouble was easily overcome after first anchoring the truck with a tow-cable attached to my Rover, and then by digging and shovelling under the high side for two hours until it assumed a more reasonable angle. The ground temperature was the usual 60°C throughout this operation. We weren't going to be let off lightly until the bitter end.

Eventually each of our battered vehicles straggled into Giles, some limping along, others being towed, but at least they made it, and our faithful old grader was driven to an out-of-the-way salt-bush flat alongside the settlement and switched off. It was at last in the position — with its job done — in which I had been striving to have it for many months, as our subsequent programme called for it to be working in the opposite direction from its Christmas time resting place. Then wonder of wonders, on that first night back, clouds gathered and it began to rain, but whatever happened from now on couldn't interfere with our present feeling of freedom from the grind which had been with us constantly for the whole year. It was as if a lead weight had been lifted from our shoulders, even though to me it had been a satisfying responsibility.

It was now December, and with only 2100 kilometres to drive home, we left Giles early on the following morning to complete the last stage of our operations. All the old mulga stakes which had been driven into the tyre covers of the vehicles in the scrub began working their way right through into the tubes as we travelled faster on the harder and more

172

compacted roads and as always, the flat tyres came one after the other. Slowly creeping from camp to camp on the soft new road, the same tyres would last for a year.

No sooner had we emerged on to the Alice Springs Highway than we came upon a huge semi-trailer hopelessly bogged in the sand as he had driven off the road to change a tyre, so out came all our tow ropes again, and we combined all our wrecks to pull him out of it back on to the hard ground. He was having real difficulties.

After another day we slowly passed through Mabel Creek station, and I paused to gaze upon a bulldozed and graded lead-off from the highway heading away to the west, knowing full well and with a pleasant sense of satisfaction, to what ultimate destination it now led.

Now that the southern half of Australia had been broken up into slightly smaller segments with its system of brand new roads, attention had to be turned to the collosal area to the north of the Gunbarrel Highway. There was still 3000 kilometres of road to be made covering roughly the remainder of the Woomera centre line north-west right through to the Indian Ocean.

A point was chosen on the first road to the Giles meteorological station as a junction for a future road to the north extending into the Northern Territory, and being nearly 400 kilometres long gave a possible access to Alice Springs from where supplies could be obtained.

When this had been achieved, a road had to be then made 1000 kilometres in length right across the Great Sandy Desert northwest to the Indian Ocean. The earlier road north from the Giles area would then form a 'T' union with the latter and the author gave this the appropriate name of Sandy Blight Junction, for he had contracted an eye ailment prevalent in the desert when carrying out the astrofix to plot its position. The northern access subsequently took on the name of "The Sandy Blight Junction Road".

After 350 kilometres of construction north-west from Sandy Blight Junction, the party's road grader broke down irrepairably and had to be towed 800 kilometres back along the newly made roads to Giles with the bulldozer, at the speed of 3 kilometres an hour. No sooner had they left on this mammoth towing operation than disaster struck . . .

174

17
Hot Water Laid On

With a startling burst of energy completely unexpected from one of his size, Quinny sprang into the air off the dust heap on which he'd been sitting. His black cloud of flies, having so suddenly lost their target, turned to a less concentrated grey as they dispersed and milled about, and a yell erupted from the still-airborne figure. The loud 'Gosh almighty!' broke up the former quiet of the searingly hot spinifex plain where Frank Quinn and I had been relaxing in the scanty shade of a lone mulga tree alongside our recently-made road. Several months earlier I had purposely made the road close to that scraggy tree with a view to its helping some future traveller to boil his billy and have his 'dinner camp' in the twelve per cent protection it afforded from the blazing summer sun. As we waited for the rest of our little convoy to catch up with us, we had been idly watching a pall of black smoke boil up out of the shimmering horizon high into the brassy sky, in the direction from which we had just come.

Our new road would eventually extend for 1600 kilometres north-west across Australia, from the Centre to the Indian Ocean. It was to skirt the northern extremity of the Gibson Desert and cut right through the heart of the Great Sandy Desert in Western Australia, finally linking up with the Mid-Northern Highway in the vicinity of Marble Bar.

So far we had reached a point about 560 kilometres on our way, but the scorching November sun had given us thoughts of suspending operations until the New Year, leaving the summer inferno of the desert to get along without us. My Gunbarrel Road Construction Party had, as

175

usual, been out in the bush since the previous February, weathering all conditions from raging dust storms to ice in our water tanks. By the end of the year the half-dozen of us were beginning to show signs of tiredness, and so was the battered machinery. The intense heat now magnified any weaknesses normally hidden in the colder months. Radiators boiled and simmered like pressure-cookers throughout the day, and our comparatively meagre water supplies were hard put to keep up with their constant need for 'topping-up.'

By now Quinny had returned to earth, only to continue his extraordinary behaviour with a bellowed 'This is absolutely terrible!' When I asked him what on earth could possibly have brought about this shattering disturbance, he beckoned me to where he was standing in his worn-out, dust-covered sweaty clothes, staring at the rear end of his long-distance supply truck. I left the doubtful shade cast by the tree and brought over my own set of worn-out, dust-covered sweaty clothes, adding my swarm of flies to his. I had stopped my Land Rover in front of his truck, and both vehicles were showing the torture to which we had subjected them since they had last seen a workshop a year ago.

After a minute of giving me the opportunity to discover for myself the cause of his concern by studying me silently from under his battered,

Top: Explorer William Tietkens carved his name and the date on this bloodwood tree at the foot of Mount Leisler in May 1889. Author's sign plate tells future travellers the story. *Bottom:* A desert tragedy took place at the Leibig Bore when the windmill broke down

oily hat-brim, he asked me incredulously why I couldn't see what was wrong. My examination roved over the back of his truck from the tailboard to the rear tyres, then back to the shiny towbar and spring shackles, and I had to admit I saw nothing amiss. Quinny's hat-brim was pulled down so low over his eyes as to half cover them against the white glare of the sun reflecting off the spinifex tops, but now he cuffed it back on his bald, nut-brown forehead and thundered his distressing question: 'Where in the blazes is that great caravan I was pulling?'

At the head of the road to date, just as we were considering calling a temporary cessation to the year's work, the grader had decided to make up our minds for us. Scotty, the operator, was placidly grading the initial cut made by Doug on the bulldozer when a most expensive-sounding crunch from somewhere down in the transmission reverberated through his machine, bringing the whole thing to a grinding halt. After the dust had settled it became quite apparent that the grader would move no more under its own power. Without help, it would have to remain right where it was.

We had already made several contacts with Aborigines in the area, and as they were more than 900 kilometres away from the nearest habitation of any kind they were a wild-looking collection. Five or so at a time, or sometimes one alone, they would come over the sandhills to watch us once they heard the sounds of our activities in their areas. The crippled grader could not be left to their mercy standing out in the desert in the middle of the road throughout the ensuing summer. Our previous experiences had dictated that there wouldn't be much of it left to come back to. In past cases with other engines and machinery, grass, sand, and leaves had been jammed into the diesel tanks, anything bendable had been broken off to use as digging implements in the search for goannas and rabbits, and fuel containers had been bashed open with rocks in the hope that they held drinking-water.

As it was already November, the only course left to us was to tow it behind the bulldozer back along our own newly-made road to where it could be left in safety for repair work. I decided to take it to Giles near the Rawlinson Ranges, a distance of at least 800 kilometres. We had established Giles six years before as a weather station for the Maralinga atomic tests, and it was still in full operation as a remote outpost transmitting weather reports to the Bureau of Meteorology. The initial reason for its inception had ceased completely with the international agreement to call a timely halt to atomic tests in the atmosphere.

Once there, our faithful old machine could be repaired by experts who could fly out the necessary parts to land on the airstrip we had made several years before with that self-same grader. It would then be ready and

Ghost gums line the spectacular Bungabiddy Gorge in which fresh water was found by the author waiting for us to resume our work in the New Year, with all its levers and fuel lines intact, and minus a diesel tank stuffed full of leaves.

The projected towing operation would simply involve tying the steering-wheel rigid with rope and then hooking the grader behind the slow-lumbering bulldozer. The water trailer normally pulled by the dozer would have to be added to the 'train' behind, as that pontoon-type tank would have to be refilled back at Giles for the New Year, and in addition we needed to protect the arc-welding motor, also mounted on its trailer, from the Aborigines and their grass. The bulldozer's average speed was about 3 kilometres per hour, and at this rate, grinding along at 35 kilometres a day, the 800 kilometres could be covered in about a month — if no further problems arose. When a bulldozer is working at bashing down logs and piling up rocks, the wear on component parts like the Caterpillar track-rollers is much less than that caused by the action of 'walking' it over long distances. Every two hours for the next four weeks those rollers would have to be greased. But all these things were incidental and almost routine to us. We had been attacking this huge area of untouched and mostly unexplored Central and Western Australia for the past eight years, opening it up with our network of thousands of kilometres of road to provide access for our rocket range and atomic bomb projects at Woomera and Maralinga.

Before starting the return trek we decided to carry on with the next 30 or so kilometres of road using the bulldozer alone. I had already planned that distance in detail, threading the route through a bad sandhill patch ahead. In the following year, as we continued with the work, I was to be very grateful that we had made this decision.

In the week we spent working on that stretch, our camp remained where it was among a most pleasant stand of desert oak trees. Normally our practice was to move it up daily to the head of the road to conserve petrol. The heavily-laden fuel and service truck, labouring along a soft, newly-made road, managed only a few kilometres to the gallon, and this had a very real effect on our petrol supplies as the service truck needs to attend to the leading bulldozer every day. Those supplies of fuel, water, and rations were brought up to us by Quinny, who was virtually on the move all the time. He constantly had to drive back along our new road to the nearest supply source — a trip which averaged a return distance of 3000 kilometres. Of course, while he was away on these fortnight-long expeditions, we would have moved over 100 kilometres further on, so Quinny's trips became progressively longer.

Eventually, making most use of the lone bulldozer, Doug and I brought the road through the difficult 30 kilometres of sandhills and, turning the heavy machine around, headed for the camp from which our long haul was to begin. This point was in an area near to some low-lying potential swamp country — if it ever rained in this most isolated region. It so happened that between the time of that memorable turn-around and the time we finally linked the road up to the north-west, a survey party from the National Mapping Council drove along to this temporary terminus. When they reached the end of the bulldozed road they camped, dug a well in the swamp area, and discovered water (of the most awful composition but nevertheless water). They timbered the sides of the well and then covered the top with chopped logs, leaving an opening for a rope bucket. They added to this a most attractive arch of uprights supporting a heavy log cross-bar with a squared-off surface on which they carved, in very neat and professional-looking letters, the name 'Jupiter Well.' In the clear night skies over the desert this large planet stood out prominently from the congregation of other dazzling stars, and so it seemed most appropriate for the new well to be named after it. Jupiter Well has been published on subsequent maps covering the region as such, and it automatically marks the exact location of the beginning of the longest bulldozer 'walk' and towing operation in the history of Central Australia.

Back in the camp alongside the sadly immobile grader we lost no time in heading off. Everything had been refuelled, greased, and made ready (not that everything was anything *but* always ready for shifting on a day to day basis), and the bulldozer was slowly reversed, attached to the improvised towbar we had made with the welder, and bolted to the front end of the grader. The cumbersome water trailer had been pushed into position with one of our three trucks and linked up to the towing pin on the grader. As the latter was still standing where it had broken down, pointed in the north-westerly direction of Marble Bar, a huge turning circle had to be negotiated so that we could once again be lined up on the road back to the south-east. It was the most ungainly train imaginable, protesting with groans and shrieks of metal pins and steel tracks, but when all components regained the road in a straight line, Doug was finally able to throttle down and throw out the clutch lever.

We had our mugs of tea and a meal fixed by good old Paul, our cook for many long years, and decided he should slowly follow behind the Caterpillar train, leaving it to set the pace. Rex, in the mechanics truck containing all the main tools and fuel, would come last so that he could lick anyone's wounds on the trip. Quinny in his truck and I in my Land Rover would go on in front and have the meal fires for 'dinner camps' and overnight stops going by the time the others lumbered along. This meant that we had to drive a distance of about 10 kilometres and then wait until the dust cloud drew near, giving us the signal to move on a kilometre or so, or to get the fire going, according to the time of day.

The Caterpillar train was not the only one in our little convoy. Paul was towing our refrigerator trailer, which in turn pulled along a Jeep trailer with the blackened stove and iron flue tied over a pair of tables we used for our meals. Iron pegs for an awning to keep off the heat or cold while eating throughout the year, axes, shovels, grill irons, crowbars, and battered water-boilers clanked about as well in Paul's second trailer, but, at the usual speed of 6 kilometres a day, nothing suffered.

Quinny had to pull behind his truck the old aluminium caravan we had acquired at Woomera several years before, because we wanted Rex to be free to move about as running repairs demanded. I was similarly free of encumbrance in case of emergencies, and the second workshop Land Rover had nothing to drag along either. This vehicle was used by our 'cherry picker,' who followed the final grading of the road, throwing off the roots and sticks which at times became hooked around behind the grader blade. When the need arose, Eric would also used it to ferry news of breakdowns back to the camp, and Rex would soon appear, complete with his 3-tonne fitter's truck, to handle them. A month or so before this, Eric had the misfortune to show signs of a condition in his throat which clearly indicated that expert medical attention was urgently needed, so he had temporarily left our party to return to civilisation on one of Quinny's ration trips. On this epic trip, however, his workshop Rover was being driven by Scotty, who was at the present moment for once without his precious grader.

We were only four days away from the terminus camp when Quinny made his outburst, and as soon as he asked his very obvious question concerning the whereabouts of his big trailer, I could start sharing in his anxiety. Up till then it had been remarkable how we just sat there for so long without noticing such a really conspicuous calamity, but now we set about planning how to recover the lost vehicle. Of course, the only thing to do was to retrace our tracks back along the road until we discovered it. Even if Rex had already found it, a repair job would probably be needed on the draw-bar and he would need help. Meanwhile the slow bulldozer train could trundle on regardless.

As we talked it over we glanced back across the wide expanse of hot spinifex in the direction from which we had come, but no trace of the caravan could be seen in the mirage. The black cloud of smoke was still in evidence about 6 kilometres away and we both decided it was coming from one of the huge piles of dry spinifex and dirt left by the bulldozer on our way out. When making the initial cuts with the heavy blade the rubbish soon heaps up to higher than the radiator-top on the machine and has to be 'dumped.' Pulling slowly off the course of the road, Doug would push it clear and lift the blade over it, driving the great steel tracks over the top to flatten down the loose clumps so that they wouldn't blow back over the road. These mounds of dumped rubbish are to be seen at short intervals beside any new road cut through scrub or unbroken ground. In our case, to help keep the loose bits of grass and debris from moving about with the wind, one of the team would often throw in a match to burn the lot down. There were obviously too many to worry about over hundreds of kilometres of new road, but at a brief re-greasing stop a near-by pile would sometimes idly be lit.

As we turned our attention from the billowing volumes of black smoke to the bare trailer-less space behind Quinny's truck, another sight caught our eyes. A large plume of fine dust was forming between us and the smoke, starting as a pinpoint and swelling to an enormous red cloud. A vehicle was coming towards us at the fastest speed the soft new road would allow. The little workshop Land Rover was the only thing in our snail-like convoy capable of such a pace, and we both thought Scotty was coming to advise us of the fact that a stray caravan was lying dormant in the desert.

Postponing our turn-around until his arrival, we were all set to listen to his news with feigned great surprise before retracing our tracks for its recovery. Eventually the little Rover ploughed to a stop in a swirl of bulldust which temporarily obliterated it, and we heard Scotty yell out from somewhere in the miniature dust storm: '*The ration truck's gorn!*'

By this time we could actually see him through the subsiding haze, and no further elaboration was needed to boost the full impact of what he had said. The real cause of the black smoke became suddenly all too apparent. How could a harmless truck full of our food supplies catch on fire, even though the soaring temperature of the day made everything too hot to touch? As we were still over 600 kilometres from anywhere, I thought that this was definitely going to break the monotony.

Without further unnecessary conversation, I leapt for my Land Rover and we headed back along the road as fast as we could, leaving Quinny to turn slowly around and follow us to at least as far as the caravan, wherever that was. As I pushed the vehicle along the smooth powdery road the thought occurred to me that, since the previous ten minutes, things could only improve. After travelling about 3 kilometres I came to the caravan, still upright, but with its broken towbar ploughed into the ground at an angle to its normal direction of travel. A few minutes ago the loss of the caravan had been the great catastrophe, but it now receded into the background as being quite unimportant. We drove around it, hardly giving it a second glance, and soon the ration truck became visible at the source of the huge mushrooming pillar of black smoke.

We couldn't approach too closely at that moment because exploding tins of stew and bottles of tomato sauce were showering the area spasmodically with carrots and shattered glass, so I stood well clear beside Paul, just staring at it all. Without pointing out to me that his truck was slowly melting in front of his eyes, a fact he deduced I could see for myself, he did casually remark in a quiet, awestruck whisper that this was terrible. Agreeing with him readily, I volunteered the opinion, as another carton of tins blew up, that you could say that with a reasonable amount of truth.

The big tyres were spouting globules of molten rubber, leaving blazing trails behind each pellet, and beyond the conflagration around the red-hot rims, the once upswept thick assembly of heavy springs was to be seen draped downward at the shackles like a foot-thick bar of toffee. The cabin where Paul had been sitting less than an hour before, quietly driving along the road, was a white-hot shell with flames still fighting to get out of the open windows, and the windscreen had softened so that it lay draped out over the bonnet like a tablecloth. The little fridge trailer was also alight at every burnable point: engine belts, canopy, tyres, and rubber seals. The ribs which once held the canvas covering over the food supplies made the whole thing look like some large prehistoric skeleton which had been barbecued by eager hungry cavemen.

When the worst of the minor explosions had eased off, I took my camera, shielded my face with a hat, and ventured closer, hoping to try and record some of this to show the yet unsuspecting transport officers at headquarters. Even as I focused the instrument a tin of pea soup burst its seams, splattering me all over with thick pale green liquid, but I carried on with the pictures after wiping a blob of soup off the lens with a piece of what was left of the pocket-lining in my old shorts.

The rest of the party had by now arrived and Doug was brought back from his bulldozer train to share in the spectacle. Rex saw the engine he had faithfully serviced for so many months lying in among a blistered array of panelling as just a shapeless block of useless iron. We did see one of the wheels as yet not actually on fire, and although it was too hot to handle we attempted to take it off with a wheel spanner to save it and use it to replace a damaged one on our other truck. Jacking it up, with one hand protecting his face, Rex managed to loosen the big nuts and free the rim from the simmering brakedrum, attaching a cable to it when it fell clear. A Land Rover dragged it away across the spinifex to cool, and that became the only item salvaged. I did hear a bubbling sound coming from the 1400-litre water-tank installed behind the cabin and it occurred to me we could at least make a cup of tea. The tap had melted so I shot a hole through the side of the tank with my revolver and, finding some tea-leaves among the wreck, filled a billy from the boiling geyser. The sugar in the once-new bulk container had melted, but some could be obtained with a shovel after digging a hole into it with a geological hammer. As we poured out the mugs of tea, each of us was asked politely if he preferred one shovelful or two as a sweetener.

I asked Paul to tell us what had happened just prior to the discovery of the fire, and he explained that as he drove slowly along he became aware of a lot of popping and crashing sounds from his load. When he looked out of his window around to the body of the truck he saw that everything behind the cabin was a holocaust of leaping flames and smoke, so he thought to himself that perhaps he should amble away from it before it exploded. Any extinguisher we carried was by then seen to be useless against the hold the fire had on the truck.

Later, as he stood beyond the reach of the flying debris, Paul was heard to remark sleepily that there was something you don't often see.

When a vehicle as important as a ration truck is suddenly no longer with a camp, large-scale measures are needed to cope with the situation, especially when it happens in the most remote regions imaginable. Half a dozen men, left without anything to eat in the space of an hour, 700 kilometres from anywhere, have to be of a certain temperament to face up to the immediate variation in their diets and the little party were certainly possessed of it.

One vehicle with two drivers merely set off on a 1500-kilometre non-stop return trip south over the new road to clean out the Giles store shed while the author drove east to Alice Springs, 800 kilometres away. This all had the added advantage of three less mouths to feed in the camp, while the towing operation proceeded with its snail-like pace as if nothing had happened.

Almost every trip made anywhere in the bush is crowded with unexpected happenings and the journey to Alice Springs and return was by no means an exception. The superintendent of an Aboriginal settlement on the way had a wife who for months had been periodically plagued by a raging toothache and every time she had been forced to consent to making the long trip for help, it had miraculously disappeared.

On several occasions previously when the settlement had been visited by the road party, the toothache had vanished just the day before, but at the time of the mercy dash after the fire, the pain was at its peak and at last the suffering woman agreed readily to accept the offer of a bush extraction . . .

184

18
A Desert Tragedy

The tooth was a maxillary or upper first molar, so the first thing to be done was to demonstrate the mucobuccal fold which indicated the point of puncture for the required supraperiosteal injection. This was done by drawing downward on the mobile mucous membrane in the maxilla, and the resulting line it made with the firm mucoperiosteum would be my centre of concentration. The book had gone on to say that this should be supplemented by a posterior palatine injection placed halfway from the gingival border to the mid-line, mesial to the third molar. Together they would anaesthetise the distal and palatal roots of the tooth. So, aiming the syringe vertically and expelling the air with a drop of liquid, I began to work.

The anaesthetic in the cartridge was zylocaine mixed with Epinephrine, which latter prolonged the numbing effect, and only a percentage of the 1.8 millilitres of the contents was to be used in this injection. The remainder was to be deposited at the posterior superior alveolar nerve in the palatine region. Drop by drop in advance of the needle I injected distally and upward past the mucobuccal fold to the apex of the roots. The manual certainly set it out clearly, and as I began the palatine injection I noticed that no ballooning of the tissues resulted.

Mrs Snook didn't even know what was happening, because at that stage the ache was still in evidence, but in several minutes that marvellous anaesthetic worked to give her the first relief she'd had for days. Then came the time to test the tissues around the tooth until eventually no feeling was left and the extraction could begin.

185

The upper molar forceps are perfectly shaped for both gripping the tooth and being gripped by the operator, and as I took them up in such a way as to make them invisible to the patient, I remembered all that Bruce had explained in his Woomera clinic. The beaks of the forceps had to be pressed past the gingival border or gum-line to concentrate their action on the roots, bypassing the crown of the tooth completely. I shut out from my mind Mrs Snook's description of her last visit to the dentist as I began the gentle but firm loosening action. Although an extreme amount of effort is needed to break the roots free from the bone, this must be concentrated to very little movement, and soon the muscles on my forearm and wrist were being used to the full. Gradually I began to detect a slight movement of the tooth independent from the maxillary bone, and soon it was free enough to be released altogether. I had always concluded that after that first movement it was almost all over, and sure enough, with the fingers of my other hand placed either side of the gum, the source of many months' torture was soon out in mid-air, still held by the now stained forceps.

Throughout the previous few moments, as is the case with any such patient, Mrs Snook's eyes had been screwed shut, but now that I was clear she ventured to ask tentatively how things were going. I couldn't believe my ears; she actually didn't know the tooth was out. After I had

informed her that it was all finished she asked to see the object which had caused her so much misery. I dropped it with a metallic clang into the kidney dish, and then proffered a glass accompanied by the most professional-sounding 'Rinse, please' I could muster. In no time my patient was proudly acquainting all and sundry with the information that she had just had a tooth out and there was really nothing to it.

I had delayed long enough, and so after repacking the dust-proof box and installing it back in the Rover I plunged once more into the swirling dust. Somehow the subject of lunch hadn't cropped up, what with one thing and another; and although I still hadn't eaten a thing since leaving the fiery truck, my thoughts didn't seem to include food. Immediately following the operation we had all had a mug of tea, and during this time I happened to hear over their radio that a complete fire ban had been declared throughout the State, with a heavy penalty for offenders. I couldn't help visualising a poor unfortunate officer, complete with waterbag, struggling out west of Sandy Blight Junction through the dust storm to collect the fine at the ration truck.

As I camped in the scrub 50 kilometres from Alice Springs, I began to sense an easing in the force of the wind, and early in the night it ceased altogether. Twinkling stars appeared, although there was no moon, and it felt wonderful to lie on my swag roll in the quiet bush, with the incessant noise of the wind completely replaced by that of the empty rumblings inside me.

On arrival in Alice Springs the following morning, I drove straight to the centre of the dry, sandy expanse known as the Todd River and set up my aerial for a contact with my camp. The prearranged time was approaching and I was soon sending out my call sign, hoping the spare transceiver Rex would be using still worked. Although it was supposed to happen, I was still surprised to receive an immediate answer from the boys, telling me the call sign was plain to hear. It followed that they had been successful in actually repairing the fridge's engine and compressor to a state where it again caused the box to freeze, and everything was as I had left it, with the bulldozer train 40 kilometres further along the way. Scotty and Frank Quinn had not yet returned with their load of rations and water, but they were still all right, even if they were becoming a little peckish. Actually I suspect they had eaten more than I since I headed off two days before, so, assuring them I would be on my way back in a day with the frozen meat supply, I packed away the aerial and went in search of something to eat.

After organising the butcher across the dry creek to prepare the meat for a long hot trip, and buying in some personal items needed by Paul and the others, I called into the police station. My gun licence would be more in order if it were endorsed to allow me to have the weapon in my possession in the Northern Territory, a fact which had already been mentioned to me by the police sergeant in Woomera. I discovered as I dropped my revolver on his desk that the Alice Springs inspector, McKinnon, already knew of me and our activities out west. However, he ignored the formalities for the time being and turned his attention to the revolver. It was too good an opportunity to miss, he said, as he carried it outside for some target practice and aimed across the street to where some empty cans lay in a heap. I really thought he was going to blaze away, turning the town into one straight out of the Wild West, but eventually he lowered the gun, muttering that in the old days he would have tested it by firing out of the window without moving from his desk.

While I camped overnight in the creek-bed the meat had time to turn solid in the butcher's deep freeze, and first thing in the morning saw us rolling it up in a canvas campsheet together with loads of dry ice. With this huge bundle roped to the roof of my Rover, I pointed the radiator to the west and headed off. I had about 600 kilometres to go and had hopes of arriving back at the camp in the early hours of the following morning when the meat would still be frozen and the transfer to our refrigerator box could be achieved before the flies knew about it. A further tragic interruption was to throw that plan to the winds.

During the trip to Papunya the Central Australian November sun beat down mercilessly, and at any waterbag stops I made, the armies of flies had taken over in force from the stinging dust of a day ago. After finally pulling up outside the Snooks' house, I found that quite a different atmosphere now surrounded the place. The family hurried down to greet me and this time the first thought was lunch. My ex-patient was in exuberant spirits. However, not long after we had all sat down to eat, there was a knock on their door and when it was opened the forlorn figure of the station cook was to be seen clutching a small cloth bag. His usual smile had gone and a toothless mouth informed us that he had just broken his upper dentures. The word had obviously spread. As my repertoire, supplemented by the tuition of the Alice Springs expert, Ray Meldrum, included the repair of such useful items we asked him to leave his little white bundle and we would attend to it.

After our meal the dust-proof box was again opened, and the dental plaster, sticky wax, and jars of Paladur powder and liquid were laid out together with a Dappins mixing glass. In a reasonably short time the two halves of the plate were fused together again. As soon as the job was done I thought of the meat on the Rover roof and lost no time in 'hitting the trail' for Liebig Bore, where I planned to empty lots of basins of water over myself before starting the last leg of the trip.

188

By mid-afternoon the outline of the big fan on top of the windmill tower at the bore began to take shape, and the big black stock tank at its base presented itself soon afterwards. A very slight air movement was causing the blades to revolve lazily, but with such a good-sized tank usually brimming with excellent quality water from the sub-artesian supply, the long trough would be full for the mobs of cattle and horses which congregated there. The ball valve assured that the need for supervision — which entailed making the long trip from Papunya — was kept to a minimum. As was the case with our bores at Giles, also close to sizeable mountain ranges, the underground supply was prolific.

Visions of basinfuls of cold water kept coming into my mind's eye as I stewed in the vehicle with a combination of sweat and fine dust covering seats and steering wheel. The shimmering expanse of bare open dirt was finally all that separated me from the airy bathroom, and the mirage at this distance made the whole scene appear to be floating in mid-air a metre off the ground. Soon the junction of tank and mill became clearer, and it was only then I began to sense that something was very wrong.

I had expected to see the stock jostling for position on either side of the strong trough in the furnace-like heat of the flat, but there was not even one animal standing near it. Dozens of bullocks lay about in the dust, and several horses with heads drooping to the bare ground stood under an almost dry mulga tree 100 metres away. As I drew closer I noticed the awkward way the bullocks seemed to be lying: legs up in the air, faces buried in the dust. Their bloated appearance immediately told its own story, and in a minute I was out of the Rover and gazing about at the scene of utter devastation.

Dead and dying cattle lay everywhere, but why? I looked into the trough, and saw that it held only a few dry sticks and a deep layer of dust. Then I climbed on to the outlet pipe and looked over the searingly hot rim at the emptiness on the inside of the tank. A few centimetres of green slime covered the bottom below the pipe, and although the fan blades were turning, not a drop of water was coming from the mill. I couldn't believe my eyes. I remembered that when we had joined our road from Sandy Blight Junction to Liebig Bore, this tank had been overflowing with clear water, and we had even stopped the spinning mill-blades with the 'pull out' gear to save their unnecessary action.

Making for the actual bore situated in the centre of the square formed by the legs of the tower, I found what had happened to cause the death and suffering of so many animals. The connecting rod joining the axle to the pump had broken at the threads where the big brass nut was located at the head of the bore casing so that, as the fan revolved, the loose wooden stem with the stump of threaded bar attached rose and fell in mid-air.

The vital pump rod remained stationary, but by a miracle it had been prevented from dropping down the hole and out of sight because the huge nut had become caught on the lip of the steel bore-casing. As a result the water remained right where it was, deep down in the earth, with the motionless pump valves immersed in it yet unable to transport it up and into the tank.

With the initial feeling of stark catastrophe all about me still implanted on my brain, I roused myself into the action which was obviously needed as quickly as possible. After a study of the broken union, I noticed that a little over a centimetre of thread remained on the swinging stub, and that the nut was quite a thick one. If I could anchor the rods from the bowels of the earth to prevent them from slipping down, and raise the whole column to meet the loose end from the top of the mill tower above it, then I might be able to use the nut to join them together. Half the thickness might hold the lower piece and half the upper to serve as a temporary union, but taking into consideration the great weight of the long string of rods, would only half a nut be strong enough? I had only limited tools with me on the Rover. It was possible that when the strain was applied the threads would simply shear off, allowing the lower string of rods to drop away out of reach forever. But one more glance around at the surrounding ruin was sufficient to convince me that I should try.

The first thing to be done was to prevent any possibility of that nut slipping off the steel rim. With infinite care I managed to encircle the rod under the nut with as many turns of heavy fencing wire as I dared, before forming a loop with a figure-eight knot. My Land Rover hydraulic bumper jack was just the shape for this operation, and in a matter of moments I had placed it firmly on the steel jack-plate with the adjustable cast-steel tongue engaged in the loop. As I slowly worked the handle, the nut lifted above the rim and for an agonising instant swung clear into the centre of the circle of casing. But the old bush standby of fencing wire held, and as I levered, the rod gradually emerged up from the hole until the nut was half-a-dozen centimetres above the casing. Luckily I carried an apparatus consisting of two parallel steel bars bolted together for use in clamping broken spring assemblies. With one bar either side of the precariously-hanging rod and resting on the rim, I screwed the clamping nuts on to the heavy bolts until they closed together around the rod like a vice. It was only a friction grip, but I put on the greatest strain possible short of stripping the threads, and tentatively relaxed the lifting jack. Once again it held firmly and I could breathe more easily at last.

The first mishap occurred as I began to operate the 'pull out' gear to stop the fan turning. The 'pull out' gear consists of a ratchet and cog winch which, joined by a light cable to the sail, moves the blades at the correct angle to catch the wind. If this vane is moved to a different direction from the plane of the fan, the breeze cannot catch the blades and the whole action stops, even in quite a strong wind. As I wound the handle the cog assembly snapped, rendering it useless, so I took a length of rope from the bundle of frozen meat on the roof of the Rover and climbed up the narrow ladder to effect repairs. Once I reached the apex of the tower I clung there precariously, endeavouring to grab at a blade as it rushed past. From the ground the revolving appeared quite lazy, but now that I was within centimetres of it, things looked very different.

Eventually, by working around the top clear of the knife edges slashing through the air, I was able manually to close the angle of the sail and so stop that potential guillotine from moving. Once stationary it was a simple matter to rope it in such a way that the hanging wooden pole was at its lowest point. Back I went down the ladder, and with the combined aid of the jack and holding blocks, I finally brought the two stub ends together. Now, with the use of my largest shifting spanner, I was ready to turn the nut. Hoping that the threads would mesh, I scratched on the stump of the rod a line half the thickness of the nut so that if it was screwed upwards to that point, then both ends would supposedly be held equally. Luckily all this went as it should, and I was now ready to carry out the final crucial test.

After I had unwound the fencing wire from the rod and removed the clamp I was elated to find that the join remained intact, so it was back up the ladder to untie the holding rope. With the fan once more turning, the whole string of rods began to go up and down. This meant that the flap valves at the deep end in the pump were doing their job. The water would once again begin to be elevated and would finally spill out of the feed pipe into the tank.

The heat was terrific out there in the open, and the thought of the water made me aware how parched I had become myself. It was only then that I made the rounds of the tortured cattle which weren't yet dead. Some, completely unable to move at my approach, were breathing heavily with their enlarged nostrils half buried in the dust. Some were able to make a feeble attempt to protest at my proximity and others just rolled their dilated eyes in agony. I counted forty dead already, and dozens were in the last stages of dying; but now, with the water trickling out of the inlet pipe, an attempt could at least be made to revive some of them. I realised that before the water level in the tank rose enough to reach the outlet pipe to the trough, many more of the animals would be dead, so I set to work immediately. After I had splashed handfuls of water into their mouths some of the stricken beasts rallied enough to drink the life-giving liquid from a tin basin pushed under their muzzles, and I had the satisfaction of seeing several actually struggle to a standing position. Others were quite obviously too far gone to try, and after an hour of carrying basinfuls of water from the small stream out of the pipe to the prostrate array of bodies scattered about I obtained a fair impression of their chances for survival.

Revolver in hand, I returned to four of the more unfortunate steers and terminated their suffering. One big bullock in particular wasn't responding, but I decided to persevere on into the early evening. The brutal sun was at last beginning to dip in the brassy sky and there was a hope that air currents resulting from the change in temperature might cause the windmill to pump at a faster speed. The thin trickle would then develop into a fuller steady stream, and at last the dust-coated trough would fill. It was ironical that the wind necessary to activate the watering system had also been the cause of the breakdown, for I concluded that this had taken place at the height of the gale-force winds battering the mill two days before. The supersonic speeds to which the fan had been whipped up had obviously proved too much for the rods.

The next step, before taking a shovel to clean out the debris and sand from the choked-up trough in preparation for the water which should soon be flowing in, was to call up the outside world on my transceiver and have a message relayed to Papunya. I had to advise them of the situation at their Liebig Bore and tell them that my repair attempt on the mill was only temporary. Although I hoped it would last to cope with the immediate crisis, a more permanent fix would be needed to forestall any repetition of the calamity. First I would have to send a message to my base communication centre at Woomera, and Ron could then repeat it all straight away to the Alice Springs Flying Doctor base. Once in Alice Springs, the emergency system would go into operation and Papunya would know about it within the hour. I contemplated this wonderful system and the marvels of progress as I transmitted my call sign to old Ron.

Although I was becoming dog-tired from the previous week's activities, there was little sleep for me that night, camped as I was beside the windmill. When I wasn't making periodical visits to the helpless bullocks with my basins of water, I couldn't keep my eyes from the rotating fan. In the early hours of the morning I was elated to feel a strengthening of the air movements, and soon, sure enough, the blades of the big fan began to blur together as they gathered speed. The resulting flow half-filled the inlet pipe and the water level began to rise. It had almost a metre to go before the trough would begin to fill, but as I studied the assortment of pipes and joints I devised a way of reducing that depth by half. By screwing the outlet goose-neck through an arc of about a right angle, I could make the nozzle half a metre lower than it was in its upright position, and with the aid of a sheet of loose iron the flow could be directed back to the trough.

So it was that after I had worked throughout the night, the trough actually began to fill, and by the time the first streaks of daylight appeared, silhouetting the stately peak of Mount Liebig, the water had risen to almost 20 centimetres. I dragged some of the younger calves bodily to the trough and pushed their muzzles into the cool water. One or two couldn't drink at all, not having even a spark of energy left in their weak little frames, but others did. Eventually, sensing the activity, the drooping horses plodded over to join in. I kept well away from the magnetic attraction of this long wet trough and was fully gratified to see a succession of animals gathering, their agony at an end.

When I revisited the big bullock with which I had persevered for half the night, I found him to be dead. I could only hope that I had brought him at least some measure of relief in his last few hours of life.

My task here was done. After I had at last emptied those lots of basins of water over my grimy, sweaty body, I replaced the rope on the load of meat and climbed into the driver's seat of my faithful Rover. It looked like being a good day, I thought, as I watched the stock jostling for position at the trough, the spinning fan on the windmill, and, more important, the pump rods rising and falling at every turn.

Transferring my gaze to the now illuminated foothills of Mount Liebig and the majestic bulk of it rearing up into the burnished morning sky, I had a multitude of mixed thoughts as I slowly drove away and on to the start of my road out west.

Place names have a wide variety of origins, and events of seemingly no consequence to anyone but those concerned can give birth to a name which often becomes a household word. When a surveyor has the acute malady of conjunctivitis and endeavours to observe stars all night through a theodolite telescope, it is easy to imagine the title of 'Sandy Blight Junction' being attached to the site of the astrofix.

Then there was Mount Leisler. An interested party in Glasgow decided to finance an expedition of exploration into the present Sandy Blight Junction area in 1889 and selected one William Henry Tietkens to lead it. Tietkens had been a main stay in the Giles expeditions fifteen years earlier and was an experienced bushman. He also kept journals of his battles with that country. When the Gunbarrel Road party were operating in that section of the country where again no one had been since, the diary of Tietkens was loaned from the Adelaide archives and read.

During the reading an outstanding mountain was given much attention which had been named for Louis Leisler, Tietkens' benefactor from Scotland. Rising 500 metres above the otherwise almost featureless spinifex plains, it certainly would be a site for one of the follow-up survey trig stations.

Adding that he had carved his initial and date on a blazed bloodwood at the easternmost foothills of this 'noble bluff,' Tietkens unknowingly marked a definite spot past which the Sandy Blight Road would be constructed — if it could be discovered after all this time on a forward reconnaissance . . .

194

19
Tietken's Tree

When at last we began to close the distance between the head of the road and the mountain which I had first observed a month and a half before, I planned a day-long trip to work out the details of where to guide the bulldozer.

An open spinifex plain lay between the Davenport Hills and Mount Leisler, and I travelled over this for about 20 kilometres before I saw several low, rocky hills followed by a small belt of sand ridges. Then for a kilometre or so the way became clear to the actual foothills of the main bluff, only sparsely covered with occasional trees and scrub. Quite close to the foothills, where the rocky ground began its sweep up to become vertical near the top, the scrub thickened — a result of the water which cascaded down the slopes after the showers which deigned very occasionally to fall on this parched, forsaken region. Several hundred metres further on, open, stony flats took over. The whole area was dominated by the cliff towering up to 500 metres above the plain, and altogether it was a very pleasant locality.

On one particularly open area under the eastern shadow of the peak stood a bloodwood tree, bordered on its western side by a dry waterway along which a heavy patch of growth formed what was almost a hedge. Although not a wonderfully healthy specimen, with some dry branches attached, it was noticeable because it appeared different from the rest of the immediate scrub.

With great excitement in the anticipation of the imminent discovery, I approached this tree carefully, so as not to destroy any possible evidence of Tietkens' presence seventy years before, and climbed out of the Rover. On the southern face of the tree a partially grown-over blaze was plainly visible; and on the original trunk, still exposed and in perfect condition, was a cleanly-chiselled number 5. The words from Tietkens' journal came back to me — a T above the numbers 5.89. There was absolutely no doubt whatever that the T and the 89 would lie beneath the healed-over blaze, covered by several centimetres of solid wood and bark. Since the time when William Henry Tietkens had stood at this very tree with his wood chisel and hammer in hand, carefully cutting in his initial and the date, seventy years' gradual growth had been taking place.

The new road could easily be directed this way before progressing onward, and as no more reconnaissance was needed that day, I turned again for the camp.

It was with mixed feelings that, four days later, I guided the bulldozer to the tree. I wondered what the earlier explorer could possibly have thought about all this. In his day, motors in general were yet to be invented, but here we were carving a road past this particular tree, singled out from countless others, in order that all sorts of people could come in their vehicles and carry out their assortment of reasons for being here. The survey parties from the National Mapping Council would lead the field of subsequent users, the first of hundreds I have known who have since made the journey, all of whom must have stopped to examine Tietkens' marked tree.

So that we need not damage or mutilate the immediate surroundings any more than absolutely necessary we passed by the tree and continued on for a kilometre before turning the machine around to widen out the cut. After a 15-tonne machine has screwed itself around, the area is left pulverised, and the resulting devastation was not what we wanted in any proximity to this landmark. On the way back, Doug had climbed down from his idling machine and plodded over to view it, after which he grudgingly conceded that here in fact was a point of interest after all.

When the blaze on the tree was opened up fully to reveal the remainder of the markings, they were to be seen as plainly as the day they had been carved. They had been protected from the elements for so long that the wood had not been allowed to harden, as was the case with the 5. I knew that the now-exposed portion would rapidly degenerate until nothing remained.

In chopping open old survey blazes, as we had done so often in the past, we always cut a deep groove into the overgrowth, well clear of the estimated position of the concealed carvings. When the cut is deep enough, the slab will fall away easily after leverage with the axe, often in one piece. Then, as the new growth takes place, the slow creeping of the bark and wood will once again follow the contour of whatever lies beneath, faithfully reproducing every microscopic blemish as nature endeavours to heal the wound. Therefore, when our gaze finally dropped to the loose slab lying face upward at the foot of the tree, a further thrill was waiting for us. A perfect mirror image of a T over the figures 89 was in full view, standing out in bold relief from the curved interior of the hard bloodwood surface. Although from that moment onwards the years of the original carvings on the trunk were numbered — sad as it was to admit it — here was a permanent relic that would last forever.

I had gathered all our spare onion bags from the ration truck, and I spread them out by the tree, reverently placed the treasure on them, and wrapped it up carefully. I would carry it in a safe position in my Rover for months until finally returning to civilisation, where I could relate the story to unfortunate city dwellers who couldn't come out to see for themselves. William Tietkens celebrated his twenty-ninth birthday while on the Giles expedition in 1874, so this would make him forty-four years old when he had carved this tree.

After the road had been widened and graded, we moved our camp up to the point where the dozer had turned around, and each member of the camp was forced to stop and marvel at the discovery whether he wanted to or not. Most of the boys were impressed but again old Paul and Quinny stayed only long enough to satisfy me before continuing on to our new campsite.

Knowing that in less than a decade the markings except for the 5 would probably be lost and unreadable, I had long before decided to leave a signpost behind. This would be one of the usual aluminium plates nailed to a mulga post, with the exact information I had seen with my own eyes recorded on the tree punched on to its surface. With a cold chisel I fashioned the shape of the blaze around the letter and figures left by Tietkens, adding a note with the alphabet stamps to record all that was plainly visible when the new road progressed past this point. I finished with the date, 29 June 1960.

The camp on that freezing cold night was now 350 kilometres from where we had tapped our original Gunbarrel Highway, 30 kilometres east of Giles weather station.

Quinny and I now stopped at the tree to wait for the arrival of the bull-dozer train, and while he sat in his cabin reading, I walked over to relive the story surrounding this area. So as not to waste time I opened my ever-ready pot of white paint and brightened up my signpost beside the road. As usual it had had around its base one of the old Land Rover's staked tyres, also painted white. In due course the rumblings drew nearer and the dust cloud became larger until it was time for us to move on.

We would soon be crossing over the Tropic of Capricorn, where yet another aluminium plate adorned a heavy mulga post complete with lead capping to inform travellers of the fact. Although this sign had no particular use, it was at least ornamental, and I had erected it to add to the many other points of interest this particular road had to offer. As we were building the road north of the Davenport Hills, we neared the latitude of 23°30′, and the thought had occurred to me that this was

TROPICAL FRUIT SALAD

Len Beadell

the value of the Tropic of Capricorn. I just could not pass over it without leaving a permanent monument at the point where the road turned tropical. An observation to the sun helped bring me near enough to carry out an accurate astrofix from which I could arrive at the spot to place the sign. Actually any latitude and longitude readings obtained on these roads were used by cartographers to produce new maps, and as all my figures were supplied to them, it wasn't entirely wasted.

I well remembered the cold, windy night when I stood at the theodolite to observe the stars at this point. Being late June it was cold enough already, without the exasperating stiff wind which, although not strong enough to shake the instrument, helped numb my fingers until they could barely turn the screws. When I had finished, late in the night, I packed up and returned to camp to sit huddled up in the back of the Rover, calculating the results. I meant to fix the signpost before moving from the region of the astronomical station, and so while Eric and Scotty went off the following morning to look for a large mulga post, I hammered out the aluminium plate. Another post on the other side of the road completed the effect I hoped to have on travellers, which was to make them think they were actually crossing over a line into a new climate. This done, they were both painted the inevitable white.

The point was a distance of 328 kilometres from the start of the road, and we had crossed over this invisible latitude line of Capricorn in longitude 129°20'38", which information all appeared on the aluminium plate for the edification of passersby. Even Quinny's dog, Lassie, had her name recorded in the list of members of our camp at the time.

For tea that night, old Paul with a flourish had opened a tin of tropical fruit salad to celebrate the occasion. He insisted he felt decidedly warmer now that we were in the tropics.

Six months later our train groaned its way south between these posts and now, at this fiery time of the year, we were all pleased to leave the tropics behind. But as Ernest Giles would have said, 'Herr Gabriel Daniel Fahrenheit still did not (con) descend to fall below a warm 108 degrees' (42°C).

Six kilometres further south of the sign, and almost within sight of it, a huge rounded boulder was to be seen gleaming white through the ground heat shimmer, forming yet another monument at the roadside. Quinny and I, as usual in front of the convoy, stopped here to repaint it while the opportunity presented itself, even knowing that after the bulldozer train had passed by, the dust pall would again coat it in chocolate-coloured dust. This rock, weighing almost a tonne, was located exactly on the 322-kilometre point from the start of the road. This fact was made meaningless by the introduction of the metric system, but at the time of construction it was quite important. That monolith marked the even 200-mile point on the road since leaving the Gunbarrel Highway and served us as a landmark on many occasions, such as the time when the ration truck failed to return. A radio message would state whether the rock had been reached or not, and this helped us plan how far back we had to go for salvaging operations. Actually it had all started out as a joke, when we wondered how future travellers might puzzle over how such a large rock just happened to be so neatly and conveniently placed alongside the road at precisely the 200-mile point. A sort of little Stonehenge in the Australian desert. Nobody would ever know that we had placed it there ourselves.

As we had approached this even mileage, I had thought that we might erect at the spot a signpost with the information attached, but as we were very close to the tropical crossing, which would mean so much more, I decided against it. When the first cut of the bulldozer was made I did mark the spot with a small cairn, but no sooner had we passed the spot than the idea of the rock came to me. A kilometre north of the cairn, a series of submerged rocks needed to be negotiated right on our line. Not wanting to upset the long straight section of road aiming directly at the eastern highest bluff on Mount Leisler, we marked out its course over and beyond the outcrop. As the rocks could not be left where they were, the bulldozer returned to them and we began the operation of moving them out of the ground. With the slight movement they had made as the machine drove over them, this procedure appeared possible. Had they been joined to exposed bedrock, then a detour around them would have been necessary.

The great steel blade had gently ploughed into the ground just short of the first boulder and lifted half of it out at the first try. One after the other followed easily, although each must have weighed a tonne; and the next move was the job of filling in the resulting holes with blades full of desert. As this was going on I noticed that one of the largest rocks had on its otherwise rounded shape an unusual flat surface upon which a sign could be painted. This was it! Huge as it was, I was sure we could somehow get it to the 200-mile point. When Doug had repaired the road to a stage where Scotty could grade it, I had a conference with him. We decided that if we used the steel tow cable carried on the front of my Rover, we could actually tie the great rock on to the bulldozer blade, which, when raised with the powerful winch, should also be able to lift it clear of the ground. If we were successful, then the whole thing could be driven slowly back to what we hoped would be its final resting-place. After lowering it on the spot we could use the bulldozer to nudge it carefully into position, with the flat surface facing the road.

As always Doug was eager to carry out such jokes, in this case our 'Operation Stonehenge.' After roping the rock into place we found that although the winch was able to raise it, the whole machine almost toppled forward again with the weight. It wasn't a recommended practice, we thought, after consideration of the front track roller and idler bearings, but out here on the spinifex plains nobody could possibly worry. After a very slow trip back, travelled in reverse, the load was eventually lowered, much to the relief of the bulldozer, and pushed into place. The rest of the camp had arrived during this exercise, and Paul came over to ask how long it would be before we had a spell from the bush. He was sure it was getting to us.

It took almost a tin of white paint to 'ice' the rock, and afterwards it resembled a huge round cake. On a subsequent trip, after the paint had dried hard, I would sign-write in black a bold '200 Miles' on the flat surface which 'happened' to be facing the road. I have since been asked by puzzled travellers just how we managed to make the road conform to those figures so accurately; so the whole operation had the desired effect.

We were now in the hemisphere south of the tropics, and the sun lit up this great white mass like a jewel on the spinifex prairie. As Quinny and I waited at the rock, I could be sure that this little joke of ours would soon be relived by Doug, driving that same bulldozer at the front of his dust-enveloped train.

From here the Davenport Hills could be clearly seen at a distance of only a further 6 kilometres. These, our next port of call, were the last of a succession of relatively small hills we had encountered before reaching Mount Leisler with the road.

It had been about here that Eric, who usually drove the workshop Rover, had begun to be affected by a soreness in his throat which slowly worsened by the month. At first only a slight swelling was noticeable, but, far from easing, this had enlarged to alarming proportions. He seemed sound enough otherwise and repeatedly declined the offer to return on one of Quinny's supply trips to have it seen to, as I guessed he suspected that this might put a stop to his activities with us. The prospect of leaving this work for good and being subjected to possible operations was not a very inviting one, and I knew at the time that I would strongly have resisted any such idea had it been myself.

While nothing really affected him or his activities we gave the swelling a chance to go away by itself, but the fact remained that something was very amiss. After a couple of months even Eric was thinking more about it, but being a former share-farmer he doggedly carried on until a visible loss of weight began to take place. Usually well built, solid, and the picture of health, he now contracted an associated stomach disorder. At first I could make no headway with him in making him see the sense of returning for expert help, but he now at last agreed that it might be advisable. Of course, I knew all the time that I could send him off even if he didn't agree. The only thing that forestalled this action was my understanding of how I would have felt in his place, and I wanted most of the decision to come from him.

It wasn't until four months after we had noticed the first symptoms that we were all convinced he should leave our camp on the very next ration trip, which I arranged to be made direct to Alice Springs. We had progressed with the road almost 300 kilometres west of Sandy Blight Junction, and as it was the last day of October, with the blazing heat already upon us, we were all aware that our year's work was drawing to a close anyway. Rolling up his swag for the last time in our camp, Eric weakly climbed up into the ration truck and it pulled out back along the new road to the east, bound for Alice Springs and the doctors.

After our long time together in this remote part of the country, it was depressing to lose one of our members, but we all knew as well as Eric that it was for his own good. When he eventually arrived in the Alice, Quinny had driven him straight to the hospital. A message sent over my transceiver was already waiting with the medical staff there. The resident doctor at Woomera, with whom I had already discussed this case, had on my request arranged a signal worded in medical terms to be transmitted to Alice Springs. I also sent a letter with Eric, outlining the circumstances which had brought about our decision for this step and describing what had transpired over the previous few months.

I heard later that the doctors at the hospital had taken one look at Eric and the large swelling on his throat and wanted to operate there and then. They spoke of thyroid glands and long hospitalisation, but Eric requested his return to Adelaide first so that he would be closer to home before all this took place. They reluctantly gave in and alerted the doctors down south that an urgent case was on the way and that no time was to be lost in effecting treatment on arrival.

The news had come back to me out at Jupiter Well, over our Woomera communication base station with whom I kept in much closer contact than ever before. As soon as the plane landed in Adelaide an ambulance had whisked Eric off to hospital, and I believe he was operated on that same day. I relayed the news to the camp after packing away the aerial. We all thought that we would never see him again in our little camp and I personally was very sorry about that, as he had always been a very willing and able worker, and easy to get along with. His background enabled him to turn his hand to almost everything, including assisting Rex with the big repair jobs on the machinery and driving the grader for a spell after Doug had damaged his hand. Apart from this, he always helped Paul in his daily chores of chopping firewood and packing.

Happily enough these gloomy thoughts proved to be short-lived, thanks to modern medicine, which could now handle his condition in a relatively simple manner. A book in old Paul's cook truck 'library' described the trouble in detail, stating that in the not so distant past, operations to correct these swellings involved removing two glands. The unfortunate patient was often left a helpless moron as a result. Now, however, the same beneficial effect could be achieved by only partial removal, and the complete recovery of the patient was more or less a certainty.

So it was that as soon as the operation on Eric had been performed, his troubles were over, and he regained his former health and weight in an amazingly short time. In the years to follow, he returned to the bush with us and carried on as if nothing had happened.

When camping and working in previously unknown country, each day is different and the definite knowledge that no other white man has ever trodden in the area gives a constant feeling of satisfaction. Every object and feature — be it geological, botanical, zoological, or ornithological — is new to the outside world and of course to the explorer himself.

A discovery of any kind which is outstanding will serve to stimulate interest for months afterwards and the excitement of further possible finds completely overrides physical hardships encountered. One such occasion came about on a rocky outcrop named by Tietkens, the Davenport Hills, where a colony of black-flanked rock wallabies was discovered, which are almost extinct in those regions.

Under the shadow of the Davenport Hills named for the then president of the South Australian Branch of the Royal Geographical Society, Sir Samuel Davenport, and situated 20 kilometres south of Mount Leisler, the road making came to a temporary halt while a variety of weighty mechanical repairs were effected.

Everyday activities which are accepted without question or even thought in normal civilisation become major problems in the bush and are coped with in a multitude of ways depending on the ingenuity of the individual. The usual act of sleeping is one that is hardly considered in houses where everything is the same night after night, but although a team constantly camping in the open in whatever weather in all four seasons may start out very primitively, improvements can always be devised given time . . .

20
Bush Bedrooms

Over the years each one of us had developed his own scheme of sleeping arrangements, and even now, during this shattering deviation from our usual routine, we all put in the night as before, as if nothing had happened. Even old Paul, suddenly minus his faithful ration truck, was still to be seen lying out in the open on his iron, hospital-type army bed with its wire mesh top.

When this project had first begun, we had all camped on the ground among the saltbush prickles, thorny spinifex, and powdery bulldust. As our campsite was changed almost every night, we gave less and less attention to preparing a sleeping area, and only the sharpest rocks in stony places were thrown aside. In khaki-burr patches, some of the spiky little balls of needles would inevitably become embedded in the blankets, leaving behind hair-like needles even when the main bulk was removed. After rainy nights, even though the swags were rolled in protective canvas camp-sheets, it would be days before we could dry out the covers, holding them up to large fires before we used them again.

We made a big concession when, several years earlier, pillows were brought in lieu of heaped-up clothes and towels; but during the winter months the dew would gradually penetrate them, and after a shower of rain they became quite unusable. The only way to restore them to a dry state was to empty the stuffing out on to a canvas sheet on the next sunny day, and after constant turning over it would eventually be fit to replace. Most of the pillow bags in our little camp showed the evidence in rows of 2-centimetre-long 'homeward bound' stitches as a result.

As a further refinement, and throwing to the winds the problem of space for carrying, we began to think that, if we wanted to take the trouble to handle them every day, thin mattresses could smooth out to a degree the larger of the rocky lumps in our desert beds. Larger canvas squares were needed so that the complete bundle, including blankets and pillow, could be rolled for transport, and these were ordered from the canvas worker at Woomera. The amount of room taken up by these great bed-rolls was phenomenal, but we persevered, and eventually rough but strong wooden shelves were added to our vehicle bumper bars to carry them. The wisdom of our determination to include these with the sleeping gear was the subject of serious doubt on one gloomy sprinkling morning after a night of constant heavy rain. The swirling waters had discovered a minute entrance into Scotty's canvas cocoon and unbeknown to him had been trickling into his wondrous mattress all night long. When he finally emerged from the completely enclosed depths of his boudoir after somehow realising that a new day had begun, we heard him mumble something about 'thirty gallons' to no one in particular.

A year of living like this had passed before the idea of a new and devastating innovation crept into our minds. The colossal bulk of a mattress only served to cover the ant-beds and rocks so they could be lain on with more ease; so, what if we were to sleep several centimetres *above* the ant-beds and rocks? The sensation of sleeping on beds had become completely foreign to us, but our thoughts were turning in that direction and the prospect was decidedly attractive. No more dusty blankets embedded with burrs, no more lying on iron-hard ant-beds or stones, and no more grappling with an ungainly mattress-roll every morning. It was so positively effeminate that no member of our small party was brave enough to be the first to mention it.

At long last a heavy equipment fitter, who was with us at the outset, actually broached out loud the subject which was already uppermost in our thoughts. The adjective 'heavy' not only applied to the equipment he fitted but also to himself, and over the months the uneven ground had surely made more of an impression on him than on us. As though nobody had ever thought of it, we agreed that perhaps some use could be made occasionally of the small canvas stretchers which we had noticed in the bulk store at Woomera. The very next trip 'down south' saw us signing for half a dozen of these items and storing our mattresses in a shed as they 'might come in handy' one day.

The first night back to the bush was one of unaccustomed excitement. The new beds were unfolded, and after a number of attempts, according to the varied mechanical ability of the boys, they were assembled and the much-diminished swag-roll placed sedately on top. There we were, up out of whatever surface that particular campsite presented, and what was more, the beds were capable of accommodating the entire assortment of contours with which a human body is made. It proved the most restful evening we'd had for years. Now that they had arrived on the scene, the beds were there to stay. Or so we thought.

Unfortunately, everything we owned and carried had, of necessity, to be of rugged construction throughout, and these stretchers were obviously designed for holiday campers. Their average use would normally be in the order of a fortnight per annum, in which case the fabric could be expected to last for years. In our case they were intended to be *idle* for only two weeks per year. However, those problems hadn't as yet cropped up.

After a dozen nights of blissful sleep a slight fraying began to be noticeable along the side rails which in themselves, although apparently quite flimsy, had, up till now, survived the heaviest of us.

Small holes followed the fraying, and it seemed sensible to start treating the beds with respect, gradually easing on to them, remaining throughout the evening as immovable as is possible after a day's work, and gingerly rolling off them in the mornings. Instinct dictated that to concentrate the strain on any one point, as for example in the act of sitting upon them, would be disastrous. Although they were only 10 centimetres clear of the ground, that was already becoming preferable to our former height of zero centimetres, so our newly-acquired treasures rode in pride of place among our prized possessions and were treated accordingly.

One night, not much later, our heavy equipment fitter had his first major mishap. Ambling over from the fire with the misguided idea of going to bed, he carefully manoeuvred his weight on to the unfortunate little stretcher and reached for his blanket covering. The noise of the ripping canvas and the following thud could be heard throughout the camp, but his groans could be heard much further, as well as his matter-of-fact statement, 'Down on the ground again.' His was only the first of a series of identical episodes which put us all back to where we started, even before the mattress era.

One day a tree branch caught in the canopy of one of the trucks, leaving a suitable-sized rectangle dangling from it after the vehicle had gone past. I happened to be the next to pass the spot, and, taking down the 'flag' by standing on the roof of the Rover, I put into operation the idea which had flashed into my mind the instant I saw the cloth flapping in the breeze. That night my stretcher, with its truck-canopy reinforcement, complete with 'homeward bound' stitches strongly sewed with plumb-bob string, was the only one that kept its user off the ground.

The next innovation clearly must involve something stronger than

canvas, and iron with heavy wire mesh was the only material acceptable. Thus our little group entered into the army-hospital-bed age, which remained with us for the rest of the project. With the U-shaped legs folded up, the beds could be hung on appropriate hooks welded to the sides of the trucks, but the problem of the hard mesh was soon found to be worse than the ant-beds and rocks. Back came the 'handy' mattresses with their bulk, and at last we all had our sleeping problems solved. My bed hung from hooks looped over the bush-bashing framework on the Rover, with its bottom rail strapped to an iron D bolted to the panelling to stop it flapping. As a station boy once said, it did look as if I was carrying a gate around with me.

Of course, during the long forward reconnaissance trips I was back to a canvas square on the ground. The bed would never last long on the side of the Rover as I plunged through the dense scrub, and apart from this its iron mass would greatly affect the oil-bath compass mounted in the cabin. So on these occasions it was placed under a mulga tree and all my surplus gear was heaped on it to wait until I returned.

As we had penetrated further into unbroken country 1000 kilometres from the nearest habitation, our initial complement of one truck and two Land Rovers proved to be hopelessly inadequate. Apart from the bedding, the rations and bulk fuel drums for the machinery just wouldn't fit. Another truck was added to our retinue, and not long afterwards a third truck was found to be essential for ferrying supplies to keep us going. The complete number of three big trucks, two Land Rovers, a bulldozer, and a grader made up our camp for many years — not including the assortment of trailers.

On one 'end-of-the-year' visit to civilisation Scotty and Doug even asked about the feasibility of adding a caravan to our string. Many of these were available at Woomera, and so the following year saw us on our way with a gleaming three-berth model in tow. When it arrived in our camp (if it survived the 2000-kilometre trip), the plan was for the grader, being the only vehicle capable of dragging it over the new roads, to lug it from camp to camp. On larger sand-ridge crossings the bulldozer was always there to pull it over when the grader wheels lost their grip. The two plant operators and the cherry picker would be using the caravan, as Paul, Quinny, and I spurned the idea of being caged in at night and preferred to carry on as usual.

The 1400-litre water-tank and the 450-litre auxiliary petrol tank installed behind the cabin of each truck gave a large flat area on their combined tops, and this was as close as Quinny ever came to a bedroom. Paul always slept out in the open with only the dome of stars over him, even when they were replaced with ominous-looking rain clouds. He did this for the entire eight years, except for one or two exceptionally wild nights, one of which had occurred at a camp 50 kilometres on our way west from Sandy Blight Junction.

I had, up to this time, remained faithful to the shorter version of the Land Rover, thinking it could force its way through some of the thicker scrub by turning in smaller circles. This left me out in the elements with Paul. On this particular October night even I was beginning to think about other methods of sleeping, and as my Rover was due for a replacement anyway, I determined that my new vehicle would be of the long wheelbase variety. This would make it possible to actually sleep indoors, although I would have to overcome my repulsion of cages, and put up with larger turning circles. As it eventuated, my new vehicle went with equal ease over any surface anywhere the others would go, and at last I could obviate the need for the never-ending rolling up of a swag every day. But it had taken this particular night in question to turn the tables.

When we had started work that day a stiff wind had sprung up, and this increased gradually in force by the hour. At first fine dust filled the air, then came heavier dirt and sand followed by ironstone gravel which peppered our little group with the violence of a shot-gun and remained unabated during the daylight hours. Black clouds appeared about midday, and one or two spots of rain spattered on to the windscreens to combine with the dust into droplets of mud. The wind ripped through the mulgas and spinifex with such frenzy that complete trees were uprooted, and those already bulldozed aside were spun around and carried bodily in the direction the gale was travelling. Anything not firmly anchored down didn't stand a chance of remaining where it was, and even the big trucks rocked on their springs.

It was impossible to do anything but seek refuge from the storm by crouching in the cabins of the vehicles. The three caravan occupants swayed about in their cubicle so dangerously that I wondered if it would stay upright on its wheels, so we moved it to a position end-on to the blast. The noise of the gravel hammering on to the aluminium walls of the van was deafening when you were on the inside, but the few minutes I spent there were very welcome. We decided against trying to prepare anything to eat but each made a small meal from our assortment of tinned food while crouching wherever we could out of this fury.

When it was time to turn in, Quinny even roped down the canvas canopy flap next to his perch on the petrol and water tanks, and as the fitter had a similar position on his truck he followed suit. Paul rolled out his swag among the ration boxes in the back of his vehicle, for once leaving the iron bed right where it was on the hooks outside, after first turning his 'trolley,' as he called it, side-on to the battering wind.

210

The elements had gone completely mad already, but now a further catastrophe descended upon us. The few sizeable drops of rain were slowly being augmented by others, and by what appeared to be late afternoon a wall of water had enveloped everything. The rain was torrential, and within seconds rivers formed in our wheeltracks and boiled along the ground to the lower areas, with spray being whipped up by the wind as they went. Without reference to watches only a guess could be made as to the time of day. It looked like being a very long night.

Having the smallest vehicle in the camp, I was the only one without any shelter apart from canvas squares, but I was determined that I would not invade the inner sanctums of any of the others. My old routine would carry on regardless. However, I did think I might reinforce the one camp-sheet with a second which I carried in case it might 'come in handy.' If it didn't come in handy that night, then it never would.

I usually slept with my head towards the back wheel of the Rover as a sort of protection against weather in general. There wasn't much else to be protected from. Often the pad tracks of dingoes searching for food were plain to see in the dust around my swag, but as silently as they came, they crept away, never molesting me in the slightest. I had often woken to notice one or two in the flesh staring motionlessly at my lone camp, only moving when I stirred — a situation which sometimes caused me to sleep alongisde my rifle. Nothing else to cause concern lived in these outback deserts apart from scorpions and centipedes, and these were only around after or during rain.

The wheel kept the bright light from the full moon out of my eyes on several nights a month and the very early morning sun in summer months away from me until I deigned to 'balance on one end.' Each morning this end-of-the-year sun brought with it not only soaring temperatures but also the accompanying black mist of flies. If I slept on the eastern side of the wheel during those months they would ensure my premature rising by swarming into my eyes, as the intense early heat caused me to discard my blanket.

During the winter, the later daybreak and the sun's warming rays were more than welcome after a freezing night, so I never slept west of the wheel. The most awkward combination of sun, moon, winter, and summer was consistently found to be on wintry evenings when the moon was full. As the sun set, the huge silver orb of the moon would appear in the east, sparkling down on the bush through the crisp dewy dusk and remaining to illuminate the scene almost to daylight intensity throughout the night. Trying to sleep with this phosphorescent floodlight on the exposed eastern side of the wheel burning into my eyes until the shadow of the vehicle took over at midnight was a problem I never solved before the advent of the long wheel-base Land Rover. I either fell asleep in the shade on the western aspect and froze away from the sun in the morning, or I stayed fitfully awake half the night to welcome the warmth of a new day. I usually decided on the latter course, with its added advantage of a sun-dried swag to roll up in place of an otherwise dew-soaked one.

The arrival of an evening wind added to the complication of deciding on a sleeping orientation because, in the case of wind, the feet end of the turned-under canvas swag must point into the direction from which it came, otherwise covers would be either blown away completely or impregnated with the accompanying dust and saltbush prickles or spinifex tops. If the wind was coming from the south on a summer night with a full moon, then the worst evening's sleep could be expected. If I lay on the south side of the vehicle, the last rays from the blistering sun as it set would continue to play on the already heated swag, there would be no shadow from the moon all night, and the first boiling shimmer would resume at dawn.

One way and another the science of merely stopping for an overnight camp developed into an exacting art only coped with after years of trial and error, with the error predominating.

Where could I sleep, therefore, on this memorable October night? With this unprecedented situation I decided to discard all the scientifically-accumulated rules, so I forced open the door of the Rover and waded around to the iron bed hanging on its hooks. Extreme tiredness dictated that I couldn't huddle upright in the driver's seat all night long. I quickly had the bed in place against the wheel, but by the time the canvas swag was unrolled on its wire top I was thoroughly drenched. Out came the handy extra square of canvas. I had thoughtfully spliced rope ties to each corner of it, and after battling with it in the wind I managed to fasten the corners securely to the underside legs of the frame, all but one corner which I raised a few centimetres to tie on to the iron D on the panelling.

With my boots pushed under the mudguard and on top of the wheel, both to prevent them from floating away in the night and to halt the procession of centipedes from invading them, as I had so often found before during rain, I levered myself into the structure. The saturated shirt and shorts had to go and were wedged on top of the boots in a sodden lump before I managed to complete the operation and finally install myself in the tube. I gained consolation from the fact that I would not suffer from moonstroke or sunstroke if morning ever arrived again, and there were certainly no banks of flies. In some ways I was really very well off.

The howling wind and driving rain hammered on my canvas with such uncontrollable energy that I could feel them on my body as though they were blows from a threshing machine. Another thing in my favour was that because it was October, the temperature was not actually freezing, even though the wind-blown rain caused a decided crispness to be felt.

No sooner had I encased myself, thankfully up off the swirling ground waters at least, than I was shaken to see through the slight crack in the canvas flap that the surrounding bush, camp, and country were suddenly illuminated to bright daylight. Momentarily the deluge of rain could be clearly seen as it beat on to the surfaces of everything about, and then, seconds after the pitch blackness returned, an ear-shattering explosion jolted its way through the night.

After that inaugural and savage eruption, the lightning and thunder swelled in intensity with violence surpassing any man-made nuclear device, and rampaged through the heavens for hours to come. Forked lightning laced the sky preceding crashes of thunder until thoughts of the splintered, blazing tree which had been struck near my camp eight years before leapt into my brain, and I began to doubt that I would ever see another sunrise. The metal of the bed and vehicle could attract such electrical forces but I hoped that the water cascading down over it all would serve as a conductor if necessary. At the same time I hoped everyone else was surviving safely.

Somehow and at some time during the night I must have succumbed to the effect of the day's battering and fallen into a merciful coma, finally emerging back to consciousness at a time when I could see my surroundings without the aid of lightning flashes. There was not much indication that the weather was abating apart from the fact that the bursts of light and explosions of thunder were missing. Wind and rain were still in much evidence, but, having had enough of the clammy blankets, I retrieved my hobs and clothes from under the mudguard and roped down the flap of the camp-sheet.

My appearance in the caravan reflected in the expressions of the three caged but wonderfully dry occupants as they looked at me with apprehension. Some people after an evening such as that might have become somewhat disconsolate, tending to suppress a smile, but I was so pleased it was over that I couldn't feel at all dejected. I did, however, venture a comment that the weather seemed to have the appearance of being a trifle boisterous.

That was by far the wildest night I've ever endured out in the open in the bush, but it was not necessarily the most uncomfortable. Lashing dust storms filling eyes, ears, nose, and blankets with powdery red dust, and nights of insidious invasions by billions of black specks of ants into swag-rolls made other occasions more nightmarish, but one thing was certain. The memory of that October camp will remain with me as clear as it was on that morning for the rest of my life. Even now, when I see a night storm raging outside any shelter I might be lucky enough to be in at the time, I never fail to register a feeling of gratitude.

Doug summed it up later by remarking, after a discussion of the event, that he 'didn't get a wink of sleep all night anyway worrying about me.' Only one day later saw me at my theodolite carrying out a sun observation in preparation for an astrofix the following night. The purpose of this was to establish a sign for the crossing of the Western Australian border where we left the Northern Territory behind. It was surely an incredible country.

Quite a while before this, Quinny, who would sometimes even beat Paul up out of bed in the mornings before the faint glow of an approaching day could be detected, made a discovery. He informed the camp of it when we all rose. It concerned the rather unusual way in which our cook dressed himself before preparing breakfast. It seemed that Paul would stand on his head to pull on his old charcoal-blackened trousers, even before he hit the ground. A long time ago he had met with an accident which had broken his legs, but apart from a difficulty in walking it hadn't

really affected him. Consequently he had obviously found it easier to allow gravity to aid him in donning his clothes, and with feet in the air, the trousers could slide down to his waist. When the operation was reversed, his shirt would react accordingly.

This morning, as we camped with our road train at the Davenport Hills, I happened to rise for once even before both of them and for the first time witnessed this phenomenon for myself. Old Paul had apparently seen the glow of the breakfast fire I had lit, so although it was still dark he decided to get up and, not having his customary ration truck as a screen, began to dress.

We would soon be on our slow way with our towing operation, but not before Paul balanced on one end, even though it was the wrong one.

When working on a project as enormous as that undertaken by the Gunbarrel Road Construction Party, State boundaries are often crossed and on such occasions where possible, the actual spot where the road cuts the border can be marked. This helps not only cartographers in plotting the new accesses on maps but serves as an object of great interest to future travellers. Also in cases of Aboriginal reserves and activities of oil exploration companies, their boundaries are immediately evident as they drive along the only existing road in their region.

The location of the borders can be determined by a series of astronomical observations and calculations for latitude and longitude to fix the position of the surveyor, from which the already known values of the borders can be measured. The state boundary between Western Australia and the rest of the continent is the longest and as the Sandy Blight Junction Road crossed it midway throughout the latter's length, a special effort was made to indicate the intersection for all to see. A line of desert oak posts were arrayed either side in line with the north south border straddling the new road, and an aluminium plate attached to the one nearest the edge told the story in letters stamped separately with steel punches.

Being on the Northern Territory section of the border, the crossing was in a particularly desolate and remote locality and when a tribe of Aborigines was discovered nearby, it was a safe bet they wouldn't have had previous contact with white men ...

216

21
The Discovery of a Desert Tribe

Even if only a few kilometres over the border, the camp that night was once again in Western Australia and within sight of the Bonython Range. Only the upper half of the rocky outcrop of which the range is composed could be seen, protruding above the high sand ridge to the north. We had been paralleling that same wall of sand from well back into the Northern Territory, as it didn't recognise such a thing as a State boundary. It had been the factor governing the course the road was made to take as we had battled our way northward through the maze of sandhills during construction. This insurmountable barrier reared up to protect the range from invasion as a moat protects a castle.

This overnight camp was at the turning point in the road where I had finally conceded a victory to the sandhills by turning easterly with the survey. I remembered endeavouring to cross over it on the original reconnaissance, having deflated all the tyres to a point where any further slackness would have rolled them off the rims. After a dozen futile attempts, a lower saddle to the east had finally allowed the charging Land Rover admittance to the rocky range beyond, and I could at least climb to its beckoning summit. From the high vantage point I hoped to scan the skyline in the direction we wanted the road to take and thus help in its final location.

I knew that we would not be putting the new access over this gigantic mound of sand because, even if we did, very few future travellers could have used it. The sand would have surely blown back to cover the tracks, leaving an access open only to specially-equipped vehicles.

The effort involved in eventually reaching the highest point of the range, with the last steep pinch being only negotiable on foot, paid dividends of paramount importance. It offered me that first exciting glimpse of the huge blue bulk of Mount Leisler far off to the north-east and made me decide then and there to which immediate destination the road was bound.

Months before, when we had arrived at this turning point with the bulldozer, I had abandoned the Rover on my 'expedition wheeltracks' and climbed up on to the heavy machine with Doug. We were going to test whether the high sandhill could halt a dozer with its great steel Caterpillar tracks. We soon found that even these wouldn't pull the massive weight up the sharp incline ahead, as there was a complete absence of grip in the soft sand. A spot slightly to the west looked more feasible, and after much churning and manoeuvring, the multi-tonne giant sat balancing on the top of the ridge. That this was the first such event in the history of the sandhill and indeed for this area in general since the world began was indisputable.

We stood on the engine cowling, which was rumbling with the steady beat of the pulsating motor beneath, to view the scene spread out in front of us. Voicing the sentiments for both of us as we beheld the stark wastes of dead trees scattering the otherwise bare sand, Doug uttered the first description of it ever made by white man: 'Gosh! what a desolate joint!'

On that first survey trip, I had covered 200 kilometres return from our camp at the current head of the road only 50 kilometres away. Weaving and circling through that dreaded belt of sandhills searching for a route to make the road accounted for the extra 100 kilometres of exploratory bush bashing. A comment I had made in my little diary at the end of the expedition stated clearly that there were millions of them, a figure which I suspect was grossly inaccurate but summed up my feelings at the time. At the close of each day I would sit on my opened swag by the Rover and briefly record the happenings on that date. Although some of the information such as the foregoing could not stand up to scrutiny, the general atmosphere would be obvious on later reading.

One day, when I was the furthest distance from my camp on that particular survey, I remembered seeing volumes of black smoke spiralling into the sky ahead coming from somewhere beyond the Bonython Range. This smoke, which continued to rise throughout the afternoon, would have originated from Aborigines' fires as they burnt off large areas of spinifex during their hunt for food. Small lizards inhabit the bases of the spiky hummocks as in summer months they are the only source of shade, and the sharp needles of the dreadful *Triodia* also protect them from eagles and other forms of danger.

218

These lizards are only about 15 centimetres from head to tail and dart with lightning speed from clump to clump. As we drove over seemingly endless plains of spinifex with bare red sand separating each mound, we found that these energetic creatures were forever part of the scene. Some would dart across the metre-long expanses of clear sand with their lower legs only, the front legs and the majority of their little bodies in a vertical position. As their rear legs churned over the ground with supersonic speed the action so closely resembled that of a cyclist that the logical name of 'bicycle lizards' resulted. They are in evidence throughout the entire year in all seasons, surviving the longest droughts, and as such they provide a constant source of food for Aborigines.

Some Aborigines can actually catch these creatures by hand, but to obtain them in sufficient numbers for eating, they merely light the spinifex up-wind and as the fire spreads the lizards are laid bare. Enormous areas of the resin-loaded hummocks are persistently burnt all over Central Australia by the few scattered Aboriginal tribes, and the billowing clouds of dense smoke are a characteristic betrayal of their presence. From long experience, I have concluded that these aerial indications could originate at a distance of anything from a kilometre or less to 50. In one particularly remote area in the Gibson Desert we saw great smoke activity at a distance which seemed to be only a sandhill or two removed from us. After beating over sandhills in that direction for over 20 kilometres in a Land Rover, with the smoke still appearing to be the same arm's length away, we gave up and returned to camp before darkness fell.

On this day of reconnaissance, as I became entangled in the convolution of piles of sand, I noticed that the smoke columns kept erupting from an area in exactly the direction of my planned destination, so I discarded the compass in favour of the signals and simply made for them. By the time I reached the final mountainous wall of sand, with the rocks of the range well in view on the other side, I was surprised that I hadn't yet caught up with the actual fires. Nevertheless, when the sun had set and intense darkness had settled over my lone camp in the quiet bush, I sensed I must be quite close to my unseen neighbours.

No sound came to me through the stillness of the crisp night air, and the blackness of the near-by range added to the eerie gloom surrounding me, but I could feel the nearness of other human beings. Having come across so many of their camps, I could see in my imagination the naked shapes of the Aborigines huddled close to their microscopic campfires, extending a hand now and then to feel the warmth. Nothing but an occasional whisper would pass between them as one by one they would lie down among the spinifex on the frosty dew-soaked sand to simulate what their pampered white brothers would call sleep.

As I put my little diary back into the leather survey bag which was my constant companion in the Rover, and crawled into the canvas-covered swag-roll, my thoughts dwelt totally upon those freezing Aborigines. How near to me were they in this limitless expanse of wilderness, and had they ever set eyes on a white man with a motor vehicle? Never in this part of the country: of that I was quite certain. We were 500 kilometres in a straight line to the nearest settlement of any kind, and that in itself nestled in a very remote locality. Nothing whatsoever would be found for twice that distance to the west or south.

When I pulled the cold canvas over myself I found that it was already soaking wet, and as I lapsed into oblivion after the long hard day of crashing through the scrub, my last reflection was how soft we had become. Remove the camp-sheet, take away the blankets and raggy clothes, and I would be the same as the Aborigines, lying out in this frigid atmosphere without protection of any kind. They didn't even have the contents of a tin of bully beef in their stomachs as I had, but only some scraps of a lizard or so which they might have been lucky enough to burn out of hiding. They would certainly have heard the engine as I charged over the sandhills and would know of my presence as surely as I knew of theirs. Their keen sense of hearing would have told them a foreigner was at hand, and how far away he was, with much greater accuracy then I was capable of when I tried to guess at the distance of the smoke.

I couldn't help the predominant feeling that I might have visitors before the time came for me to move on in the morning. After dark the Aborigines generally remained at their fires, but I had experienced incidents where definite evidence of their silent infiltration into my camps could be discovered. A bag of flour ripped open or an empty water-tank on my Rover with the tap full on over a patch of wet mud were the sort of things I had previously encountered. Of course, the loss of the water gave the greatest concern, and I only hoped that the same thing was not about to happen this night. Taking a length of fencing wire and a pair of pliers to the unprotected rear of the vehicle, I took the precaution of clinching a strong loop over the handle and under the outlet pipe in such a way as to render it immovable by hand, before finally encasing myself in the swag. As always, the water provided my only means of returning to the far-away camp, leaving the food to rank a quite insignificant second. Radiators just won't work on tinned meat.

Awake at first light next morning, I threw back the stiff, frosty canvas, being anxious to get a warming fire going as quickly as possible. Although I had not actually lain shivering throughout the night I was by no means over-warm, and the frozen open-top hobnailed boots into which my bare feet were thrust didn't fail, as usual, to reduce the temperature even further. In less than a minute, the match dropped into the nearest clump of spinifex had converted it into a roaring inferno on to which I deposited an armful of debris from the bonnet of the Rover. The accumulation of sticks from dry mulga trees and bushes as I pushed through the scrub would heap up daily until it resembled an eagle's nest, but I always left it intact for use as morning wood, except when it piled higher than my line of sight through the windscreen.

Only after I had stood by the fire for a few minutes did I thaw enough to inspect the sand around my airy camp to see if any nocturnal visitations had occurred. However, the crisp white frost lay all about quite undisturbed. There was no need even to look at the water tap, but when something so vital to survival is at stake, I did cast a quick glance in that direction before hurrying back to the source of warmth. The strong wire clinch was in place. As I stood soaking in the warmth of the flames I looked to the north past the rocky range. Sure enough, the hunting fires were still issuing their columns of smoke. If the terrain in that direction had been at all favourable I would definitely have attempted to make contact with the hunters, but as it was I had already pushed the little vehicle as far north as it would go — a fact proved by the way I had had to close the final gap to the summit of this range on foot.

There had been much to do that day, as I had far from discovered a satisfactory route to make the road up to this point. The normal procedure I had evolved was to endeavour to sort it out on my return trip. With this in mind I rolled up that soggy swag and with no thought of breakfast started up the engine once more. I cut the wire safety device from the tap with my pliers and huddled over the dying embers of the fire for a last warm-up before climbing into the refrigerated cabin. I had already wiped a rag over the icy windscreen in order to see through it, and was soon moving slowly over the hummocks, tossing like a cork on a rough sea, in the general direction of camp. I had been pleased to notice the absence of any flat tyres which so often opened the day's proceedings, thanks to the lack of hard dead mulga roots and branches. These had given way to more open spinifex since the last session of patching the day before.

As it was early winter, the sun quickly dispelled the biting cold of the evening, and by mid-morning I was warm enough to discard my old army overcoat as I battled with the steering wheel. The engine helped to defrost the cabin, and with an occasional glance behind, I could see the columns of smoke becoming less and less distinct as the morning wore on. I was never to see smoke in that direction again, and I frequently wondered who the people were, how many there were of them, and how far they actually were from my lonely camp in the sandhills.

Two years later, after the completion of that road, an incident happened which caused me immediately to remember those smoke spirals and to wonder if in fact I had at last actually made contact with one of those mysterious hunters.

We had joined our road at Jupiter Well with another coming down from the opposite direction and originating from Gary Junction, the northern terminus of the Gary Highway. Having thus paved the way for a 500-kilometre loop access back to the Gunbarrel Highway, it became necessary to drive on past the burnt-out truck to Giles via the Sandy Blight Junction Road for more supplies. We intended then to connect Gary Junction to Australia's Highway One near the Indian Ocean, a distance of some 500 kilometres further away to the north-west.

During the drive from Jupiter Well I had Scotty with me in the Rover. We had left his grader in readiness at Gary Junction to be guarded by Paul, Eric, and Doug at our camp there. As usual they were quite content to await our return. Quinny of course came with us, bringing his supply truck to be loaded with fresh rations and fuel for our next lunge into the Great Sandy Desert.

As we drove past the burnt shell of our old ration truck and approached the border signpost, we were actually only about 60 kilometres due north of our former camp near the Bonython Range. The distance removed from my original estimation of the location of the hunters' smoke fires was therefore only 40 kilometres, which isn't very far when you are speaking of nomadic Aborigines in search of food.

We both saw it together. Away to the south and from behind a bank of high sandhills erupted a long, thin column of black smoke in the exact direction of the rocky range where I had camped alone with a strong wire clinch on the Rover's water tap. The events of that night leapt into my mind. The coincidence of the proximity of both sightings, although seen from vastly removed standpoints and with the space of two years separating them, was far too strong to ignore.

Grinding along the still relatively new road, I repeated the story of that last experience to Scotty. No sooner had I finished than, as if in answer to our combined curiosity, a naked black figure appeared from the far side of the nearest sand ridge, running as fast as it could go. We had been wishing for time enough to negotiate the sandhills in the direction of the smoke so that we could try to bring about a meeting with these people, but now that looked to be unnecessary.

There was a clearing on the crest of sand several hundred metres from us, with scattered scrub and low bushes covering the intervening distance. It was in this clearing that we first saw the movement, and it was obvious that the Aboriginal was racing in a line towards the road in such a direction that he would be able to head us off several hundred metres in front. No Aborigines had ever been seen in this locality in the years we had been working there. As we closed the distance between the Rover and the running figure we caught an occasional glimpse of the athletic form as it flashed between the bushes. Then, in almost no time, our eagerly searching eyes beheld the wiry frame of an Aboriginal standing on the road ahead, barring our way. I was surprised at his boldness, as in most such instances these people are quite timid in their approach.

He waited until we stopped, and we could see no evidence of his having just raced at least half a kilometre. No panting or gasping for breath, not a sign of tiredness as he strode around to my door, and no obvious traces of sweating. Had an untrained white man extended himself to such a degree he would have been slumped down with his head between his knees, fighting for air and soaked in perspiration. We were soon to discover that although visible evidence of exertion was lacking, this didn't comprise the whole description of our audacious friend.

I began to open the door as the wild-looking Aboriginal reached it, blocking the action, and instantaneously the space between us through the open window was converted into a dense seething mass of flies. For a time I could barely see him through the haze from which emitted such a din as to drown the sound of the engine. Each individual fly must have been screaming at full pitch and the noise was deafening, but this wasn't even half of the disruption to our former comparatively serene drive. Forcing its way through the fog came a fragrance with such impact as to cause my passenger, anxious as he was to view our visitor at close range, to vacate his seat forthwith. The operation as he rocketed out of the cabin was performed with such downright alacrity that I was scarcely aware of being alone in so microscopic a period of time.

I was a metre closer to the source of the aroma, and this didn't help a bit. Furthermore, I was trapped in the confined space of the driver's seat, and any attempt at retreat was foiled by the radio transceiver box installed in place of the middle seat. Forward evacuation was thwarted by the door which, although slightly ajar, was held by what easily could have been a hand, obscured completely by the flies. When the time came to breathe inwards once more, after exhaling for only half a minute, I just had to push open the door enough to permit my escape.

Admittedly the day had been warm, but as there hadn't been much rain for about a year and with the bathing facilities as scant as they were in the desert, the likelihood of even a personal rinse since the last good downpour was extremely remote.

Not a word in either of our languages had as yet been uttered, as conversation necessitated periodic inhalations which, as well as the

scented atmosphere, would have drawn in a hatful of flies with every breath. The Aboriginal, still gripping the door to save himself being knocked over as I plunged out into the open air, thrust the swarm of insects on his shoulders in through the window, obviously in search of anything edible. How he could see beyond his eyelids eluded me. At last, standing 10 metres away over the windrow of dead spinifex, I could regain my breath. It seemed reasonable to give him a tin of water from the tap at the back of the Rover, and as I turned it on, I thought of the wire twitch with which I had locked that very tap two years before.

Could this have been one of those mysterious hunters against whom I had guarded my meagre but precious supply of water on that frosty night at the Bonython Range? Would he have been the one who might have crept silently into my camp and caused my failure to regain the party at the head of the road? After all, it was only 40 kilometres or so from where we stood at that moment. My own answer to these questions was that definitely, here in the flesh, in the midst of that mound of flies, an original member of that same tribe was drinking the proffered water from that self-same tap.

After several futile attempts to discover the number of his companions still concealed behind the sand ridge, we indicated that we were about to

224

make our departure and leave him to return to his people, taking with him his personal cloud of flies, quaint perfume, and all. Even after the flies had receded into the background and we had resumed our drive, it wasn't until we reached the campsite that the last haunting traces of that unforgettable stench had finally dissipated and it again became possible to breathe *inside* the cabin.

Right now, all this was in the future. My momentous meeting with one of those remote nomadic hunters was still to come, and at this time I could only cogitate over their existence. As I lay on my swag in the intense heat of the Central Australian summer, only the memories of those earlier smoke sightings and the reasons leading up to the enforced change in the direction of our road filled my mind. Complete quietness had replaced the former screeching and banging of our bulldozer train, and it now stood on the road alongside our little camp, waiting to resume its towing activities in the morning.

But on every subsequent trip past this point on the road, following that first meeting with the aromatic tribesman, I have always recalled that it was about here that another happening well worthy of mention had taken place.

Although some missions can have the appearance of going on indefinitely, such as oceanography and meteorology, most operations usually come to an end however large or difficult or lengthy they have been to accomplish. Constant dripping will wear away a stone and if an almost impossible project is taken in small stages, its completion must eventually be assured. Even to dragging a string of crippled vehicles from the desert, a distance of 800 kilometres at a speed of 3 kilometres an hour.

It is specially rewarding when that operation is performed over the very road which owed its newly acquired existence to the equipment being salvaged, which became the absolute first user of the new access. It wouldn't be long before the original cleared campsites, reused by the party, would all be lost forever as the desert winds and growth took over, but now this was all too new.

Features which were taken for granted when the roar of the bulldozer amid clouds of dust was the only thing which occupied the party's thoughts, could now be studied from an entirely different aspect: that of an impartial traveller. Why was that curve made? What was the reason for crossing that sand ridge? How did the road negotiate that rocky outcrop in the distance?

The answers were all there in the minds of that little band of men as they crept along week after week; answers that could not be duplicated by any other person ever attempting the same journey in the years to come . . .

226

22
Bungabiddy and Home

W ithin half a day of pulling out from our overnight camp between the sand ridges east of the Robert Range, the train emerged from the valley. As we rounded the last of the dunes, the Walter James Range was at last in full view. The Robert Range, located 10 kilometres west of that historic upward turn in our road, was named by Ernest Giles in 1874 after his brother and was for us the last main topographical feature before Walter James.

On my solitary reconnaissance to discover a break through to the north, I had camped relatively close to the Robert Range in a deep basin completely ringed by high steep sandhills. After a battle with Lake Hopkins I came upon some rocky bluffs, a little too far to the west, as the memories of those salty swamps had been fresh and I had been endeavouring to give them a greater berth than was necessary. These vertical cliffs were named the Wallace Hills and the huge belt of impassable sand ridges bordered them on their western side. Of course at the time I hadn't known this. I was unwittingly about to find it out the hard way.

Beating through the scrub and sand until the sun had long since set, I decided before camping to tackle the one large ridge in front of me at the time in the gloom of dusk. After a dozen attempts I felt elated at finally winning and slid down the other side to the flat valley in a cascade of sand, knowing full well I could never retrace my tracks back in that direction. I couldn't see further than a few metres, but once on the level surface, I soon found among the spinifex a clearing on which to settle down for the night. I needed a clearing as I had two flat spare tyres to mend, but I decided against the need for an astrofix on that spot.

Too tired after the day's bush bashing and repairs after dark to think of eating, I lay down in my swag over 100 kilometres from the rest of the boys waiting at the current head of the road at Walter James. Before long — or so it seemed — daylight had begun to approach once more in the form of a faint glow over the dunes to the east. Up and anxious to be on my way, I rolled my blankets in the semi-darkness of the hollow as the sky became lighter by the minute, and looked about me. Ahead lay a high and very steep sandhill. This curved around to the north to connect to the huge one I had slid down in the darkness of the previous evening, barely 100 metres away. Tracing the outline to the south, I was amazed to discover that it followed an almost identical course, arcing right back again to the one behind. I was in a deep basin completely surrounded by a circular wall of sand, with every avenue of escape apparently blocked off. Searching in vain for an outlet in any direction, I realised that without knowing what I was doing in the dark I had landed myself in a drastic predicament by allowing the gallant little Rover to be carried by the moving sand to the bottom of the dune. I was so far from the nearest living thing that any possibility of walking was out of the question, and I knew straight away that this was going to mean a lot of hard work if I was to ever see my camp again. Even if I did manage to emerge from this bowl, there were still 100 kilometres of as yet unknown country to penetrate before I could reach the rest of the party, for so far on this expedition I had only succeeded in discovering an impossible route through Lake Hopkins. The final location for my road was as yet an unknown quantity. With this in mind and with the daylight by then almost fully upon me, I studied the details of my amphitheatre.

At one point to the south-east I noticed that the barrier was slightly lower than it was for the remainder of the entire circle, and I concluded that my exit route would have to be over this section or not at all. As I approached it, my hopes faded, for the potential crossing seemed to increase in height with my closer proximity. Nevertheless I selected the appropriate gears on the Rover and tried. That first attempt barely lifted the vehicle over its own height from the floor of the arena and I knew then that this was going to get worse before it could get better. Backing the Rover in a straight line well clear of the pathetic little progress of that first effort, I climbed out and deflated all my tyres to a point beyond which they would fall off their rims. They had already been slackened to a stage which made it possible for me to get into this dish in the first place but that clearly wasn't enough for this do-or-die operation. I considered unloading and dragging each item over the barrier on foot to lighten the vehicle, but decided that often a little weight adds to the traction if any. This plan would be kept for a last-ditch effort. The thought of a further method waiting for me always goaded me on and raised my spirits sufficiently to tackle the one in hand.

Using my little shovel, I started work on making a road in the same way as the early convicts in Australia built them. The only things missing were the leg-irons and the harsh boss with his flogging whip. Smoothing the hummocks of spinifex and replacing the dissected tussocks evenly on the route, I worked for hours to attain a smooth, if steep, grade to the top where initial momentum might carry me over. How I longed for the bulldozer resting quietly back in my camp with its huge gleaming blade in front of those great Caterpillar tracks.

At long last, and with the sun by then beating down on me as I worked, I had managed to construct a twin set of tracks from the front of the Rover to the summit of the ridge. Then, looking hopelessly around me at the circle of even higher dunes, I clambered into the driver's seat. This attempt brought me a third of the way and left a good straight set of tracks. Replacing the disturbed spinifex and smoothing out the small hillock which had built up in front of the wheels at their furthest point, I repeated the process to gain another metre.

With renewed hope and after fifteen more attacks I knew that the next one should clear the crest. I had already climbed to the top to ascertain if I had an outlet on the other side, or if another such basin awaited me there. If that had been the case I might have been able to remain on the razorback crest and follow it around, but after that early inspection I found that all was well.

Carefully replacing the moved herbage back on to the tracks, which by this time were quite deep, I returned to the vehicle only to find a front tyre absolutely flat on the ground. The torture had proved too much for it in its slackened state. Thankful for the previous night's mending, I replaced it with a newly-patched 'spare' and sorrowfully allowed all the air, which I'd laboured to pump in by hand only hours before, to escape. If this last charge was successful I would gladly reinflate all the tyres as I couldn't afford to waste petrol by using the engine plug pump.

I don't think anyone has expected more from a motor than I did when the vehicle was within a metre of that virtually unattainable crest, but the length of run-up and the gradual consolidation of the deep wheel-tracks won over, and with the engine screaming at full pitch, I found myself on top. I didn't lose momentum until the whole weight was at last on the downhill slope, when I stopped and trudged back for my shovel. I hadn't dared pack it away or take it upon myself to assume success until it was positively achieved.

Now, with those Wallace Hills only a memory and with the Robert Range receding to make way for the Walter James Range, I had an increasing feeling that the worst of our long haul was over. The spectacle of the red quartzite cliffs held a much more friendly atmosphere for me. It had been here that I had finally returned to camp after a successful expedition on which I had discovered a route through almost impossible country for this part of the Sandy Blight Junction Road.

I had first set eyes on this range on a similar journey to survey ahead a course for the road which at that time reached only to the easternmost termination of the Schwerin Mural Crescent. Between there and the Petermann Range further to the east existed a complete break in the range system which extended from 140 kilometres to the west through the Rawlinson Range. The Petermanns took up almost as soon as the Mural Crescent left off, and the Rebecca Creek, also named by Ernest Giles, threaded its dry course between them.

The presence of this pass had led me to decide on a starting point for my new road north into the Northern Territory. I came to this decision only after much laborious work testing a route through the only other western outlet at the Giles meteorological station. We had established this weather station on the southern side of the Rawlinsons only 6 kilometres from this break (named by Giles as the Pass of the Abencerrages), and I endeavoured at the time to continue my road through it. After several long, hard expeditions during which I constantly ran into barriers of rocky outcrops and dense sand ridges, I was forced to the conclusion that such a route was not easily possible, so I decided to make use of the only other outlet to the north at the Rebecca. As it turned out I have often been glad I did, for the quiet little station set in its most pleasant surroundings would have been continually beset by plagues of future travellers, each expecting help in one form or another.

With a view to people one day coming up from the south on my original road to the station, I selected a point which made most use of its northerly trend before curving westward to form what is now known as the Gunbarrel Highway, and created a junction. A pleasant stand of desert oaks 30 kilometres short of the station made an ideal camp for our initial base on the existing road, and this has now become a junction well known to countless travellers.

With the new road and my camp at its head on the banks of Rebecca, I had need of a detailed knowledge of the country to the north to guide the road, so, as on so many occasions before, I plunged off alone into the scrub ahead. The north-westerly trend of the Rebecca governed the first 10 or so kilometres of the route because I didn't want the main access to cross it, and immediately after leaving the watercourse I became entangled with the rough rocky outcrops of the Anne Range. Fresh from failure at discovering a route through the other pass, I wondered if such a road was to be feasible at all; but happily and after days of exploration small outlets among mazes of sand belts appeared at the right places to admit the width of a road.

After clearing this rocky obstacle I pushed through the thick bush once more on a northern course, seemingly for the time being unmolested by topography in this completely unknown section of Central Australia.

Soon I could see another mountain range towering above the comparatively diminutive one I'd just negotiated, and in 10 kilometres of heavy scrub bashing I felt I was level with it, although still 5 kilometres distant. I thought that the extreme troubles I had encountered close to such huge outcrops for almost every kilometre of progress to date must fade as I moved further away from them, but at the same time I often stood on the Rover's roof with binoculars to study this newest example. After all, the road was initially meant to provide access for a trig survey for Woomera, to help with the mapping of areas hitherto uncharted because of their extreme remoteness, and trig and tellurometer stations could only be established on hills giving line of sight between each other. The closer the road was built to high outcrops, the easier it was for the following survey parties.

Late one afternoon, as I scanned the eastern face of this Walter James Range through the glass, with the low sun's rays highlighting prominent features, an exciting deep black crevasse held my undivided attention. I knew instantly that I must go to it, so I jumped from the roof of the Rover and turned the vehicle towards it. In the cabin it was immediately obscured by scrub, but after an hour of beating the gorge could be seen at ground level, only half a kilometre distant. My feeling of excitement mounted as I contemplated the imminent visitation of such an isolated and remote feature. The depth of the crevasse could not even then be ascertained, and it looked more intriguing by the minute.

Finally, with my further progress blocked by rocks fallen from the towering cliffs after eons of weathering, I abandoned the Rover and continued on foot with the noise of my hobnailed boots echoing eerily in the otherwise silent canyon. Within half a kilometre, by moving in the only possible direction allowed by the vertical walls, the waterway elevated me to a level ledge across the entire width. Although the heat was intense at that time of the year, I quickly climbed the last few metres to the top of the stone barrier.

I could hardly believe my eyes at the sight spread out in front of me. A triangular-shaped smooth rock basin a dozen metres across had been formed naturally in the cleft between high cliff walls, and it was brim

Len Beadell

full of crystal-clear rainwater. The clear bottom receded into the depths at the centre. Hurrying down to the water's edge, I scooped up handfuls of the purest liquid I'd seen for months and drank gratefully. Only minutes before I'd been forcing my way through kilometres of dense hot dry bush, covered as I always seemed to be in a mixture of sweat, dust, and spinifex gum, and here in this hidden gorge lay an oasis too perfect to conjure up even in dreams. After so long away from plentiful water, and feeling as I did, the urge to plunge into this cold pool overcame all thoughts of preserving it, and soon I was diving into it from a rock ledge above, trying to reach the bottom at its centre. After several attempts I found I could not dive deep enough to feel a floor and concluded that this must be an almost permanent supply. It would be filled after even a small shower once or twice a year, catching the quick run-off from the hundreds of square metres of smooth rock all around. The sun's rays would seldom reach it, and with this depth at their disposal, Aborigines for countless generations would have survived the longest droughts.

Climbering further up the gully, I found that yet another and even bigger and better pool was located at the base of a most spectacular unscaleable fold in the rock formation. By now daylight was fading, and

232

I was suddenly brought back to earth, realising I had a long way to go if I was to rejoin my camp that night. I couldn't easily reach my old shorts and hobs resting on the far bank of the first pool without a last plunge and swim over to them, and soon afterwards I was on my way back down to the Rover. As I clambered over the rocks I decided that wherever else it went, our road would be located as close as possible to this spot. With that in mind I drove off only as far as was necessary to clear the foothills before turning south to my outgoing wheeltracks.

Back in my hot, sweltery camp I sprang out of the simmering vehicle and informed the small group that I had just been for a swim in an almost bottomless stone tank, after diving from a high rocky platform. But nothing I could add would make them believe me, and I might as well have tried to convince the dusty hot mulga scrub around us that I hadn't completely taken leave of my senses. All I was rewarded with was tolerant smiles of agreement and a friendly word from Paul that of course I'd been swimming in the desert. 'What else?' Quinny was for once without comment and retired to his swag on the water-tanks in his truck. Scotty gave his opinion that intense heat often does this sort of thing to people, while Doug just ignored me politely. Eric followed Quinny's example and escaped into the caravan. I smiled smugly to myself and said inaudibly, 'You'll all soon see.'

So it was that a week later our new road skirted the lower slopes of the Walter James Range, and with a view to obtaining water, even though it would have to be hand-carried to help our meagre supply, we bulldozed a short access from the main road to the entrance of the gorge. Only then did the party begin to have a suspicion that something might be there after all. Clearing a small area with the grader against the actual mountain the camp settled down for the night; and next morning with a flourish I led everyone, including Paul and Quinny, up to my discovery.

My credibility rating with the boys as a result of this episode lasted for months after this memorable contact with the Bungabiddy Rock Holes, to give them their official Aboriginal title. My standing seemed to wane at the Mount Leisler area but the unusual collection of huge red rounded boulders there served to revitalise it. These things contributed to the story of our lives during our eight years together on our monumental project.

As our bulldozer train lumbered on past that little offshoot into Bungabiddy, I, and I'm sure most of the others, relived the time eight months before when the Sandy Blight Junction road had progressed no further than that spot. Now here we were, almost the first to make use of our own road, limping back from the far-off deserts with what was left of the equipment that had made it. In one way it was as if it had dug its own grave. But we all knew that once we were back at Giles, it would all be repaired ready for our fresh onslaught into the bush in the new year.

That night, after clearing Bungabiddy and the Walter James Range, we camped again on our old area by Rebecca Creek, right between the two main range systems. Scotty, Quinny, and I even found a water soak in its bed. At that time of the year and in this area, the sight of water other than from hidden rock-holes was remarkable and meant that some little shower had fallen — though we certainly hadn't seen it.

The Schwerin Mural Crescent which now reared up alongside us had been also named by Giles after the Princess of Schwerin, who was married to the Emperor of Russia. Along its length was Vladimir Pass, named after their son. However he thought of such people when naming these features completely eluded me as I couldn't think of any connection whatsoever. More to the point was the name of Rawlinson given to the main range to the west, after Sir Henry who was president of the Royal Geographical Society in London.

The next day, as our train groaned along, still protesting in vain at the long drawn-out effort, we slowly passed the beautiful ghost gum alongside which we had carved the road, with the first of our aluminium signplates for this section installed on the blaze. Having no distances as yet to add, and no need of astronomical values for latitude and longitude, it merely gave the names and vocations of our party, the date when the new road had reached the spot, and the usual note added to inform future users that the Gunbarrel Road Construction Party was to blame for it.

In the background, a few kilometres away and standing remote from the main crescent, the curious formation of Gill's Pinnacle reared up abruptly from the scrub-covered level ground. Giles had named this after his nephew — a rather closer relation than the Emperor of Russia's wife.

The next overnight camp on this incredible and unprecedented towing operation was, almost sadly to say, to be our last. For almost a month this slow progress had become a way of life for us, and although it had been a gruelling experience, we were somehow sorry to see it coming to a close. I selected for our final stopover the same site among the desert oaks at the junction where we had camped when we began this whole year's work, mainly as the timing would be right after the distance from the Rebecca had been covered. Another reason was that I planned to erect a signpost to advise newcomers of the ultimate destination of our brand-new road, together with other relevant information, and I would be on the spot to complete it.

In anticipation of this I chopped a long straight length from one of the magnificent stands of oaks which at the outset we had reluctantly been forced to clear 17 kilometres on our way. Lead capped, the post should last for many years, I thought, as I attached the plate which I'd spent an hour happily punching out, and painted the whole thing the usual white.

During that night, as we lay spreadeagled on top of our swags in the oppressive heat, endeavouring to gain the greatest possible degree of relief from a gently moving air current, I had cause to think that this was not only to be my last project, but my last night on earth. Through the fog of a restless attempt at sleep, a crawling sensation across my throat brought me back to cold reality. Motionless, I felt this slow movement across my bare shoulder and over my neck. I was quite sure that a deadly spinifex snake was making its lethargic way over me, and that one flicker of movement on my part would send poison fangs sinking into my pulsating veins. I lay there for what seemed like hours, not daring to even swallow. The incessant creeping persisted until a weak increase in the breeze caused an immediate corresponding flutter across my chest, transferring the contact from my throat. At that instant I thought it was now or never. I leapt up in what must have been the most rapid movement I had made for years, and looked down on my moonlit swag. There, alongside my grimy pillow, lay the old ragged shirt I had shed prior to collapsing for the night, with a willowy shred of material surging slowly about at the will of the breeze.

Paul was the only one who ever heard about that, as the others would never have let me forget it.

Seven hours after moving off saw our desert cavalcade at the foot of the stony rise upon which we had sited the weather station a half dozen years before. Once on top Doug manoeuvred the train to an out-of-the-way position and kicked out the master clutch-lever for the last time that year. Then, climbing down with an air of great importance, he threw down the decompression lever and that faithful big diesel engine died immediately.

Eric made for the bore-water shower room while Paul unceremoniously headed for the kitchen to help the station cook cope with meals for the swelled numbers. Quinny was all set to turn around and return to the desert again, a feeling I shared with him, and Scotty joined Rex to inspect the still simmering train whose dust had barely settled. We had come 800 kilometres from the end of the new road, which right then terminated at an inconspicuous mound of spinifex deposited by the bulldozer before turning around.

As if to soften the traumatic blow of this most abrupt cessation of the lifestyle which had motivated us for nearly a year, several incidents occurred in quick succession to occupy our minds in the following few days.

Firstly, one member of our group came to me with the separate pieces of his upper denture which had somehow not stood up to the pounding in his shirt pocket as he did his washing; so once again out came the little dust-proof box. The plate had to be repaired quickly, as he wasn't to be left out of the enticing new food available. Then, seeing that the box was open with its contents spread out, one of the meteorological observers thought he might as well have a temporary filling installed as well.

The second excitement came the following morning when an Aboriginal woman limped in with a mangled toe for treatment. It was an obvious case of gangrene, and this meant a long radio conversation with the doctor at Woomera. Following the detailed instructions relayed to me, I performed an amputation, surrounded by Aborigines clutching bunches of spears. I wrapped the toe in paper and returned it to her, as it was hers anyway, together with the opinion that if she put it in a glass of water overnight, the fairies might pay her a visit.

Then, as if to completely erase any lingering depression at being in comparative civilisation again, if only temporarily, a Bristol Freighter which was due with supplies landed on the near-by airstrip that we had located and constructed ourselves when starting Giles, only to be crippled

236

after a high-canopied station truck drove into its wing-tip. The pilot made the somewhat heated but quite unnecessary statement that it was a good plane when he landed but now it was useless.

One thing was certain: the Sandy Blight Junction Road would never be forgotten by our little party, if only for the fact that we had completed what just had to be one of the longest and most arduous towing operations in the history of Australia, if not indeed for the rest of the world.

Len Beadell